WORLD HISTORY BY ERA

Classical Greece and Rome

═══╣ VOLUME 2 ╠═══

Don Nardo, *Book Editor*

Daniel Leone, *President*
Bonnie Szumski, *Publisher*
Scott Barbour, *Managing Editor*

Greenhaven Press, Inc., San Diego, California

Every effort has been made to trace the owners of copy-
righted material. The articles in this volume may have been
edited for content, length, and/or reading level. The titles
have been changed to enhance the editorial purpose.

Library of Congress Cataloging-in-Publication Data

Classical Greece and Rome / Don Nardo, book editor.
    p. cm. —(World history by era; vol. 2)
    Includes bibliographical references and index.
    ISBN 0-7377-0577-9 (pbk. : alk. paper) —
  ISBN 0-7377-0578-7 (lib. : alk. paper)
    1. Civilization, Classical. 2. Civilization, Ancient.
  I. Nardo, Don, 1947–   II. Series.

  DE59 .C56 2002
  938—dc21   2001016157
                                                    CIP

Cover inset photo credits (from left):
Corel Professional Photos; Photodisc; Corel Professional
Photos; Corel Professional Photos; Planet Art; Digital Stock;
Photodisc
Main cover photo credit: Réunion des Musées
Nationaux/Art Resource, NY
Dover, 201, 209
North Wind Picture Archives, 38, 52, 76, 91, 219
Prints Old and Rare, 108

Copyright © 2002 by Greenhaven Press, Inc.
10911 Technology Place, San Diego, CA 92127

Printed in the USA

CONTENTS

dides, pitted the two most powerful Greek states—
Athens and Sparta—along with their respective
leagues of allies, against each other for twenty-seven
agonizing years.

was the most powerful nation in the known world
and Carthage was wiped from the face of the earth.

Chapter 3: Beyond Europe: New Cultures, Nations, and Empires

FOREWORD

The late 1980s were a time of dramatic events worldwide. Tragedies such as the explosions of the space shuttle *Challenger* and the Chernobyl nuclear power plant shocked the world out of its complacent belief that humankind had mastered nature and firmly controlled its technological creations. In U.S. politics, scandal rocked the White House when several high-ranking officials in the Ronald Reagan administration were convicted of selling arms to Iran and aiding the Nicaraguan Contra rebels. In global politics, U.S. president Ronald Reagan and Soviet president Mikhail Gorbachev signed a landmark treaty banning intermediate-range nuclear forces, marking the beginning of an era of arms control. In several parts of the world—including Beijing, China, the West Bank and Gaza Strip, and several nations of Eastern Europe—people rose up to resist oppressive governments, with varying degrees of success. In American culture, crack cocaine and inner-city poverty contributed to the development of a new and controversial music genre: gangsta rap.

Many of these events were unrelated to one another except for the fact that they occurred at about the same time. Others were linked to global developments. Greenhaven Press's World History by Era series provides students with a unique tool for examining global history in a way that allows them to appreciate the seemingly random occurrences as well as the general trends of human progress. This series divides world history—from the time of ancient Greece and Rome to the end of the second millennium—into ten discrete periods. Each volume then presents a collection of both primary and secondary documents that describe the major events of the period in chronological order. This structure provides students with a snapshot of events occurring simultaneously in all parts of the world. The reader can then see the connections between events in far-flung corners of the world. For example, the Palestinian uprising (*Intifada*) of December 1987 was near in time—if not in character and location—to similar

protests in Beijing, China; Berlin, Germany; Prague, Czechoslo-
vakia; and Bucharest, Romania. While these events were different in many ways, they all involved ordinary citizens striving
for self-autonomy and democracy against governments that
were attempting to impose strict controls on their civil liberties.
By making the connections between these events, students can
see that they comprised a global movement for democracy and
human rights that profoundly impacted social and political systems worldwide.

Each volume in this series offers features to enhance students'
understanding of the era of world history under discussion. An
introductory essay provides an overview of the period, supplying essential context for the readings that follow. An anno-
tated table of contents highlights the main point of each selection. A more in-depth introduction precedes each document,
placing it in its particular historical context and offering bio-
graphical information about the author. A thorough chronology
and index allow students to quickly reference specific events
and dates. Finally, a bibliography opens up additional avenues
of research. These features help to make the World History by
Era series an extremely valuable tool for students researching
the rise and fall of civilizations, social and political revolutions,
cultural movements, scientific and technological advancements,
and other events that mark the unfolding of human history
throughout the world.

AN EMERGING GLOBAL SOCIETY

First and foremost, it is essential to understand what is meant by the term "classical world." The word "classical" is often used to denote a period in which a people or nation reached the zenith of its cultural advancement or output. The era lasting from about 500 to 323 B.C., for example, is called the Classical Age of ancient Greece because it was in these years that Greek political scientists, philosophers, architects, dramatists, and others created works and achievements of extraordinary excellence. And the period of about A.D. 320 to about 540 is referred to as ancient India's Classical Age for the same reason.

The word classical has come to have another, larger definition, however. When the ancient Romans conquered the entire Mediterranean sphere in the third through first centuries B.C., they absorbed the Greek kingdoms and city-states in that sphere into their growing empire; and large-scale Greek autonomy ended, not to be revived until the nineteenth century, when the modern nation of Greece emerged. Yet the glories of Greek culture did not die. This was because the Romans, who had a tradition of borrowing the best ideas from conquered peoples, were mightily impressed with Greek art, architecture, literature, mythology, and philosophical ideas. And they readily absorbed and copied these cultural elements, adopting them to their own needs and in the process becoming thoroughly Hellenized. (The Greeks called themselves Hellenes, so the process of adopting Greek culture is known as Hellenization.) The fusion of Greek and Roman cultures, which survived the fall of Rome and exerted a profound influence on later European peoples and cultures, came to be called classical civilization.

The classical world, therefore, is the Greco-Roman world. Chronologically, it encompasses the main periods of dominance of both peoples, beginning with the Greeks' major victory over the Persian Empire in the early fifth century B.C. and ending with the fall of Rome in A.D. 476. Greek and Roman ideas and institutions formed the principal basis of later Western culture, the collection of European-based societies that grew on the wreckage of classical civilization. Thus, it is only natural that Greco-Roman history and culture remain of primary interest to those who live in Western societies, including the vast majority of readers of books like this one.

Yet it would be a foolhardy and unfortunate mistake to focus all of one's attention on the Mediterranean sphere, as if it was the only region in the world that was civilized and prosperous during the thousand years in question. In fact, during the ascendancy and eventual decline of ancient Greece and Rome, high civilizations arose in several other sections of the globe—in Africa, the Near East, India and China in the Far East, and in Central America. With the exception of the latter, the Greeks and Romans were aware of the existence of and carried on trade with all of these cultures. To gain a clear understanding of how the ancient precursors of the Western world fit within the larger framework of an emerging global society, one must consider the founders of the Eastern world and other non-Western precursors as well.

THE STUFF OF LEGEND

Actually, it was a major confrontation between Western and Eastern cultures that launched the Mediterranean classical world in the first place. In the sixth century B.C., the Persian Empire rose in the Near Eastern region now occupied by Iran and Iraq and soon expanded eastward to the borders of India and westward to the coasts of the Aegean and Mediterranean seas. The Persians controlled the major trade routes leading from the Far East to the Mediterranean, and they had regular contacts with various Indian and Chinese states. It is possible that, had things gone better for Persia, it might have continued to expand eastward, absorbing part or all of India. However, this scenario never transpired because the Persian colossus, the largest empire the world had seen up to that time, made the mistake of attempting to expand westward into Europe; in the process it came up against the tiny but tenacious Greek city-states.

In the face of the Persian threat, the Greeks, for whom freedom and independence (from one another as well as from non-Greeks) was their life-blood, staged a desperate and heroic resistance that has become the stuff of legend. The stories of the charge of the Athenian hoplites (infantrymen) against a much larger Persian army on the plain of Marathon in 490 B.C.; the destruction of the mighty Persian fleet in the Bay of Salamis ten years later; and the almost total annihilation of the invading Persian land army at Plataea in 479 B.C. have thrilled Western school children through the ages. (By contrast, Persian children were taught, with some justification at the time, that these were nothing more than small skirmishes on the distant borders of a vast empire that was in no way threatened by such minor losses. This shows how the annals of history are invariably colored by the personal and local viewpoints of those who write them.)

Whichever viewpoint one chooses for the Greco-Persian conflicts, the fact is that following the Greek victory no other Persian army ever entered Europe again. Moreover, in a twist no one could have predicted at the time, Greece's darkest hour proved to be an important stimulus to its subsequent development of cultural grandeur. The victory instilled in the Greeks a feeling of immense accomplishment. They had demonstrated to the world—and also to themselves—that they were capable of glorious deeds; and the defeat of the world's greatest empire seemed only the first step toward other, equally noteworthy achievements. In this way, historian W.G. Hardy remarks, the victory over Persia became "the torch to set fire to the brilliance of the great age of the Greeks. There was a tremendous upswelling of confidence . . . [and now] the Greeks felt that there was nothing they could not attempt."[1]

THE RISE OF ATHENS

As the wealthiest and most populous Greek city-state, Athens felt and demonstrated this new confidence more than any of its neighbors. With amazing energy and boldness, in the decades following the great patriotic war, the Athenians generated a prodigious flurry of political, economic, and cultural creativity. Athens had emerged from the conflict as one of the two most powerful and prestigious Greek cities (the other being Sparta, in southern Greece); and it quickly exploited that power and prestige by taking the lead in the establishment of the Delian League, a confederation of over a hundred city-states intended to guard against further Persian incursions. In the decades that followed, the audacious and increasingly aggressive Athenians transformed the alliance into their own lucrative maritime empire. And the considerable moneys generated ended up funding the ambitious and expensive building programs that became one of the chief hallmarks of Athens's golden age.

The highlight of these programs was the creation of a majestic complex of temples and other structures atop Athens's Acropolis. The new works owed their inspiration and political backing largely to Pericles, a leader of extraordinary intelligence, vision, and imagination, as well as keen political skills. What better way to demonstrate that Athens was the marvel of Greece, he asked his countrymen, than by celebrating and honoring the city's patron deity, Athena (goddess of wisdom and war), whose divine favor had been instrumental in Athens's rise to greatness? Building new, grand, and beautiful temples to her would ensure her continued protection, he proposed. At the same time, a new and magnificent Acropolis complex would be the ultimate symbol of Athenian imperial greatness. Indeed, as the first-century A.D. Greek biographer Plutarch would later write, this ambitious project was seen, both at the time and by posterity, as Pericles' and Athens's greatest achievement:

> There was one measure above all which at once gave the greatest pleasure to the Athenians, adorned their city and created amazement among the rest of mankind, and which is today the sole testimony that the

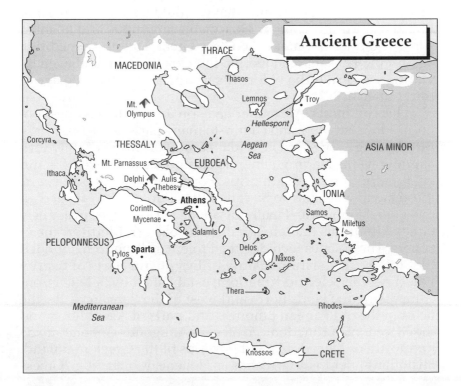

tales of the ancient power and glory of Greece are no mere fables. By this I mean his construction of temples and public buildings.[2]

PHILIP, ALEXANDER, AND THEIR SUCCESSORS

Athens's golden age was relatively short in duration, however. In 431 B.C. the Peloponnesian war broke out between Athens and Sparta and their respective leagues of allies. And the twenty-seven-year-long war ended with Athens's defeat and the exhaustion of all involved. More squabbles among the leading Greek states followed; and these left these states open to outside aggression. This time, however, the threat did not come from Asia, as it had in the previous century, but from Macedonia, a kingdom in extreme northern Greece. In the mid-fourth century B.C., a brilliant and capable young king, Philip II, rapidly united the Macedonian tribes, forming a strong nation with a powerful army. Eventually Philip set his sights on making himself master of all the Greeks. And over the course of a mere two decades he did so by employing a highly effective combination of diplomacy, deceit, and naked aggression.

The city-states now found themselves swept along in the tide of Philip's grandiose plans for invading Persia. The Western and Eastern worlds were once more about to clash, again with momentous, far-reaching results that no could have foreseen. After Philip was assassinated in 336 B.C., his ambitious and talented son, Alexander III (later called "the Great") led the expedition against the Persians, conquering their entire realm and even invading western India before his untimely death at the age of thirty-three in 323 B.C.

In his conquests, Alexander had spread Greek language, political administration, and culture to many parts of the Near East. But the huge kingdom he had created was immediately torn asunder as his leading generals and governors faced off and eventually came to death grips. For the next forty odd years, these men, who came to be called the "Successors," waged almost unrelenting war. Finally, by about 280 B.C., three major new Greek kingdoms had emerged in the eastern Mediterranean sphere. These states included the Ptolemaic Kingdom, founded by Ptolemy, consisting mainly of Egypt and parts of nearby Palestine; the Seleucid Kingdom, established by Seleucus, encompassing the lands north and west of the Persian Gulf—the heart of the old Persian Empire—and parts of Asia Minor; and the Macedonian Kingdom, created by Antigonus Gonatas, made up mostly of Macedonia and portions of the Greek mainland. Historians refer to these realms as Hellenistic, meaning "Greek-like," since their societies often consisted of Eastern languages, customs, and ideas overlaid by a veneer of Greek ones.

Historically speaking, this era was the last period of major Greek political independence in antiquity. This was primarily because the Hellenistic Greeks proceeded to repeat the same fatal mistake the city-states had; in short, they constantly argued and fought among themselves. And this inevitably reinforced their disunity and led to weakness and vulnerability to an outside power. In the mid-third century B.C., as they squabbled, oblivious to the potential consequences, far to the west that power— Rome—was rising steadily and ominously.

MASTER OF THE MEDITERRANEAN

For an undetermined number of years, Rome, a small city-state occupying only a few square miles of territory near Italy's western coast, was a monarchy ruled by kings. Then, in about 509 B.C., the kingdom's leading landowners threw out their king and established the Roman Republic. Roman citizens could now vote for their leaders, including the chief administrators, the consuls, who also commanded the army. However, the new government was largely controlled by a legislature, the Senate, whose wealthy, elite members set the policies the consuls acted on.

The Republic rapidly expanded in power and influence. Its increasingly highly skilled and disciplined armies conquered first its neighbors on the Italian peninsula, then the maritime empire of Carthage (centered in north Africa), and in time Spain, Gaul (what is now France, through the later conquests of the gifted military leader Julius Caesar), and the Greek states and kingdoms clustered in the eastern Mediterranean sphere. In the three Macedonian Wars, lasting from 214 to 168 B.C., the Romans defeated and finally dismantled the Greek Macedonian Kingdom. And in 146 B.C. a Roman general destroyed the once great mainland Greek city of Corinth as an object lesson to other Greeks who might contemplate rebellion against the new master of the Mediterranean world.

These wars were soon followed in the first century B.C. by more rounds of blood-letting, this time a series of devastating civil wars that killed hundreds of thousands of people and left the survivors fearful and war-weary. From this strife, one man finally emerged victorious—Octavian, Caesar's adopted son. After he had defeated his last rivals, the Roman general Mark Antony and Egypt's Queen Cleopatra, in the naval battle of Actium (in western Greece) in 31 B.C., Octavian was the most powerful man in the world. Bowing before that power, the now humbled and fearful Senate conferred on him the name Augustus, "the revered one." And immediately he began building a new, more autocratic Roman state on the ruins of the now defunct Republic. Though he never personally used the title of emperor, Augustus was in fact the first ruler of the political unit that became known as the Roman Empire.

THE ROMAN PEACE

Augustus and most of his immediate successors were thoughtful, effective rulers who brought prosperity and relative peace to the Roman world. And the period of their combined reigns, lasting from about 30 B.C. to A.D. 180, became known as the *Pax Romana,* or "Roman Peace." The five emperors who ruled from 96 to 180—Nerva, Trajan, Hadrian, Antoninus Pius, and Marcus Aurelius—were particularly capable and enlightened. They brought Roman civilization to its political, economic, and cultural zenith, prompting the great eighteenth-century English historian Edward Gibbon to remark:

> If a man were called upon to fix the period in the history of the world during which the condition of the human race was most happy and prosperous, he would without hesitation name that which elapsed from the accession of Nerva to the death of Aurelius. . . . Their united reigns are possibly the only period of history in which the happiness of a great people was the sole object of government.[3]

Under Trajan (reigned 98–117), the Empire was larger than it had ever been or ever would be. It stretched from the Atlantic Ocean in the west to the Persian Gulf in the east and from north Africa in the south to central Britain in the north, a colossal realm encompassing some 3.5 million square miles and 100 million people.

ANARCHY AND DECLINE

But in the centuries following the *Pax Romana,* despite some notable military and cultural successes and high points, the Romans were ultimately unable to stem the increasing tide of northern European tribal peoples across the continent and into Roman territory. In the decades following Marcus Aurelius's passing in 180, the Empire's political, military, and economic problems rapidly increased. And in the third century the realm entered what historians often call the "anarchy," a severe crisis in which its political and economic stability was shattered. At times it appeared that the Empire might collapse from an inability to deal with a prolonged onslaught of serious internal problems and external threats, the main such threat being large incursions of German tribes into the northern provinces.

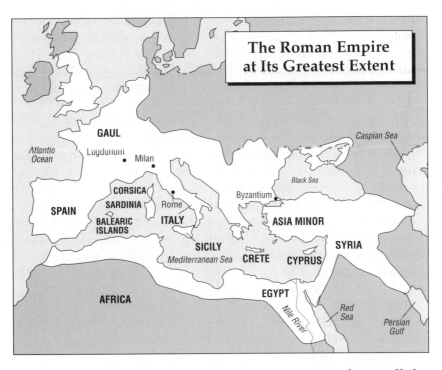

The Roman Empire at Its Greatest Extent

Disunity, chaos, and enemy incursions appeared to spell the end of the old Roman world. However, beginning in the year 268 a series of strong military leaders took control and, in the words of the prolific historian Michael Grant, "in one of the most strik ing reversals in world history, Rome's foes were hurled back."[4] With the Empire reunited and minimal order restored, in 284 a remarkably intelligent and capable ruler named Diocletian ascended the throne. Modern scholars often refer to the new, grimmer, ultimately less-stable realm that emerged under his rule and lasted until Rome's fall in 476 as the Later Empire. Diocletian drastically overhauled the provinces, the economy, and the military, giving the realm a new lease on life.

That lease turned out to be only temporary, however. This was because the pressure of tribal peoples on the northern borders, which had existed on a lesser scale for centuries, now grew to epic proportions; and Rome, with its economic and military apparatus unable to cope, was overwhelmed. The human flood from the north began in earnest in the mid-370s. The Huns, a fierce nomadic people from central Asia, swept into eastern Europe, driving the Goths and other Germanic peoples into the Roman border provinces. The advance of the Huns set in motion the greatest folk migrations in history, as the Goths, Vandals, Burgundians, Franks, Saxons, and many other tribes spread across the continent in search of new lands. The fertile valleys of Roman

Italy, Gaul, and Spain beckoned to them; and the Roman army, now not nearly as strong, disciplined, and mobile as it had been in the Empire's heyday, was increasingly unsuccessful in stopping the invaders. The province of Britain had to be abandoned in about 407 and in the succeeding decades various tribal peoples settled permanently in other western provinces.

The western Empire eventually shrank to a pale ghost of the mighty state of the *Pax Romana* days. The last few western emperors ruled over a pitiful realm consisting only of the Italian peninsula and portions of a few nearby provinces; and even these lands were not safe or secure, for claims on Roman territory continued. In 476, a German-born general named Odoacer, who commanded what turned out to be the last official Roman army in Italy, marched into Ravenna (in northern Italy), then capital of the western Empire, and without striking a blow deposed the young emperor Romulus Augustulus. No emperor took the boy's place, and historians have come to see this event as the fall of the western Empire (although life in Rome went on as usual for a while under German rulers and the eastern Empire, centered at Constantinople, survived and steadily mutated into the Byzantine Empire).

Important Religious Developments

Greco-Roman culture did not cease to exist, of course. One of its most important survivals, both in the west and east, was Christianity, which had begun as a small Jewish sect in the first century A.D. and slowly risen to control the apparatus of the Roman state by the late fourth century. The faith owed much of its success to Constantine I, who ruled from 307 to 337. His predecessors, Diocletian and his co-emperor Galerius, were the last Roman rulers to stage a large-scale persecution of the Christians, who made up only about 10 percent of the Empire's population in the year 300. Constantine became a strong supporter of Christianity (although he did not actually convert to the faith until he was on his deathbed). The Edict of Milan, which he and the eastern Roman ruler, Licinius, issued in 313, guaranteed absolute toleration for the Christians and provided for the restoration of all the property they had lost in the persecutions. Thanks largely to Constantine's efforts, Christianity went on to become the principal faith of medieval and modern Europe.

Meanwhile, other religious developments during the Greco-Roman centuries had helped to transform the world. The Jews, who had inhabited Palestine (on the Mediterranean's eastern coast) since the second millennium B.C. and whose religion—Judaism—had given birth to Christianity, rebelled against Rome in the first century B.C. The Romans crushed them, destroyed their great temple in Jerusalem, and they scattered across the known world. More fortunate was Buddhism, which emerged in India in the fifth century B.C., at the same time that Athens was rising to greatness in Greece. In the centuries that followed, Buddhist missionaries carried the faith's message of righteous living and tolerance to China, Japan, and much of southeast Asia.

BEYOND THE GRECO-ROMAN SPHERE

One reason that Buddhism found a receptive audience and fertile ground in China (beginning on a large scale in the first century A.D.), was that by this time China was a united, relatively stable state with a strong centralized government. This was its legacy from the Ch'in, a short-lived but highly influential dynasty that came to power in 221 B.C. The Ch'in quickly united the many separate Chinese kingdoms, which had been warring among themselves for centuries, into an empire, the region's first; and later Chinese dynasties more or less followed the administrative structure they created. The Ch'in knew of the Greeks and Romans through periodic trade contacts. But the Chinese leaders had no clear picture of the size and extent of Europe; nor could they have realized that while they were erecting the Great Wall of China to prevent war, far away the Romans were fighting the largest and most destructive war the world had yet seen (the Second Punic War, against Carthage).

Moreover, China and Rome were not the only areas of major activity at this time. During the reign of the Ch'in, the Parthians, an Asian people from the region near the Caspian Sea, were pushing the Greeks out of the Near East and consolidating the old Persian territories into a powerful new realm. Still again East met West head-on, as in the next two centuries the Parthians and Romans became major rivals and repeatedly fought for possession of what had once been Mesopotamia. These centuries also saw the Romans supplanting the Ptolemies, the Greek rulers of Egypt, and turning that once mighty ancient land into a Roman province.

The glories of African kingdoms were far from over, however, for in the first century A.D. another strong realm, Axum, rose in what is now Ethiopia (south of Egypt) and grew rich and prosperous by trading with the Greeks, Romans, Parthians, Arabians, Indians, and others. Among the Indian leaders the Axumites dealt with were the Guptas, who came to power about the year 320, shortly after Constantine granted the Christians tolerance. Both the Guptas, who presided over India's classical period of art and literature, and the Axumites were destined to outlive the Romans by almost a century.

The only great civilization of the classical world that had no knowledge of these European, African, and Asian peoples and realms (nor they of it), was that of the Maya in Central America. The Americas, which Europeans would later come, rather arrogantly, to call the New World (since it was hardly new to its native inhabitants), still existed in isolation. Unlike the peoples mentioned above, the Maya built a highly civilized social and religious order without any influence from the cultures of other continents. And this fact makes their achievement all the more remarkable. The late, great modern historian Arnold Toynbee pointed out that the many ruins of Maya cities that still dot the dense jungles of southern Mexico speak quite

> eloquently of the intensity of the struggle with the physical environment which the creators of the Mayan civilization must have waged in their day. In her very revenge, which reveals her in all her gruesome power, tropical nature [which eventually reclaimed the Mayan cities] testifies to the courage and vigor of the men who once . . . succeeded in putting her to flight and keeping her at bay.[5]

Indeed, creating and maintaining a network of cities in the jungle is one of the most impressive accomplishments of the millions of people who inhabited the wider, very diverse, and often fascinating world that existed beyond the edges of the Greco-Roman sphere.

NOTES

1. W.G. Hardy, *The Greek and Roman World.* Cambridge, MA: Schenkman Publishing, 1962, p. 11.

2. Plutarch, *Life of Pericles,* in *Rise and Fall of Athens: Nine Greek Lives by Plutarch.* Trans. Ian Scott-Kilvert. New York: Penguin, 1960, p. 177.

3. Edward Gibbon, *The Decline and Fall of the Roman Empire.* First published 1776–1788. 3 vols. Ed. David Womersley. New York: Penguin Books, 1994, vol. 1, pp. 101, 103.

4. Michael Grant, *The Fall of the Roman Empire.* New York: Macmillan, 1990, p. 3.

5. Arnold Toynbee, *A Study of History.* New York: Oxford University Press, 1947, p. 81.

Classical Greece: Crucible of War and Culture

CHAPTER 1

THE GRECO-PERSIAN WARS USHER IN GREECE'S CLASSICAL AGE

SARAH B. POMEROY, STANLEY M. BURSTEIN, WALTER DONLAN, AND JENNIFER T. ROBERTS

Most modern historians see the surge of confidence that infused the Athenians and many other Greeks after their tremendous victory over the Persians in the early fifth century B.C. as a major factor in the subsequent explosion of Greek political and cultural activity. The trouble began when the Greek cities of Ionia (along the western coast of Asia Minor) rebelled against their Persian overlords and Persia's king, Darius, responded. Much of what we know about the ensuing war, including the famous heroic defense of the pass of Thermopylae by a band of Greeks led by Sparta's King Leonidas, comes from the *Histories* of the fifth-century B.C. Greek chronicler Herodotus. The following overview of the Greco-Persian conflicts, which forever decided the fate of Europe, is by the authors of the absorbing *Ancient Greece: A Political, Social and Cultural History.* The book's authors include Sarah B. Pomeroy, of Hunter College; Stanley M. Burstein, of California State University, Los Angeles; Walter Donlan, of the University of California, Irvine; and Jennifer T. Roberts, of the City University of New York Graduate Center.

In 499 BC revolt broke out among the Ionian Greeks. Discontent in Ionia was considerable; taxes had gone up when the Greek cities were transferred from Lydian to Persian hands, and the Greeks resented the system of puppet tyrants the Persians had imposed. . . .

[Athens and her neighbor, Eretria, decided to help the Ionians after Sparta refused]. The Athenians were . . . more adventurous people than the Spartans, they were not constrained by fear of a slave rebellion in their absence. . . . [Also], access to grain and other resources in the Black Sea area was precious and deserving of protection. They agreed to send twenty ships; the Eretrians to the north were willing to send five.

The unsuccessful rebellion of the Ionian Greeks ended in a major naval defeat off the island of Lade near Miletus in 494 BC. Greek morale had fallen. . . . Miletus was defeated, its women and children enslaved, and the men relocated to the mouth of the Tigris. In the course of the rebellion, however, the capital city of the western Persian empire, Sardis, was burnt, whether accidentally or on purpose.

Darius would not forget the burning of Sardis, but neither would the Greeks forget the annihilation of Miletus. Home of the philosophers Thales, Anaximander, and Anaximenes . . . Miletus had been one of the most cultured cities in the Greek world. When the poet Phrynichus produced a tragedy on its fall entitled *The Capture of Miletus,* the Athenians fined him one thousand drachmas for reminding them of their misfortune. The story of the Athenians' outrage reveals a growing sense of identity among the Ionians and perhaps among the Greeks more broadly. The Athenians had withdrawn from the rebellion in its early stages, after the burning of Sardis, so that Athenian soldiers had not been involved in the collapse of Miletus; yet they identified passionately with it in its final hour.

There was reason to believe that the fate of Miletus could soon be that of cities in mainland Greece. Under the leadership of a rising politician named Themistocles, who had just been elected archon, the Athenians began to fortify the three rocky harbors of Piraeus and convert them into a naval and commercial base. . . . Acutely sensible to the Persian threat . . . Themistocles served Greece well at this critical time.

DARIUS' INVASION OF GREECE

Darius had been interested in Greece for some years before the Ionian rebellion, and the desire to avenge the burning of Sardis had added an additional spur to his ambition. In 492 BC he sent his son-in-law Mardonius west at the head of a large force.

Though Mardonius successfully restored Persian prestige in northern Greece, conquering Thrace, Thasos, and Macedonia, the fleet was wrecked off Mount Athos on the Chalcidic peninsula, and Mardonius was forced to turn back. Darius promptly began mobilizing for another expedition, one that would sail straight across the Aegean, avoiding the treacherous promontories of the north. Mindful of the fate of Miletus, many Greek cities yielded to the demand of Darius' heralds for earth and water, the proverbial tokens of submission that signaled recognition of the king's supremacy on land and sea. The islanders felt they had little choice, and on the mainland Argos and Thebes went over to the Persians. Sparta and Athens, however, remained steadfast in their opposition.

Darius' first order of business was to punish Athens and Eretria for their role in the Ionian rebellion. In fact, it may have been the primary purpose of his expedition. In the summer of 490 his fleet arrived in Greece, commanded by his nephew Artaphernes and Datis, a Mede. . . . Datis and Artaphernes may have had twenty thousand men with them, one of whom was the aging Hippias, the exiled ruler of Athens whom they hoped to reinstall as both Athenian tyrant and Persian vassal. . . .

After a siege of less than a week, Eretria was betrayed from within. The Persians burnt the Eretrians' temples in revenge for those destroyed at Sardis and deported the population in accordance with Darius' orders. . . . From Eretria the Persians moved down on Marathon in . . . northern Attica.

The Athenian assembly immediately voted to dispatch their forces to Marathon, and a runner, Pheidippides (or perhaps Philippides) was sent to Sparta, covering, so the story went, fully 140 miles by the next day. The Spartans, however, could not take advantage of the speed with which the message was delivered, for, they explained to the breathless Pheidippides, they were celebrating a festival of Apollo, the Carnea, and were forbidden to march until the full moon. As the Spartans were deeply religious and no cowards in war, their explanation may have been sincere.

Herodotus' figures are probably erroneous, but it is likely that the Athenians were outnumbered, if not as outrageously as he suggests then at least by a factor of two to one. The Persians had the more versatile force, with cavalry, archers, and skirmishing troops, but the Athenian force consisting essentially of hoplites was more heavily armed. The most serious problem faced by the Athenians was the lack of a commander, for all decisions lay with the ten strategoi [elected generals] . . . deliberating as a body. As some wanted to wait for the Spartan reinforcements expected after the full moon and others thought delay risky, there was danger that a deadlock in the Athenian camp would throw the victory to the Persians and Greece would be overrun. When the Athenians learned that some of the Persian troops and cavalry were missing and suspected that part of the Persian forces were heading for Phaleron, it seemed to several generals that the moment to strike had come, even though the moon was full and the Spartans could be expected shortly; any delay could be fatal. The strategos Miltiades seems to have played a key role in saving Greece. . . .

And so, early one morning in late September of 490, under Miltiades' command, the Athenians, flanked by some Plataeans, ran down the hill on which they had encamped, covering the mile or so that divided them from the Persians at double speed despite the weight of their hoplite armor. Aristides and Themistocles commanded their tribal contingents in the center, while Callimachus commanded on the right wing and the Plataeans held the left. Knowing they were outnumbered, the Athenians packed their wings as tightly as they could, concentrating as many men as possible on the outer ends of their formation, even though it meant leaving the center thin. Despite their numerical superiority the Persians were unable to withstand the disciplined and determined hoplites fighting in defense of their freedom. (The Greeks also had better armor and longer spears.) In the flight to their ships, many of the Persians were bogged down in the marshes.

Arriving too late to participate in the fighting, the Spartans visited the battlefield and surveyed the Persian corpses. Herodotus maintained that the Athenians lost 192 men, the Persians 6400. The Greek statistic is probably correct, for the names were inscribed on the battlefield; they included Callimachus. The dead were cremated where they had fallen, and a monument was subsequently erected on the site. . . .

THE THREAT OF A NEW PERSIAN INVASION

Darius raised taxes in the summer of 486, thus arousing suspicion that he was gathering resources to finance a new invasion of Greece. He would probably have some support in northern Greece—Thessaly, for example—and no doubt in the south as well. By this time the Persians were well aware how divided Greek cities were among themselves . . . racked by internal conflict. . . . Darius' project had to be delayed, however, because of a rebellion in Egypt sparked by the increase in taxes. In the fall of 486 BC he fell ill and died.

Darius' son and successor, Xerxes (Cyrus' grandson on his mother's side) was at first ambivalent about carrying out the invasion, but by 484 BC he had made his decision, and the Greeks learned that ships were being built in large numbers throughout

The Greco-Persian Wars, 494–469 B.C.

Important battle sites

the ports of the extensive Persian empire from Egypt to the Black Sea. Engineers and laborers were dispatched to the Hellespont, where they bridged the crossing with boats, and to northern Greece where they cut a canal across Athos so that the shipwreck Mardonius had suffered in 492 could be avoided.

Fortuitously, at this very time the Athenians working the silver mines of Laurium in southeastern Attica for their modest yield hit upon an extraordinary lode of silver previously undiscovered. The new vein was so rich that it yielded well over 2 tons the first year alone. In Athens, voters were divided about what to do with it. Aristides led those who wanted to partition it among the citizens, but Themistocles advocated building ships. . . .

The ships the Athenians built with their windfall from Laurium were triremes, light, fast, maneuverable warships with three banks of oars. Although the first triremes had been built, probably in Corinth, as early as the seventh century, they were expensive vessels to construct, and it took some time for the trireme to replace older, less efficient models as the Greek warship par excellence. By the fifth century, however, the trireme had established itself as an indispensable tool of war. A long, slender vessel, the trireme was about nine times as long as it was wide, about 120 feet by 15 feet, and was powered by 170 rowers. . . .

While the Athenians busied themselves constructing warships, Xerxes' heralds arrived in Greece seeking earth and water, and many states complied. Thessaly, Thebes, and Sparta's inveterate enemy Argos could not be counted on. Athens and the Peloponnesian League would have to take the lead, and in concert they called a congress of delegates at Corinth in 481 BC to plan the defense of Greece. There the thirty-one states that were determined to resist the Persians formed themselves into a league historians generally call the Hellenic League. . . . The high command on both land and sea was conferred on Sparta. Troops would be sent north, though not so far north as to be in territory bound to go over to Persia, but the Greeks probably placed their greatest hope in their fleet. After an abortive expedition to Thessaly, they established their ground forces at the pass of Thermopylae on the Malian Gulf while the fleet settled in at nearby Artemisium off northern Euboea. At the instigation of Themistocles, the Athenians probably voted to evacuate Attica and wait out the war on the island of Salamis and in nearby Troezen in the Peloponnesus. . . .

The information center of the Greek world, the Delphic oracle knew enough about Persian might to discourage resistance—the combined forces of the rich king contained many thousands of men, perhaps as many as a quarter million—and both the Spartans and the Athenians had received glum oracles. Themistocles argued that the "wooden wall" that Delphi conceded might save Athens was in fact the navy; Spartans were told that their only chance lay in the death of a king. The oracle may in part explain King Leonidas' tenacity in holding the Thermopylae pass against all odds. It is also true, however, that hard calculation called for a land operation, however unpromising, to buy time for Greece while the fleet off Artemisium could cripple the Persian navy. . . .

THE BATTLES OF THERMOPYLAE AND SALAMIS

Leonidas marched into Thermopylae with about seven thousand men, a fairly small force; possibly the Spartans were ambivalent about taking a stand so far north. But for their dependence on the Athenian fleet, some of them might have been content to limit their defense to the Peloponnesus. The Phocian contingent, which was most familiar with the local terrain, was charged with defending the hidden road over the mountains against the chance that Xerxes would be lucky enough to find it. Lucky he was: a Greek traitor revealed the existence of the road and led Xerxes' commander Hydarnes up it with the crack troops known as the Immortals. For some reason Leonidas dismissed the bulk of his forces. He may have doubted their loyalty, or perhaps he knew his position was hopeless and wished to save as many soldiers as he could for future battles while still inflicting damage and delay on the enemy. Only the Thebans, Thespians, and three hundred Spartans remained. Leonidas and his men defended the pass heroically and fell fighting, having slain many "Immortals" including two brothers of Xerxes. On Xerxes' orders the body of Leonidas was decapitated and displayed on a cross. . . .

Their victory at Thermopylae opened central Greece to the Persians, whose confidence was boosted by the knowledge that they had killed a Spartan king. Swiftly they moved their land forces down on Athens. From Salamis just off the western coast of Attica, where the opposing fleets had taken up their position, the Athenians could see the smoke of the burning Acropolis all too easily, and those who had regarded the fortifications on the hill as the saving "wooden wall" touted by Delphi were forced to admit their mistake. Dissent racked the navy. Some of the Peloponnesians wanted to cut back to the isthmus, while the Athenians were determined to stay where they were and fight in the narrows. Xerxes was apparently tricked into taking action by a message from Themistocles, who purported to be on his side and urged immediate attack before the demoralized Greeks could disperse to their various homes. In reality, many Greeks were thinking of doing just that, and Xerxes' decision to attack was a foolish one. . . . By arranging for the contest to be decided in the narrows, Themistocles maximized the chances that the lighter, more maneuverable Greek ships could worst the heavier Persian vessels. From his high perch on the shore Xerxes watched the course of the battle, in which the Greeks had the additional advantage that, as nearly all of them had grown up near water, they could swim; many of Xerxes' sailors could not. By sundown the Persians had lost two hundred ships and the battle. Rather than confront the foolishness of his decision to fight, Xerxes reacted to the defeat by executing his Phoenician captains for alleged cowardice in the battle, thus depriving himself of Phoenician naval support for the future.

Retreating with his navy to Persia in order to secure the Hellespont, Xerxes left Mardonius in Greece, where in the spring of 479 he faced the largest Greek army ever to have taken the field. Theban support bolstered the Persian cause, but it was insufficient to ensure victory. At the town of Plataea near the border between Attica and Boeotia, Mardonius ended his long years of service to Persia. Led by the Spartan Pausanias . . . the Greeks managed to win the hard fought battle, and in the fighting Mardonius fell. The Theban leaders who had "medized," that is, gone over to the Persians, were subsequently executed without trial. Around the same time—tradition claimed that it was the very same day as the battle at Plataea—the Greek fleet that had pursued the Persians eastward defeated their navy at the Battle of Mycale off the coast of Asia Minor, in part because the Ionian Greeks deserted from the Persian side.

THE WAR THROUGH GREEK EYES

Victors usually record the history of their triumphs. The vanquished reduce the same events to trivial, easily forgotten incidents. . . . Foremost among the ancient literary sources that established this perspective has been the *Histories* of Herodotus, who highlighted the unexpectedness of the Greek victory against all odds and searched for the causes in the fundamental institutions of Greek and Persian society and government. . . .

Herodotus' *Histories* was only one reflection of the extraordinary burst of energy that erupted among the Greeks after their surprising victory over the wealthy and powerful empire that had sought to bring them into its orbit.

The Athenians later celebrated their triumph over the Persians in the relief sculptures of the Parthenon, the temple built to honor their goddess Athena. The reliefs on the four sides of the building showed battles: the gods against the giants; the Greeks against the Amazons; the Lapiths (a Greek people) against the half-human, half-horse males known as Centaurs; and the Greeks against the Trojans, a reference to the struggle against the Persians, who also lived in the east. Thus the Athenians elevated their victory to mythical status. . . .

The unanticipated success of the little city-states over the monolithic empire had little impact in Persia, but in Greece it would give birth to a civilization of extraordinary brilliance and originality.

AN EYEWITNESS DESCRIBES THE GREEK VICTORY AT SALAMIS

AESCHYLUS

In his play, the *Persians,* first produced in 472 B.C., the Athenian playwright Aeschylus, who fought in the sea battle at Salamis, describes how Greek sailors and soldiers, after gaining the advantage in the narrow strait of Salamis, slaughtered the terrified Persians by the thousands. In this excerpt, a messenger tells the astonished Persian queen mother about the unexpected Greek victory.

M ESSENGER: Had Fortune favoured numbers, we would
have won the day.
Three hundred vessels made the total Hellene [Greek]
strength,
Not counting ten picked warships. Xerxes had, I know,
A thousand in command, of which two hundred and seven
Were special fast ships. That was the proportion. Now,
Do you say we entered battle with too weak a force?
No. The result shows with what partial hands the gods
Weighed down the scale against us, and destroyed us all.
It is the gods who keep Athene's city safe. . . .

At last
Over the earth shone the white horses of the day,
Filling the air with beauty. Then from the Hellene ships
Rose like a song of joy the piercing battle-cry,

Excerpted from *Prometheus Bound and Other Plays,* by Aeschylus, translated by Philip Vellacott (Penguin Classics, 1961). Copyright © 1961 by Philip Vellacott. Reprinted by permission of Penguin Books Ltd.

And from the island crags echoed an answering shout.

The Persians knew their error; fear gripped every man.
They were no fugitives who sang that terrifying
Paean, but Hellenes charging with courageous hearts
To battle. The loud trumpet flamed along their ranks.
At once their frothy oars moved with a single pulse,
Beating the salt waves to the bo'suns' chant; and soon
Their whole fleet hove clear into view; their right wing first,
In precise order, next their whole array came on,
And at that instant a great shout beat on our ears:
'Forward, you sons of Hellas! Set your country free!
Set free your sons, your wives, tombs of your ancestors,
And temples of your gods. All is at stake: now fight!'
Then from our side in answer rose the manifold
Clamour of Persian voices; and the hour had come.

At once ship into ship battered its brazen beak.
A Hellene ship charged first, and chopped off the whole stern
Of a Phoenician galley. Then charge followed charge
On every side. At first by its huge impetus
Our fleet withstood them. But soon, in that narrow space,
Our ships were jammed in hundreds; none could help another.
They rammed each other with their prows of bronze; and some
Were stripped of every oar. Meanwhile the enemy
Came round us in a ring and charged. Our vessels heeled
Over; the sea was hidden, carpeted with wrecks
And dead men; all the shores and reefs were full of dead.

Then every ship we had broke rank and rowed for life.
The Hellenes seized fragments of wrecks and broken oars
And hacked and stabbed at our men swimming in the sea
As fishermen kill tunnies or some netted haul.
The whole sea was one din of shrieks and dying groans,
Till night and darkness hid the scene. If I should speak
For ten days and ten nights, I could not tell you all
That day's agony. But know this: never before
In one day died so vast a company of men. . . .

SLAUGHTER ON THE ISLAND

But there is more, and worse; my story is not half told.
Be sure, what follows twice outweighs what went before. . . .

The flower of Persian chivalry and gentle blood,
The youth and valour of our choice nobility,
First in unmoved devotion to the king himself,
Are sunk into the mire of ignominious death. . . .

Opposite Salamis
There is an island. . . .
There Xerxes sent them, so that, when the enemy,
Flung from their ships, were struggling to the island beach,
The Persian force might without trouble cut them down,
And rescue Persian crews from drowning in the sea:
Fatal misjudtement! When in the sea-battle Heaven
Had given glory to the Hellenes, that same day
They came, armed with bronze shields and spears, leapt from
    their ships,
And made a ring round the whole island, that our men
Could not tell where to turn. First came a shower of blows
From stones slung with the hand; then from the drawn bow-
    string
Arrows leapt forth to slaughter; finally, with one
Fierce roar the Hellenes rushed at them, and cut and carved
Their limbs like butchers, till the last poor wretch lay dead.

This depth of horror Xerxes saw; close to the sea
On a high hill he sat, where he could clearly watch
His whole force both by sea and land. He wailed aloud,
And tore his clothes, weeping; and instantly dismissed
His army, hastening them to a disordered flight. . . .

The captains of surviving ships spread sail and fled
In swift disorder with a following wind. On land
The remnants of the army suffered fearful loss,
Tortured by hunger, thirst, exhaustion. . . .
He who died Quickest, was luckiest. The handful who survived,
Suffering untold hardship, struggled on through Thrace
To safety, and now at last have reached their native earth.

So, well may Persia's cities mourn their young men lost.
I have spoken truth; yet all I have told is but a part
Of all the evil God sent to strike Persia down.

ATHENS RISES TO GREATNESS

CHESTER G. STARR

After the stunning Greek defeat of Persia in the early fifth century B.C., Athens was the largest, most populous, and one of the two strongest city-states in Greece (the other being Sparta). Athens had also recently instituted the world's first democracy, a reflection of the political boldness and vigor of its leaders and citizens. The energetic Athenians took full advantage of these attributes, first by becoming the leader of the Delian Confederacy (or League), an alliance of over a hundred cities formed to guard Greece against further Persian incursions; and second, by turning the Confederacy into what was essentially a powerful eastern Mediterranean Empire controlled by and chiefly benefiting Athens. As the late, noted classical scholar Chester G. Starr explains here, under the leadership of Pericles a goodly portion of the funds from the Confederacy went to beautify Athens, which rapidly became an important center of artistic and cultural endeavors and democratic experimentation. The city displayed its newfound grandeur in the construction of public buildings atop its central hill, the Acropolis, and in its splendid yearly religious festival, the Panathenaea. And in Pericles' words (as reported by his younger contemporary, the historian Thucydides), Athens became the "school of Greece" (i.e., an example for other Greeks).

T he evolution of democracy at home was intimately connected with the increasing imperialism of Athens abroad. The commercial and industrial elements, which benefited from the growth of seaborne trade, were a bulwark of the Assembly. In turn, the general unity of all classes made it possible for Athens to exert greater strength abroad. The result was a sea-based empire spread over much of the Aegean.

THE FIRST IMPORTANT WESTERN EMPIRE

This empire had begun 40 years earlier as a voluntary associa-tion of Greek states, the Delian League, which wanted to keep back the Persians after their invasion of Greece in 480–479 B.C. Athens was by far the largest member of this league and more or less unconsciously converted the voluntary into an involuntary bond over the next three decades.

At its height the Athenian empire covered some 170 Greek communities on the north and east coasts of the Aegean, reach-ing from Byzantium down to the south coast of Asia Minor. The empire had a population of some 2 million people; but Athenian naval power was an important factor all the way from Sicily to the Black Sea. Almost all subject states paid an annual tribute to-taling about 400 talents a year (1 talent had 6000 drachmas, and a drachma was more than a day's pay for a worker). Much of this money was spent as soon as it came in; the surplus was stored on the Acropolis at Athens.

The dependent states also had to follow Athenian foreign pol-icy; use Athenian weights, measures, and coins; and send major lawsuits to Athens, which thus could protect its local friends. Generally the subjects could have any form of government they wished, even tyranny so long as it was loyal; but if they revolted, Athens was likely to favor institution of a democracy on recon-quest. Loyalty to the imperial master was also encouraged by the presence of Athenian colonies or garrisons at certain points and by a variety of traveling inspectors; ultimately obedience was forced by the Athenian navy, the costs of which were paid by the tribute of the subjects. In peacetime some 60 triremes, each with a crew of 200 men (150 rowers and others), would be at sea for eight months of the year.

Just as the Athenians created the first great democracy, so too they developed the first important empire in Western civilization. They argued about building an empire far more openly and fiercely than have subsequent imperialists (who sometimes have not been aware they *were* imperialists). Athenian subjects, how-ever, had only limited opportunity to enter the debate; if they ex-pressed any disagreements by revolts or failure to pay tribute, they were treated ruthlessly by Athens. Many subjects felt that their position was one of "slavery," but traders appreciated the security of the seas brought by the Athenian navy and also the prosperity of the period.

MIGHT MAKES RIGHT?

Many Athenians, however, were troubled. They felt uneasy at the free manner in which Pericles used the tribute of the empire to beautify Athens itself; the subjection of fellow Greeks seemed unjust; conservative landowners did not like the way the naval empire encouraged the trading and industrial lower classes. In an ostracism contest in 443, the anti-imperialists tried to get rid of Pericles; but the result was that their leader was ostracized. Cleon and his friends were too proud of Athenian power and wealth to give up foreign rule. Even the Parthenon was a product of imperialism: tributes had paid its costs.

Later the historian Thucydides drew a grim picture of how the Athenians equated might and right, grew increasingly vindictive in killing rebels, and dreamed of ruling all the Greek world. Democracy at home made imperialism abroad more inevitable and ruthless, and Athenian imperialism in time led to the mighty fall of Athens in 404 [in the climax of the Peloponnesian War, fought against Sparta and its allies]; for the free Greeks who lived in Sparta, Corinth, and elsewhere eventually became deeply alarmed by Athenian expansion. But no one in the period of Periclean prosperity could foresee the future.

There is, however, another view of the picture to be kept in mind, for imperialism is not necessarily as bad an institution as it is often depicted to be. As long as Athens was master of the Aegean, its merchants were free from the danger of piracy, and the Greek world as a whole was safe from Persia. After the fall of Athens . . . Persia became more and more the ultimate judge of what happened in 4th-century Greece.

THE SCHOOL OF GREECE

In his Funeral Oration, Pericles calls Athens "the school of Greece," and certainly in the time of Pericles, Athens became the center to which foreign thinkers were drawn, as they now may be drawn to London or New York. In the same period, native-born Athenians were writing those tragedies and comedies which are the first great achievements of Western drama, and other men were turning the Acropolis into an eternal home of beauty. This artistic and literary outburst is one of the most concentrated and amazing triumphs of all human history.

Why did it take place? At any one time most men live from day to day, earning their daily bread and enduring the cares and uncertainties of human existence; if Cleon went beyond these chores, he could spend most of his time on his duties as a citizen and a ruler of a large empire. Still, all phases of life were tightly interwoven in this small, closely knit country. Artistic and literary de-

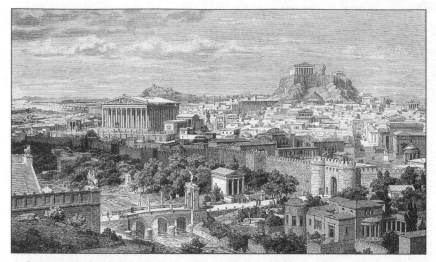

Athens as it probably appeared during the early second century A.D., *when Greece was part of the Roman Empire. The famous Acropolis rises in the distance at upper right.*

velopments, then, were not entirely separate matters for experts, but were directly tied to the religious and public life of Athens. The revenues of the empire and of Athens' growing commerce provided surplus money; the confidence and expansiveness of the age encouraged men to create boldly; most important of all, Greek civilization had developed a solid basis for great achievements.

Temples which are masterpieces of refinement and harmony were erected in the 5th century all over the Greek world. Sculptors too were busy everywhere; probably the greatest sculptural decoration of any temple is that of the Temple of Zeus at Olympia. Of the poets of this age the greatest was Pindar of Thebes, who celebrated the aristocratic merits of victors at the great athletic games in shimmering, virtually untranslatable Greek verse. Nowhere, however, was there such an outpouring as at Athens.

HIGHER LEARNING

Down to the 5th century virtually all Greek writing was in the form of poetry, but shortly before 500, prose had been developed as a literary means of expression. Sometimes it was used for scholarly work, including the medical treatises which go under the name of Hippocrates. (We do not, incidentally, know very much that is certain about this great doctor; but it is clear that Greek medicine, unlike earlier semi-religious superstitions, assigned earthly causes to human illnesses and sought to cure them by rational means for the first time.) Other prose work of the 5th century included the great histories of Herodotus and Thucydides, philosophical essays, and orations.

The busy, practical Athenians of this period were not much interested in knowledge for its own sake. The philosopher-scientist Anaxagoras, the first to know the real causes of eclipses, came to Athens and discussed his theories about the origins of the world; but when he asserted the sun, usually considered a god, was really a molten rock larger than the Peloponnesus the Athenians expelled him for irreligious thoughts. Soon after 440, however, Athens began to draw from all over the Greek world teachers called "sophists," men who could impart the useful skills of oratory and argument; these sophists were the real founders of advanced education and began the formal study of rhetoric, logic, and grammar. At the same time they were sharp critics of ancestral political and religious conventions.

TRAGEDY AND COMEDY

The greatest Athenian contribution to literature was the rise of drama. Twice a year, tragedies and comedies were performed at festivals in honor of the god Dionysus. . . .

Of the comedies, only some of the works of Aristophanes have been preserved. These are remarkably varied in subject. One play, the *Clouds*, is a bitter attack on the philosopher Socrates, who is portrayed as a sophist leading the young to make fun of their elders. Another comedy, the *Frogs*, assaults the tragedian Euripides as also corrupting the younger generation; here Aristophanes expects his audience to be able to appreciate mock quotations from Aeschylus and Euripides. The *Birds* is a marvelous fantasy of some Athenians, discontented with the lawsuits and contentions of their daily life, who try to live with the birds and set up an ideal Birdland. Others are direct attacks on major political leaders or on the war with Sparta then raging. Whatever their subject, these comedies combine lyric poetry, quick repartee, and outright obscenity in a frankness of speech rarely equaled in later ages.

The subject of a tragedy was usually a legend of the heroic age, such as the war of Argos and Thebes or the tales clustered about the Homeric heroes; but plays might also deal with historic events. The one surviving example of the latter type is Aeschylus' *Persians*, performed in 472 with Pericles as producer.

Narration of a story or legend, however, was only a means by which the author might explore the nature of mankind; and in doing so, the tragedian turned firmly away from realistic depictions of Athenian citizens to an ideal level of heroic men and women. Even the gods themselves might appear on occasion. However great, the human beings in a tragedy had flaws which led them to ruin; the authors who brought these heroes to life before Cleon and his fellow citizens sought not so much to explain how the universe operated as to illuminate the greatnesses and defects of mankind.

Although many authors vied in the annual competitions, the three who were considered the greatest were Aeschylus, Sophocles, and Euripides. Aeschylus was a deeply religious thinker, although at times he exhibits the strong hold of earlier tradition. His plays, like the *Agamemnon,* are brooding dramas of inevitable, catastrophic ruin, in which passion is still ill-restrained and in which the religious and aristocratic qualities of 6th-century Greece are powerful. His characters stand almost outside the human world, and his poetry rumbles with the thunder of bold images.

Most balanced and serene of the three was Sophocles, who was a friend of Pericles and on occasion an elected general of the Athenian democracy. He is said to have written 123 plays and won first place 24 times, but only 7 plays are preserved. The greatest of these is generally considered to be *Oedipus the King,* performed shortly after 430. . . .

With Euripides, the last of the three great tragedians, we step almost outside the boundaries of 5th-century civilization. In his lifetime Euripides was rarely successful, for he won first prize only five times. Before his death he had abandoned the tottering, bitter Athens of the Peloponnesian war and withdrew to Macedonia, where he wrote the *Bacchae* and some other plays. Yet his skepticism about the divine government of the world and his sympathetic treatment of human passion in such female figures as Medea, Alcestis, and Iphigenia made him a favorite of later ages; no ancient playwright appears more often on the modern stage than Euripides.

THE NATURE OF MAN

The 5th-century view of man is nowhere better displayed than in the Attic tragedies. Again and again a great man or woman stepped forth upon the stage, only to be stripped of pride and often to die violently in ruin. The vehicle for the ruin was a man's own flaws, for man was free; and yet behind all lay the immortal gods, who punished undue pride (*hybris*). In tragedy the moral lesson was to cultivate *sophrosyne,* a proper balance and awareness of one's true position.

Nonetheless the tragedians shared a pride in man's achievements and his independence of action. Most noble of all is the great praise by the chorus in Sophocles' *Antigone,* which begins, "Wonders are many, and none is more wonderful than man." Man crosses the sea, harnesses the earth, teaches himself word-swift thought and speech; "cunning beyond fancy's dream is the fertile skill which brings him, now to evil, now to good."

The balanced view of man; the serene, even severe temper of tragedy; the welling passion which is restrained almost unconsciously by a sense of proper form—all these are qualities of what we call the "Classic outlook." In a play such as *Oedipus the King* the tempo is slow and deliberate at the outset, but speeds up irresistibly. . . .

Like Classic art and architecture the play has an outwardly simple, austere treatment which omits the insignificant diversions, on-stage violence, and by-plots so evident in Shakespeare's plays. The whole development of *Oedipus the King* takes only 1530 lines. Yet the tight logical construction of the play, its skillful proportions, and its artistic quality are a superb example of the developed Greek mind. When Oedipus fiercely proclaimed, "I must not hear of not discovering the whole truth," he expressed the consistent effort of the Greek thinker to plunge to the heart of a problem, no matter what the cost.

PERICLES: SHAPER OF A GREAT AGE

PLUTARCH

A good deal of Athens's success in the mid–fifth century B.C. was the result of the efforts of its strong, vigorous leader, Pericles. In this excerpt from his biography of Pericles, the first-century A.D. Greek writer Plutarch tells first how his subject was an aristocrat who championed the common people and democracy. Then the narrative describes Pericles' unusual abilities as an orator (an important tool he used to sway the people and hold onto power) and the achievement for which he is most famous in the eyes of posterity—the construction of the Parthenon and other temples atop the Acropolis, works of timeless majesty.

A s a young man Pericles was inclined to shrink from facing the people. One reason for this was that he was considered to bear a distinct resemblance to the tyrant Pisistratus [who ruled Athens during the prior century], and when men who were well on in years remarked on the charm of Pericles' voice and the smoothness and fluency of his speech, they were astonished at the resemblance between the two. The fact that he was rich and that he came of a distinguished family and possessed exceedingly powerful friends made the fear of ostracism very real to him, and at the beginning of his career he took no part in politics but devoted himself to soldiering, in which he showed great daring and enterprise. However . . . at last Pericles decided to attach himself to the people's party and to take up the cause of the poor and the many instead of that of the rich and the few, in spite of the fact that this was quite con-

Excerpted from "The Life of Pericles," in *The Rise and Fall of Athens: Nine Greek Lives*, by Plutarch, translated by Ian Scott-Kilvert (Penguin Classics, 1973). Translation copyright © Ian Scott-Kilvert, 1973. Reprinted by permission of Penguin Books Ltd.

trary to his own temperament, which was thoroughly aristo-cratic. He was afraid, apparently, of being suspected of aiming at a dictatorship; so . . . he began to ingratiate himself with the people, partly for self-preservation and partly by way of secur-ing power. . . .

EMBARKING ON A POLITICAL CAREER

He now entered upon a new mode of life. He was never to be seen walking in any street except the one which led to the market place and the Council-chamber. He refused not only invitations to dinner but every kind of friendly or familiar intercourse, so that through all the years of his political career, he never visited one of his friends to dine. The only exception was an occasion when his great-uncle Euryptolemus gave a wedding-feast. . . .

Pericles wished to equip himself with a style of speaking which, like a musical accomplishment, should harmonize per-fectly with his mode of life and the grandeur of his ideals, and he . . . far excelled all other speakers. This was the reason, some people say, for his being nicknamed the Olympian, though oth-ers believe that it was on account of the buildings with which he adorned Athens, and others again because of his prowess as a statesman and a general; but it may well have been the combi-nation of many qualities which earned him the name. However, the comic poets of the time, who were constantly letting fly at him either in earnest or in fun, declare that the title originated mainly from his manner of speaking. They refer to him as thun-dering and lightning when he addressed his audience and as wielding a terrible thunderbolt in his tongue. . . .

The truth is, however, that even Pericles was extremely cau-tious in his use of words, so much so that whenever he rose to speak, he uttered a prayer that no word might escape his lips which was unsuited to the matter in hand. He left nothing be-hind him in writing except for the decrees he proposed, and only a very few of his sayings have been handed down. . . . [For ex-ample] in his funeral oration for those who had fallen in the war against Samos, Pericles declared that these men had become im-mortal like the gods: 'for we cannot see the gods,' he said, 'but we believe them to be immortal from the honours we pay them and the blessings we receive from them, and so it is with those who have given their lives for their country.'. . .

A SHREWD AND EFFECTIVE POLITICIAN

At the beginning of his career, as we have seen, Pericles had to measure himself against [his rival, the aristocrat] Cimon's repu-tation, and he therefore set out to win the favour of the people. He could not compete with the wealth or the property by means of which Cimon captured the affections of the poor; for the latter supplied a free dinner every day to any Athenian who needed it, provided clothes for the old, and took down the fences on his estates so that anyone who wished could pick the fruit. So finding himself outmatched in this kind of popular appeal, Pericles turned his attention to the distribution of the public wealth . . . and before long, what with the allowances for public festivals, fees for jury service, and other grants and gratuities, he succeeded in bribing the masses wholesale and enlisting their support in his attack on the [aristocratic] Council of the Areopagus. Pericles was not himself a member of this body. . . . Because he had thus been excluded, Pericles, once he had gathered popular support, exerted himself all the more to lead his party in a campaign against the Areopagus, and he succeeded so well that not only was it deprived of most of its judicial powers . . . but Cimon himself was ostracized [banished for ten years] on the charge of being a friend of Sparta and an enemy of the people's interests. Yet this was a man who was second to none in Athens in birth or in wealth, who had won the most brilliant victories over the Persians and filled the city with money and treasure, as has been recorded in his Life. Such was the strength of Pericles' hold over the people. . . .

The aristocratic party had already recognized for some time that Pericles was now the most important man in Athens and that he wielded far more power than any other citizen. But they were anxious that there should be someone in the city capable of standing up to him so as to blunt the edge of his authority and prevent it from becoming an outright monarchy. They therefore put forward Thucydides, of Alopece, a man of good sense and a relative of Cimon, to lead the opposition. He was less of a soldier than Cimon, but better versed in forensic business and an abler politician, and by watching his opportunities at home and engaging Pericles in debate, he soon succeeded in creating a balance of power in Athenian affairs. . . . Pericles therefore chose this moment to hand over the reins of power to the people to a greater extent than ever before and deliberately shaped his policy to please them. He constantly provided public pageants, banquets, and processions in the city, entertaining the people like children with elegant pleasures; and he sent out sixty triremes to cruise every year, in which many of the citizens served with pay for eight months and learned and practised seamanship at the same time. . . .

THE CREATION OF TIMELESS WORKS

But there was one measure above all which at once gave the greatest pleasure to the Athenians, adorned their city and created amazement among the rest of mankind, and which is today the sole testimony that the tales of the ancient power and glory of Greece are no mere fables. By this I mean his construction of temples and public buildings; and yet it was this, more than any other action of his, which his enemies slandered and misrepresented. They cried out in the Assembly that Athens had lost her good name and disgraced herself by transferring from Delos into her own keeping the funds that had been contributed by the rest of Greece, and that now the most plausible excuse for this action, namely, that the money had been removed for fear of the barbarians and was being guarded in a safe place, had been demolished by Pericles himself. 'The Greeks must be outraged,' they cried. 'They must consider this an act of bare-faced tyranny, when they see that with their own contributions, extorted from them by force for the war against the Persians, we are gilding and beautifying our city, as if it were some vain woman decking herself out with costly stones and statues and temples worth millions of money.'

Pericles' answer to the people was that the Athenians were not obliged to give the allies any account of how their money was spent, provided that they carried on the war for them and kept the Persians away. 'They do not give us a single horse, nor a soldier, nor a ship. All they supply is money,' he told the Athenians, 'and this belongs not to the people who give it, but to those who receive it, so long as they provide the services they are paid for. It is no more than fair that after Athens has been equipped with all she needs to carry on the war, she should apply the surplus to public works, which, once completed, will bring her glory for all time, and while they are being built will convert that surplus to immediate use. In this way all kinds of enterprises and demands will be created which will provide inspiration for every art, find employment for every hand, and transform the whole people into wage-earners, so that the city will decorate and maintain herself at the same time from her own resources.'

Certainly it was true that those who were of military age and physically in their prime could always earn their pay from the public funds by serving on Pericles' various campaigns. But he was also anxious that the unskilled masses, who had no military training, should not be debarred from benefiting from the national income, and yet should not be paid for sitting about and doing nothing. So he boldly laid before the people proposals for immense public works and plans for buildings, which would involve many different arts and industries and require long periods to complete, his object being that those who stayed at home, no less than those serving in the fleet or the army or on garrison duty, should be enabled to enjoy a share of the national wealth. . . .

So the buildings arose, as imposing in their sheer size as they were inimitable in the grace of their outlines, since the artists strove to excel themselves in the beauty of their workmanship. And yet the most wonderful thing about them was the speed with which they were completed. Each of them, men supposed, would take many generations to build, but in fact the entire project was carried through in the high summer of one man's administration. . . . It is this, above all, which makes Pericles' works an object of wonder to us—the fact that they were created in so short a span, and yet for all time. Each one possessed a beauty which seemed venerable the moment it was born, and at the same time a youthful vigour which makes them appear to this day as if they were newly built. A bloom of eternal freshness hovers over these works of his and preserves them from the touch of time, as if some unfading spirit of youth, some ageless vitality had been breathed into them.

THE PELOPONNESIAN WAR DEVASTATES GREECE

CHARLES FREEMAN

Charles Freeman, author of several recent widely read books about ancient Greece and Rome, begins this overview of the so-called "great war" by reviewing the immediate causes of the conflict. Then he examines the Greek historian who chronicled the war. Without Thucydides' honest reporting, attention to detail, and vivid writing, Freeman points out, later ages would be left with no record of much of the event that brought Athens to its knees and left the Greek world shattered and exhausted. He then goes on to summarize the war's highlights, including the ill-fated Sicilian expedition, Alcibiades' treachery, and Athens's eventual defeat after a decisive Spartan naval victory on the Hellespont.

The Athenians intruded with growing recklessness in the west. In 433 Athenians approached Corinth's colony Corfu, a vital staging post on the way to the west and the state with the third biggest navy in Greece, supporting her in breaking away from Corinth. A small Athenian fleet, of ten triremes, actually clashed with the Corinthian fleet, which withdrew when another Athenian force came up in support. Corfu had been defended but there was now open hostility between Athens and Corinth. Trouble then brewed in the Corinthian colony of Potidaea, which had been a member of the Delian League and thus absorbed into the empire. Athens had been worried about its loyalty and demanded the dismissal of its Corinthian magistrates.

The Potidaeans naturally called on Corinth and Sparta for help and then broke into a revolt which was joined by several of their neighbors (432). Altogether seventy Athenian triremes had to be sent to quell the revolt while Corinth retaliated by sending a force of two thousand hoplites. The Athenians were forced to settle down to a three-year siege.

These were symptoms of a deteriorating situation. Corinth was now in total opposition to Athens and was driven towards Sparta, which, Thucydides makes clear, was simmering with resentment at the continued Athenian expansion that, on her own, she could do nothing to prevent. Here at last was a chance for revenge. Athenian forces were in Potidaea, the Corinthian navy was available, and support was offered by the strategically placed Megara, which seems to have been under some trade ban from Athens. Sparta could pose as a liberator of the subject cities of the empire. These were all factors that tipped the balance. A state of war between Sparta and Athens had to be created, however, and this was done by Sparta's encouraging Thebes, one of her allies, to attack Plataea, an ally of Athens since the heady days of Marathon. It was an outrage to the sacred rules of war but it broke the tension. The Peloponnesian War (431–404), actually the second under this name, was under way.

THUCYDIDES: THE WAR'S CHRONICLER

There is a fine contemporary history of the Peloponnesian War, written by Thucydides, an Athenian aristocrat connected to Cimon's family. Thucydides was in the center of things, a survivor of the devastating plague of 430 in Athens and a general in the northern Aegean in 424. When he failed to save the trading center of Amphipolis from the Spartans in that year he was exiled and spent the twenty years to his death outside Athens. He retained contacts there but was now free to travel the Peloponnese to gather the story of the Spartan side of the war. His account had reached the year 411 by the time he died around 400 B.C.

As soon as the war began Thucydides grasped its importance in comparison to earlier wars in Greek history (he was right, the Peloponnesian War was to Greek history what the First World War was to European) and he determined to write a documentary history of events as they unfolded. He took himself and his craft seriously, contrasting himself with Herodotus whom he derided for his loose use of sources and inaccuracies. He, he insisted, was of a different stature, recording what actually happened. . . . In his penetration to the core of human motivation, his steady gaze on the horrors of war, his superb narrative power, Thucydides ranks as one of Europe's major historians.

Generally, Thucydides has been taken at his own word and the truthfulness and accuracy of what he wrote accepted. This should not mask the fact that what he chose to describe was highly selective. . . . Unlike Herodotus, for instance, Thucydides is not interested in the cultural background to the societies that fought the war, nor, as a modern historian might be, how each side raised the resources to fight it. Rather it is the events of the war themselves that interest him. . . .

What seems to have fascinated Thucydides was not just the events of the war but the way human beings reacted to the pressures these created. Here Thucydides shared one of the preoccupations of his age, intense critical interest in human nature. What conditioned the ways human beings behaved? Were there common human instincts found in every society or did society shape behavior through conventions and custom? Was the way human behaved in particular circumstances predictable, as many other aspects of the physical world were seen to be? The answers could perhaps be found from observation and in this sense Thucydides' detached narrative acts as a laboratory for the dissection of human behavior. . . .

Thucydides' world is a bleak one, made bleaker by the vicious nature of the fighting he describes. The Peloponnesian War was a war of terror and counterterror, one in which whole cities were destroyed and their inhabitants enslaved or massacred.

INITIAL STALEMATE

When the war began in 431 Pericles had been Athens' leading statesman for over twenty years, a remarkable achievement in a city that was ruled by a volatile assembly of its citizens. He is Thucydides' hero and he is portrayed as having a shrewd and realistic idea of the strengths and weaknesses of his city. What was essential, Pericles argued, was to keep the fleet intact, the trade routes secure, and the empire stable. The Long Walls constructed in 458 that ran around the city and down to enclose the Piraeus had made it impregnable from the land and allowed it to be provisioned by sea. This meant that Attica itself could be abandoned without Athens itself being lost and Pericles ordered those living there to come into the city. . . . Further pressures were added when plague swept through Athens in 430, killing perhaps a quarter of the population. Those who had come into the city and settled in closely packed huts were the worst affected. Thucydides describes the plague in one of his great set pieces, analyzing its symptoms with scientific precision but making no attempt to mask the emotional devastation it brought.

The war soon settled into stalemate. There seemed no obvious way that either side could secure a decisive victory. Athens did not have sufficient land forces to defeat Sparta, Sparta the naval forces to destroy Athens. The Spartans ravaged Attica regularly during the 420s but there was no way they could seriously weaken the city by doing so. The Athenians counterattacked along the Peloponnesian coast. . . . [Pericles] died in 429. Thucydides now records that policy fell into the hands of more unscrupulous leaders from nonaristocratic backgrounds and associates this with a more volatile foreign policy. Cleon, for instance, owner of a tanning shop, persuaded the Assembly to order the execution of all the men of Mytilene and the enslavement of its women and children after the city had revolted in 428. (After reflection, the Assembly reconsidered its decision.) However, in 425 Athens had a stroke of luck when 120 Spartans on the island of Sphacteria off the western Peloponnese were captured and taken back as hostages to Athens. Such a public surrender was deeply humiliating for Sparta and the loss of even such a small force of highly trained men important when Spartan manpower appears to have been in decline. . . . Some face was saved the following year when a Spartan general Brasidas took an expedition to the northern Aegean and captured the trading city of Amphipolis and several others before being killed in 422. (Cleon who was leading the Athenian expedition against him was killed at the same time.) Both sides were now happy to make peace (the Peace of Nicias, 421 B.C.). . . .

The peace, however, did not hold. Thucydides never believed it would; there was simply too much unfinished business. Nothing, for instance, had been done for Megara or for Corinth, which had lost several possessions in the northern Aegean and which now turned against Sparta for failing to protect her interests. By 418 Athens was again meddling in the Peloponnese, exploiting the traditional hostility of Argos for Sparta to create an anti-Spartan coalition. . . . . Once again the enormous superiority of Sparta's hoplite training and tactics was shown when at the battle of Mantineia, one of the largest hoplite battles recorded with perhaps twenty thousand men involved, she crushed her enemies. The humiliation of Sphacteria was revenged and Spartan supremacy on land reaffirmed. The survival of Sparta at this moment could, with hindsight, be seen as the turning point of the war. . . .

ALCIBIADES SWAYS THE ASSEMBLY

The Athenian intrusion in the Peloponnese had been masterminded by a flamboyant but unscrupulous young aristocrat, Alcibiades. Alcibiades was to prove a competent soldier and a skilled diplomat but these qualities were overlaid by his egotism and personal ambition. He believed that the Assembly would be impressed by his wealth, which he spent with open panache, and the recent success of his chariot teams in the Olympic Games. Some citizens undoubtedly were but others felt that such profligacy was not suited to a democratic city. Their preferred politician was the older and more cautious Nicias who had masterminded the peace of 421 with Sparta. The two men fought openly before the Assembly over what should be the next move in the war.

By chance a city of Sicily, Segesta, had appealed for help to Athens against its neighbor Selinus who was a protégée of Syracuse, the wealthiest city of Sicily (and originally a foundation of Corinth's). The fertility of the island and southern Italy was well known. So the possibility of sending an expedition to Sicily to support Athens' allies' there again and to consolidate the economic links was attractive. However, it was difficult to see how such an expedition would help defeat Sparta, except indirectly through cutting off the grain supply of the island to the Peloponnese. . . . However, a proposal to send an expedition of sixty ships was accepted by the Assembly. A fleet of this size could have been spared, but a few days later in an impassioned debate dominated by Alcibiades who played on the supposed ease with which Sicily could be conquered and the enormous wealth which would accrue to Athens if she was, a plan to send a much larger expedition was adopted by an emotionally charged Assembly. Little thought was given to how Sicily would have been held, and most important of all, what would happen if the expedition failed. Here Thucydides' assertion (reinforced no doubt by his own aristocratic perspective) that democratic assemblies were not always the best decision makers seems justified.

There were three generals appointed to lead the expedition, Alcibiades, the experienced Nicias (who, though he had always opposed the expedition, was not prepared to let his city down by refusing a command), and one Lamarchus, brought in to balance these two political opponents. One hundred thirty-four triremes and five thousand hoplites were ready to sail by the summer of 415 but the expedition's departure was marred when a number of the Herms, marble pillars bearing the head of the god Hermes and an erect phallus which acted as boundary markers in the city, were found with the phalluses (normally a sign of good luck) mutilated. No one can be sure who was behind this vandalism but the city was shaken by the experience and the fleet set off haunted by the episode.

DISASTER AT SYRACUSE

The account of the Sicilian expedition is normally seen as the high point of Thucydides' work. He places it after the episode in which the people of Melos, a neutral Spartan colony in the Cyclades, were massacred by the Athenians, perhaps to make the point that Athens deserved the disaster that followed in Sicily. And it was a disaster. The fleet arrived and found little support from the Sicilians. (Athens' allies in Sicily had exaggerated their resources to attract her support.) It was soon clear that any success would depend on the capture of Syracuse but the three commanders quarreled over how this should be done. Alcibiades' enemies got him recalled on a charge of complicity in the mutilation of the Herms (but he defected to Sparta instead, an indication of

The Spartans inflict heavy casualties as they pursue the retreating Athenians across the Sicilian countryside near Syracuse. Almost all the Athenian troops were either killed or captured.

the shallowness of his loyalty to his city) and Lamarchus was killed in skirmishing before Syracuse. Nicias, who had opposed the expedition all along, now found himself in charge. He did manage to capture Syracuse's harbor and land the hoplites but before the city itself could be taken its resolve was stiffened by the arrival of a Spartan force. Athens sent reinforcements but the original fleet now found itself blocked into the harbor by Syracuse's own navy. There was a desperate battle to break out, brilliantly told by Thucydides from the perspective of the watching Athenian hoplites:

> As the struggle went on indecisively, the Athenian soldiers revealed the fear in their hearts by the swaying of their bodies; it was a time of agony for them, for escape or destruction seemed every moment just at hand. So long as the issue of the seabattle was in doubt, you could have heard every kind of sound in one place, the Athenian camp: lamentation, shouting, "We're winning!," "We're losing!," all the cries wrung from a great army in great peril. The feelings of the men on the ships were much the same, until at last, when the battle had gone on for a long time, the Syracusans and their allies routed the Athenians and fell upon them, decisive winners, yelling and cheering, and chased them to the land. And then the Athenian sailors, as many of them as had not been captured afloat, beached their ships wherever they could and poured into the camp. The soldiers were not in two minds any more, but all with one impulse, groaning, wailing, lamenting the outcome of the battle, rallied—some of them close to the ships, others to guard the rest of their defensive wall, while the greater part of them began to think now about themselves, about how they were going to survive.

> (Translation: Sir Kenneth Dover)

After a final attempt to break out failed, the Athenian army was left with little alternative but to retreat overland. Harassed by Spartans and Syracusans they were finally cowed into surrender and herded back to imprisonment in the stone quarries which surrounded Syracuse. Altogether some forty thousand lives may have been lost as well as half the Athenian fleet.

SPARTA SEIZES THE GRAIN ROUTE

Athens was weakened in every sense by the Sicilian disaster through the loss of manpower and shipping, through the shattering of her prestige within the empire, through political turmoil at home when her democratic government was overthrown by a pro-Spartan government of Four Hundred. Sparta even set up a base within Athenian territory at Decelea from where she lured some twenty thousand slaves, many of them mine workers, away from Athens. Yet for the time being Athens survived. There were revolts by subject cities in the northern Aegean and along the coast of Asia Minor but most were subdued. Many cities in fact remained loyal largely because Persia was now reemerging as a force in the Aegean and rule by an Athenian democracy was preferable to domination by a barbarian tyranny. Ships were rebuilt and the government of Four Hundred was replaced by a more democratic one (of Five Thousand) when it tried to make peace with Sparta.

It was the reemergence of Persia that was to tip the balance in the war. Persia had the resources to help whichever side was prepared to drop its scruples and accept that something would be demanded in return. Sparta was the one who clinched the deal (411). Abandoning any pretense that it was a liberator of the Greeks, Sparta secured Persian money with which to build a fleet. . . .

As Sparta built ships and recruited mercenaries to man them, the focus of the war now shifted to the northern Aegean. If Sparta's vulnerability lay among the helots of Messenia, Athens' was in the Hellespont, the channel through which the city's essential grain supplies came. The region had now become accessible to Sparta and so the next years of the war were thus dominated by a bitter struggle between the two fleets for control of the Aegean and access to the Black Sea. Byzantium, overlooking the entrance to Bosporus and hence to the Black Sea itself, was captured by the Spartans in 411. The Athenians regained it in 408. Athenian victories in 411 and 410 nearly brought Sparta to sign peace and the city suffered another major defeat at Arginusae (near Lesbos) in 406. As the years passed, however, it was the impact of Persian gold that told as the Spartans were able to continually rebuild and man their fleet. In 405 the Spartan commander, Lysander managed to gain a safe harbor within the Hellespont itself at Lampsachus. The Athenians had no such protection and were forced to use an open beach opposite at Aegospotamae. Every attempt to lure the Spartans out to battle failed and in the end it was a devastating surprise attack on the beached ships by Lysander that decided the issue; 170 out of 180 Athenian triremes were captured and the grain routes of the Hellespont closed.

"As the news of the disaster reached Athens" wrote the historian Xenophon, "one man passed it on to another, and a sound of wailing arose and extended first from the Piraeus, then along the Long Walls until it reached the city. That night no one slept. They mourned for the lost but more still for their own fate. They thought they themselves would now be dealt with as they had dealt with others." (Translation: Rex Warner.) As the food supplies dried up, the city had little option but to surrender (May 404). Even though the city was not razed to the ground, its men killed and its women enslaved . . . the terms of the peace treaty were harsh: the loss of the empire, much of the remaining fleet, and the destruction of the great walls which had surrounded the city. Lysander then used a perceived delay in pulling down the walls as an excuse for imposing a government of Thirty Men (later dubbed tyrants by the Athenians) on the city though democratic government reasserted itself in October 403.

ATHENS HUMBLED, GREECE EXHAUSTED

The Peloponnesian War changed the course of Greek history as significantly as the First World War changed Europe's. It is hard to know for how long Athens would have maintained control of her subjects if the war had been won, but there is the possibility that victory in Sicily and the consolidation of the island's resources in the service of Athens could have produced a self-sustaining empire which would eventually have been able to tackle Sparta. With the collapse of the expedition and the defeat of Athens, Greek politics resumed their earlier course, one in which a number of city-states fought among themselves for leadership of their surrounding region without any able to effectively dominate on a wider scale. Athens did regain its democracy and independence, rebuild its fleet and, even for a short time, head a coalition of allied states, but the city's power was broken. It has been estimated that the male population in 395 was perhaps half of what it had been in 431. There were to be no more extravagant building programs on the Acropolis or in the Agora now. In fact there is hardly any evidence for new building of any kind before 350.

As the walls of Athens came down in 404, the historian Xenophon recorded that the demolishers, presumably many of them drafted by the Spartans from former subjects of the empire, danced and rejoiced to the music of flute girls, "thinking that this day was the beginning of freedom for Greece." Of course it was not to be. The power of Persia loomed again on the eastern horizon; Sparta was trying clumsily to build an Aegean empire of her own; and within sixty years a new power, Macedon, was to intrude into Greece from the north. The strain of the Peloponnesian War on the resources of Greece, the disruption of agriculture and the loss of so many men were to leave Greece vulnerable to outsiders.

THE RISE OF MACEDONIA

N.G.L. HAMMOND

The sudden, spectacular rise of the Macedonian monarch Philip II in the mid–fourth century B.C. and his subsequent mastery of Greece's leading city-states is one of history's most remarkable success stories. When he assumed power as a young man, his country was backward and divided (into Lower and Upper Macedonia, the latter being more backward than the former). And his northern borders were threatened by Illyrians (or Dardanians), Paeonians, and other fierce tribal peoples. Yet in an amazingly short time he overcame these obstacles and forged Europe's first national standing army. As detailed in this essay by N.G.L. Hammond, professor emeritus at Bristol University, it was this effective fighting force that enabled Philip to penetrate central and southern Greece. His first major victory in this strategic region was over the Phocians (of the city-state of Phocis, northwest of Thebes). The Phocians had recently seized the sacred sanctuary at Delphi (in central Greece), home of the famous oracle. Most members of the Amphyctyonic League, a loose alliance of nearby states who sent representatives to administer the sanctuary, objected and the so-called Sacred War ensued. The ambitious and crafty Philip, Hammond explains, proceeded to exploit the conflict to his own advantage.

P hilip took control in 359 not as king but as guardian of his nephew, Amyntas IV, a young boy. His country was on the verge of collapse, having lost 4,000 men in battle, while the victorious forces of Bardylis [king of the Illyrians] were in occupation of towns in Pelagonia and Lyncus and threatened to invade Macedonia itself in 358. Philip put heart into his army by holding assembly after assembly, rearming and training his infantry, and inspiring them with his own indomitable spirit. In spring 358 he convinced the assembly of the King's Men that they should take the offensive. In a decisive battle with almost equal numbers he inflicted a crippling defeat on Bardylis, established the east bank of Lake Lychnitis (Ochrid) as his frontier, and confirmed a treaty of peace with Bardylis by marrying his daughter, Audata. His victory freed Pelagonia, Lyncus and the other tribal states of West Macedonia, then called 'Upper Macedonia', from raiding and occupation by the Dardanians. He now invited the peoples of these states to abolish their monarchies and to enter the Macedonian kingdom with equal rights to those of the Macedonians. The invitation was accepted. . . .

By this act, which Philip must have taken with the agreement of the Macedonian assembly, he doubled the resources and the manpower of the kingdom. It was important to raise the standard of life in Upper Macedonia to that of Lower Macedonia, and for that purpose he founded new towns there in which young men received educational and military training. As they graduated he recruited the best of them to enter the king's army and become members of the assembly as 'Macedones'. His innovations were so successful that the number of his Companion Cavalrymen rose from 600 in 358 to 2,800 in 336, and that of the Companion Infantrymen from 10,000 in 358 to 27,000 in 336. Alexander was to inherit the most formidable army in Europe.

PHILIP'S EARLY CONQUESTS

By a combination of diplomatic skill and military opportunism Philip defeated Illyrian tribes beyond his western frontier, forced the Paeonians to become his subjects, gained possession of Greek colonies on his coast, defended Amphipolis against the Athenians and Crenides—renamed Philippi—against the Thracians, and advanced his eastern frontier to the river Nestus (Mesta), all by late 354. He was fortunate in that Athens was distracted by the war against her subject-states (357–355) and Thebes by the war against Phocis, which became the Sacred War (355–346); and he managed to make a treaty of alliance with his powerful neighbour, the Chalcidian League of city-states [on the three-fingered Chalcidic peninsula, just east of Macedonia], on condition that neither party would enter into separate negotiations with Athens. During these eventful years he confirmed an alliance with the ruling house of Larissa in Thessaly by marrying a lady of that house, Philinna, and an alliance with the Molossian royal house

by marrying Olympias in 357. . . . In that year, 357, he was elected
king in place of Amyntas IV.

The Sacred War was declared by a majority of the members of
the Amphictyonic League, of which the Council laid down rules
of conduct in religious and other matters and in particular administered the temple of Apollo at Delphi. That majority was
formed by the peoples of Thessaly, Central Greece and Boeotia;
but the minority included Athens, Sparta, Achaea, and later
Pherae in Thessaly, which all entered into alliance with Phocis.
Other states showed sympathy with one side or the other. The
Phocian occupiers of Delphi survived by looting the treasures
and hiring mercenary soldiers, and in 353 an able leader, Onomarchus, launched an offensive against Thebes and sent 7,000
mercenaries to support Pherae against the other Thessalians. This
was Philip's opportunity; for the Thessalians asked him for help
and he enabled them to win a victory. But Onomarchus came
north and inflicted two defeats on Philip. He withdrew, as he
said, 'like a ram, to butt the harder'. In 352 Philip and his Thessalian allies won a decisive victory over Onomarchus' army of
500 cavalry and 20,000 infantry, to the amazement of the city-
states. Philip paraded his championship of Apollo. For his soldiers went into battle wearing the laurel wreath associated with
the god, and on his orders 3,000 prisoners were drowned as
guilty of sacrilege. He also championed the cause of liberty and
federalism against the dictators of Pherae, whom he now expelled together with their mercenaries. His reward was election
as President of the Thessalian League, which placed its forces
and its revenues at his disposal. At this time he married Nice-
sipolis, a member of the leading family in Pherae.

CONCLUSION OF THE SACRED WAR

His chief fear was a coalition of Athens and the Chalcidian
League; for the Athenian fleet could then blockade his coast and
the armies of the two states could invade the coastal plain of
Macedonia. In 349, when the Chalcidian League violated its
treaty and entered into alliance with Athens, Philip invaded
Chalcidice and despite the efforts of Athens captured Olynthus,
the capital of the League, in 348. He held the Olynthians responsible for breaking the religious oaths which had bound them under the treaty. He razed the city and sold the population into
slavery. He destroyed two other city-states (Apollonia and Sta-
gira) and incorporated the peoples of the Chalcidic peninsula . . .
into the Macedonian kingdom.

Meanwhile the Phocians were running short of funds and also
of mercenary soldiers, and the Thebans had been hammered into

a condition of weakness. Who would administer the *coup de grâce* [deathblow]? Envoys from most of the city-states hastened to Pella, hoping to enlist Philip on their side in 346. At that time Alexander, as a boy of ten, will have watched with interest as his father found gracious words for all of them and committed himself to none. When the envoys were on their way home to their respective states, the Macedonian army reached Thermopylae, where the Phocian leader and his 8,000 mercenaries accepted the terms offered by Philip: to surrender their weapons and horses, and to go wherever they wished. The Phocian people were now defenceless. . . .

Philip had acted as the champion of Apollo. It was for him a matter of religious conviction. He therefore entrusted the settlement to the Council of the Amphictyonic League, on which his allies in Thessaly and Central Greece had a majority of the votes, and they no doubt listened to his advice. The terms for the Phocians were mild by Greek standards (one Greek state proposed the execution of all the men): disarmament, division into village-settlements, payment of an indemnity to Apollo and expulsion from the Amphictyony. In their place the Macedonians were elected members. The two votes of Phocis on the Council were transferred to the Macedonian state. . . .

THE ROAD TO CHAERONEA

Philip's aim was to bring the city-states into concord and set up a Treaty of Common Peace, of which Macedonia and they would be members. This . . . coincided with the tenor of a political pamphlet, entitled *Philip*, which [the noted orator] Isocrates published in 346 just before the capitulation of Phocis. He advised Philip as the ruler of the strongest state in Europe to bring the city-states into concord, lead them against Persia, liberate the Greeks in Asia, and found there new cities to absorb the surplus population of the Greek mainland. The price of concord was acceptance of the *status quo*. . . . Despite Philip's offers to set up a Common Peace, Athens, Sparta and Thebes went their own way in the name of 'freedom', and Philip realised in 341 that he might have to use force rather than persuasion if he wanted to exercise control.

Athens depended for her food-supply on imports of grain from South Russia, which had to pass through the Bosporus and the Hellespont. On the European side Byzantium was able to exact 'benevolences' [tolls] from shipping at the Bosporus, and Athens through her colonies on the Chersonese (the Gallipoli peninsula) could do likewise in the Hellespont. The Asian side was held by Persia, which had put down a series of revolts on the coast of the Mediterranean and could now muster a huge fleet.

Philip approached this sensitive area through a conquest of the tribes of eastern Thrace. It was during the Thracian campaign in 340 that he appointed Alexander at the age of sixteen to act as his deputy in Macedonia. From then on Alexander was fully aware of Philip's plans.

Events moved rapidly. Philip laid siege to Perinthus and Byzantium, whereupon Athens declared war. He was thwarted by Persia and Athens acting in collusion. He summoned Alexander to join him . . . and extended his control of eastern Thrace to the Danube. During his return to Macedonia in summer 339 he had to fight his way through the land of the Triballi, a powerful tribe which captured some of his booty. In Greece another Sacred War had started, and the command of the Amphictyonic forces was offered to and accepted by Philip in the autumn. The sacrilegious state which he had to discipline was Amphissa. He took his Macedonian army and troops from some Amphictyonic states not towards Amphissa but through Phocis to the border of Boeotia, in order to threaten Thebes, which though his 'friend and ally' had been behaving in a hostile manner, and to act against Athens, with which he was still at war. The envoys which he sent to Thebes were outbid by the envoys of Athens. In violation of her treaty Thebes joined Athens and sided with Amphissa. Philip tried more than once to negotiate terms of peace, but in vain. The decisive battle was fought at Chaeronea in Boeotia in August 338. The troops of Boeotia, Athens, Megara, Corinth and Achaea numbered some 35,000; those of Macedonia and her allies somewhat less.

Alexander, in command of the Companion Cavalry, pitched his tent by the river Cephissus. When his father's tactics created a breach in the opposing phalanx Alexander charged through the gap, and it was he who led the attack on the Sacred Band of 300 Thebans [Thebes' crack military unit]. The Macedonian victory was total. Thebes was treated harshly as the violator of its oaths. Athens was treated generously. Alexander led a guard of honour which brought the ashes of the Athenian dead to Athens—a unique tribute to a defeated enemy—and the 2,000 Athenian prisoners were liberated without ransom. As Philip advanced into the Peloponnese, his enemies submitted and his allies rejoiced. Sparta alone was defiant. He ravaged her territory and he gave some frontier regions to his allies; but he did not attack the city. During his return northwards he left garrisons at Acrocorinth, Thebes and Ambracia. Meanwhile the Council or the Amphictyonic League reduced the restrictions on the Phocians, made the Amphissaeans live in villages and approved the acts of Philip.

CAPTAIN-GENERAL OF THE GREEKS

The future of the city-states was in Philip's hands. He decided to create the 'Greek Community' (*to koinon ton Hellenon*), in which the states would swear to keep the peace among themselves, maintain existing constitutions, permit changes only by constitutional methods, and combine in action against any violator of the 'Common Peace', whether internal or external. His proposal, made in autumn 338, was accepted by the states in spring 337, and a 'Common Council' was established, of which the members represented one or more states in proportion to their military and naval strengths. The Council was a sovereign body: its decisions were sent to the states for implementation, not for discussion. The military forces and the naval forces at the disposal of the Common Council were defined: the former amounted to 15,000 cavalry and 200,000 infantry, and the number of warships, which is not stated in our sources, was later to be 160 triremes, manned by crews totalling some 30,000 men. Thus the Greek Community far outdid the Macedonian State in the size of the forces it could deploy. The Council had disciplinary, judicial and financial powers which were binding on the member-states. If we look for a modern analogy, we should look rather to the United States of America than to the European Community.

The next step was the creation of an offensive and defensive alliance between the Greek Community and the Macedonian State for all time. Because Macedonia was already at war with Persia, the Council declared war on Persia late in 337 and voted that the commander of the joint forces should be Philip. Within the Community his title was 'Hegemon' [supreme commander or captain-general], and the powers of his office were carefully defined. In the spring of 336 the vanguard [small, leading unit] of the joint forces crossed to Asia under the command of three Macedonian generals whom Philip appointed, and arrangements were made for the stipulated forces of the coalition to follow in the autumn with Philip as overall commander.

The brilliance of Philip's political initiative, power of persuasion and effective leadership is obvious. He brought into being the combination of a newly created Greek State, self-standing and self-governing, and a Macedonian State which was unrivalled in military power. If that combination should succeed in liberating the Greek cities in Asia and in acquiring extensive territory, it would provide a cure for many of the troubles of the Greek world. [The Greek historian] Theopompus, critical of Philip in many ways, entitled his history *Philippica* 'because Europe had never produced such a man altogether as Philip, son of Amyntas'.

THE CONQUESTS OF ALEXANDER THE GREAT: WEST MEETS EAST

THOMAS R. MARTIN

This concise overview of the exploits of Macedonia's Alexander III (later called "the Great") is by Thomas R. Martin, a professor of classics at Holy Cross. Martin covers most of the familiar main events, such as the crossing of the Hellespont (in 334 B.C.), siege of Tyre, liberation of Egypt, and major victories in Persia. He also includes several anecdotes and details that shed light on Alexander's character, such as the fact that he kept a copy of Homer's *Iliad* (given to him by his tutor, Aristotle) with him always. As Martin points out, Alexander's most immediate legacy was the chaotic scramble to carve up his newly acquired empire in the years following his untimely passing.

A disgruntled Macedonian assassinated Philip in 336 B.C. Unconfirmed rumors circulated that the murder had been instigated by one of his several wives, Olympias, a princess from Epirus to the west of Macedonia and mother of Philip's son, Alexander (356–323 B.C.). Alexander promptly liquidated potential rivals for the throne and won recognition as king while barely twenty years old. In several lightning-fast campaigns, he subdued Macedonia's traditional enemies to the west and north. Next he compelled the city-states in southern Greece that had rebelled from the League of Corinth at the news of Philip's death to rejoin the alliance. (As in Philip's reign, Sparta remained outside the league.) To demonstrate the price of disloyalty, Alexander destroyed Thebes in 335 as punishment for its rebellion. This lesson in terror made it clear that Alexander might claim to lead the Greek city-states by their consent (the kind of leader called a hegemon in Greek) but that the reality of his power rested on his superior force and his unwavering willingness to employ it.

ALEXANDER LEADS HIS TROOPS INTO ASIA

With Greece cowed into peaceful if grudging allegiance, Alexander in 334 led a Macedonian and Greek army into Anatolia [Asia Minor] to fulfill his father's plan to avenge Greece by attacking Persia. Alexander's astounding success in the following years in conquering the entire Persian Empire while still in his twenties earned him the title "the Great" in later ages. In his own time, his greatness consisted of his ability to inspire his men to follow him into hostile, unknown regions where they were reluctant to go, beyond the borders of civilization as they knew it. Alexander inspired his troops with his reckless disregard for his own safety, often, for example, plunging into the enemy at the head of his men and sharing the danger of the common soldier. No one could miss him in his plumed helmet, vividly colored cloak, and armor polished to reflect the sun. So intent on conquering distant lands was Alexander that he had rejected advice to delay his departure from Macedonia until he had married and fathered an heir, to forestall instability in case of his death. He had further alarmed his principal adviser, an experienced older man, by giving away virtually all his land and property in order to strengthen the army, thereby creating new landowners who would furnish troops. "What," he was asked, "do you have left for yourself?" "My hopes," Alexander replied (Plutarch, *Alexander* 15). Those hopes centered on constructing a heroic image of himself as a warrior as glorious as the incomparable Achilles of Homer's *Iliad*. Alexander always kept a copy of the *Iliad* under his pillow, along with a dagger. Alexander's aspirations and his behavior represented the ultimate expression of the Homeric vision of the glorious conquering warrior.

Alexander cast a spear into the earth of Anatolia when he crossed the Hellespont strait from Europe to Asia, thereby claiming the Asian continent for himself in Homeric fashion as territory "won by the spear" (Diodorus, *Library of History* 17.17.2). The first battle of the campaign, at the River Granicus in western Anatolia, proved the worth of Alexander's Macedonian and Greek cavalry, which charged across the river and up the bank to rout the opposing Persians. Alexander visited Midas's old capital of Gordion in Phrygia, where an oracle had promised the lordship of Asia to whoever could loose a seemingly impenetrable knot of rope tying the yoke of an ancient chariot preserved in the city. The young Macedonian, so the story goes, cut the Gordion knot with his sword. In 333 B.C. the Persian king Darius finally faced Alexander in battle at Issus, near the southeastern corner of Anatolia. Alexander's army defeated its more numerous opponents with a characteristically bold strike of cavalry through the left side of the Persian lines followed by a flanking maneuver against the king's position in the center. Darius had to flee from the field to avoid capture, leaving behind his wives and daughters, who had accompanied his campaign in keeping with royal Persian tradition. Alexander's scrupulously chivalrous treatment of the Persian royal women after their capture at Issus reportedly boosted his reputation among the peoples of the king's empire.

THE DEFEAT OF PERSIA

When Tyre, a heavily fortified city on the coast of what is now Lebanon, refused to surrender to him in 332 B.C., Alexander employed the assault machines and catapults developed by his father to breach the walls of its formidable offshore fortress after a long siege. The capture of Tyre rang the death knell of the walled city-state as a settlement impregnable to siege warfare. Although successful sieges remained rare after Alexander because well-constructed city walls still presented formidable barriers to attackers, Alexander's success against Tyre increased the terror of a siege for a city's general population. No longer could the citizens of a city-state confidently assume that their defensive system could withstand the technology of their enemy's offensive weapons indefinitely. The now-present fear that a siege might actually breach a city's walls made it much harder psychologically for city-states to remain united in the face of threats from enemies like aggressive kings.

Alexander next took over Egypt, where hieroglyphic inscriptions seem to show that he probably presented himself as the successor to the Persian king as the land's ruler rather than as an Egyptian pharaoh. On the coast, to the west of the Nile river, Alexander in 331 founded a new city named Alexandria after himself, the first of the many cities he would later establish as far east as Afghanistan. During his time in Egypt, Alexander also paid a mysterious visit to the oracle of the god Ammon, whom the Greeks regarded as identical to Zeus, at the oasis of Siwah far out in the western Egyptian desert. Alexander told no one the details of his consultation of the oracle, but the news got out that he had been informed he was the son of the god and that he joyfully accepted the designation as true.

In 331 B.C., Alexander crushed the Persian king's main army at the battle of Gaugamela in northern Mesopotamia, near the border of modern Iraq and Iran. He subsequently proclaimed himself king of Asia in place of the Persian king. For the heterogeneous populations of the Persian Empire, the succession of a Macedonian to the Persian throne meant essentially no change in their lives. They continued to send the same taxes to a remote master, whom they rarely if ever saw. As in Egypt, Alexander left the local administrative system of the Persian Empire in place, even retaining some Persian governors. His long-term aim seems to have been to forge an administrative corps composed of Macedonians, Greeks, and Persians working together to rule the territory he conquered with his army.

TO INDIA AND BACK

Alexander next led his army farther east into territory hardly known to the Greeks. He pared his force to reduce the need for supplies, which were difficult to find in the arid country through which they were marching. Each hoplite in Greek armies customarily had a personal servant to carry his armor and pack. Alexander, imitating Philip, trained his men to carry their own equipment, thereby creating a leaner force by cutting the number of army servants dramatically. As with all ancient armies, however, a large number of noncombatants trailed after the fighting force: merchants who set up little markets at every stop, women whom soldiers had taken as mates along the way and their children, entertainers, and prostitutes. Although supplying these hangers-on was not Alexander's responsibility, their foraging for themselves made it harder for Alexander's quartermasters to find what they needed to supply the army proper.

An ancient army's demand for supplies usually left a trail of destruction and famine for local inhabitants in the wake of its march. Hostile armies simply took whatever they wanted. Friendly armies expected local people to sell or donate food to its supply officers and also to the merchants trailing along. These entrepreneurs would set up markets to resell locally obtained provisions to the soldiers. Since most farmers in antiquity had practically no surplus to sell, they found this expectation—which was in reality a requirement—a terrific hardship. The money the farmers received was of little use to them because there was nothing to buy with it in the countryside, where their neighbors had also had to participate in the forced marketing of their subsistence.

From the heartland of Persia, Alexander in 329 B.C. marched northeastward into the trackless steppes of Bactria (modern Afghanistan). When he proved unable to subdue completely the

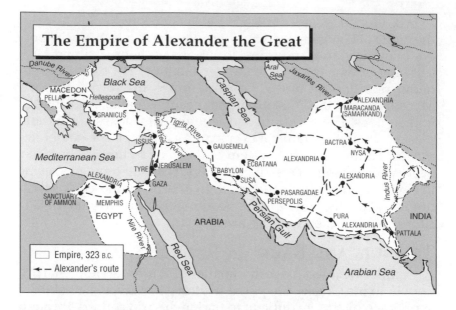

highly mobile locals, who avoided pitched battles in favor of the guerrilla tactics of attack and retreat, Alexander settled for an alliance sealed by his marriage to the Bactrian princess Roxane in 327. In this same period, Alexander completed the cold-blooded suppression of both real and imagined resistance to his plans among the leading men in his officer corps. As in past years, he used accusations of treachery or disloyalty as justification for the execution of those Macedonians he had come to distrust. These executions, like the destruction of Thebes in 335, demonstrated Alexander's appreciation of terror as a disincentive to rebellion.

From Bactria Alexander pushed on eastward to India. He probably intended to march all the way through to China in search of the edge of the farthest land on the earth, which Aristotle, once Alexander's tutor, had taught was a sphere. Seventy days of marching through monsoon rains, however, finally shattered the nerves of Alexander's soldiers. In the spring of 326 B.C. they mutinied on the banks of the Hyphasis River (the modern Beas) in western India. Alexander was forced to agree to lead them in the direction of home. When his men had balked before, Alexander had always been able to shame them back into action by sulking in his tent like Achilles in the *Iliad*. This time the soldiers were beyond shame.

Alexander thereupon proceeded south down the Indus River. Along the way he took out his frustration at being stopped in his eastward march by slaughtering the Indian tribes who resisted him and by risking his life more flamboyantly than ever before. As a climax to his frustrated rage, he flung himself over the wall of an Indian town to face the enemy alone like a Homeric hero. His horrified officers were barely able to rescue him in time; even so, he received grievous wounds. At the mouth of the Indus on the Indian Ocean, Alexander turned a portion of his army west through the fierce desert of Gedrosia. Another portion took an easier route inland, while a third group sailed westward along the coast to explore for possible sites for new settlements and harbors. Alexander himself led the contingent that braved the desert, planning to surpass earlier Persian kings by marching through territory that they had found impassable. There a flash flood wiped out most of the noncombatants following the army. Many of the soldiers also died on the march through the desert, expiring from lack of water and the heat, which has been recorded at 127 degrees in the shade in that area. Alexander, as always, shared his men's hardships. In one legendary episode from this horrible ordeal, a few men were said to have brought him a helmet containing some water they had found. Alexander spilled the water out onto the sand rather than drink when his men could not. The remains of the army finally reached safety in the heartland of Persia in 324 B.C. Alexander promptly began plans for an invasion of the Arabian peninsula and, to follow that, all of North Africa west of Egypt.

ALEXANDER A GOD?

By the time Alexander returned to Persia, he had dropped all pretense of ruling over the Greeks as anything other than an absolute monarch. Despite his earlier promise to respect the internal freedom of the Greek city-states, he now impinged on their autonomy by sending a peremptory decree ordering them to restore to citizenship the large number of exiles wandering homeless in the Greek world. The previous decades of war in Greece had created many of these unfortunate wanderers, and their status as stateless persons was creating unrest. Even more striking was Alexander's communication to the city-states that he wished to receive the honors due a god. Initially dumbfounded by this request, the leaders of most Greek states soon complied by sending honorary delegations to him as if he were a god. The Spartan Damis pithily expressed the only prudent position on Alexander's deification open to the cowed Greeks: "If Alexander wishes to be a god, we agree that he be called a god" (Plutarch, *Moralia* 219e).

Scholarly debate continues over Alexander's motive for desiring the Greeks to acknowledge him as a god, but few now accept a formerly popular theory that he sought divinity because he believed the city-states would then have to obey his orders as originating from a divinity, whose authority would supersede that of all earthly regimes. Personal rather than political motives best explain his request. He almost certainly had come to believe that he was the son of Zeus; after all, Greek mythology told many stories of Zeus producing children by mating with a human female. Most of those legendary offspring were mortal, but Alexander's conquest showed that he had surpassed them. His feats must be superhuman, he could well have believed, because they exceeded the bounds of human possibility. In other words, Alexander's accomplishments demonstrated that he had achieved godlike power and therefore must be a god himself. The divinity of Alexander, in ancient terms, emerged as a natural consequence of his power.

Alexander's overall aims can best be explained as interlinked goals: the conquest and administration of the known world and the exploration and possible colonization of new territory beyond. Conquest through military action was a time-honored pursuit for ambitious Macedonian leaders such as Alexander. He included non-Macedonians in his administration and army because he needed their expertise, not because he had any dream of promoting an abstract notion of what has sometimes been called "the brotherhood of man." Alexander's explorations benefited numerous scientific fields, from geography to botany, because he took along scientifically minded writers to collect and catalogue the new knowledge that they encountered. The far-flung new cities that he founded served as loyal outposts to keep the peace in conquered territory and provide warnings to headquarters in case of local uprisings. They also created new opportunities for trade in valuable goods such as spices that were not produced in the Mediterranean region.

NO ORDINARY HUMAN LIFE

Alexander's plans to conquer Arabia and North Africa were extinguished by his premature death from a fever and heavy drinking on June 10, 323 B.C., in Babylon. He had already been suffering for months from depression brought on by the death of his best friend, Hephaistion. Close since their boyhoods, Alexander and Hephaistion were probably lovers. When Hephaistion died in a bout of excessive drinking, Alexander went wild with grief. The depth of his emotion was evident when he planned to build an elaborate temple to honor Hephaistion as a god. Meanwhile, Alexander threw himself into preparing for his Arabian campaign by exploring the marshy lowlands of southern Mesopotamia. Perhaps it was on one of these trips that he contracted the malaria-like fever that, exacerbated by a two-day drinking binge, killed him.

Like Pericles, Alexander had made no plans about what should happen if he should die unexpectedly. His wife Roxane was to give birth to their first child only some months after Alexander's death. When at Alexander's deathbed his commanders asked him to whom he bequeathed his kingdom, he replied, "To the most powerful [*kratistos*]" (Arrian, *Anabasis of Alexander* 7.26.3).

The Athenian orator Aeschines (c. 397–322 B.C.) well expressed the bewildered reaction of many people to the events of Alexander's lifetime: "What strange and unexpected event has not occurred in our time? The life we have lived is no ordinary human one, but we were born to be an object of wonder to posterity" (*Orations* 3.132). Alexander himself certainly attained legendary status in later times. Stories of fabulous exploits attributed to him became popular folk tales throughout the ancient world, even reaching distant regions where Alexander had never trod, such as deep into Africa. The popularity of the legend of Alexander as a symbol of the height of achievement for a masculine warrior-hero served as one of his most persistent legacies to later ages. That the worlds of Greece and the Near East had been brought into closer contact than ever before represented the other long-lasting effect of his astonishing career. Its immediate political and military consequences were the struggles among his generals that led to the creation of the kingdoms of the Hellenistic world.

WHY ALEXANDER WAS A GREAT LEADER

ARRIAN

A Romanized Greek born about A.D. 90 in the Roman province of Bithynia (in Asia Minor), Arrian (Flavius Arrianus) is renowned for his *Anabasis Alexandri* (*Alexander's March Up-country*), the most complete and reliable surviving source chronicling the campaigns of Alexander the Great. The work was based largely on now lost histories by Alexander's general Ptolemy, and by Aristobulus, an engineer under Alexander; therefore, historians consider much of Arrian's well-written account to be reasonably accurate. What follows is its conclusion, in which Arrian discusses his subject's faults as well as his strong points and also suggests that Alexander desired to allow Persian customs and individuals to have roles in shaping the character of his new empire.

O nce this second crossing [of the Hydapses] was successfully accomplished, Alexander again marshalled his troops. His Royal Squadron and the best of the other mounted regiments he brought round to the right wing, stationing the mounted archers in the van; in the rear of the cavalry he posted the Royal Regiment of Guards under Seleucus, then the Royal regiment of the heavy infantry, in close touch with the other Guards divisions, according to their precedence for that day. The archers, Agrianes, and javelin-men took their position on either wing of the main body of infantry. Having thus made his dispositions, he gave orders for the infantry, nearly 6,000 strong, to follow in order of march, while he himself, with only the cavalry (numbering some 5,000) in which he thought he had the advantage over the enemy, moved forward rapidly. Tauron, captain of the archers, was instructed to advance in the rear of the cavalry with all the speed he could make.

The idea in Alexander's mind was that if Porus' army should attack in force he would . . . fight a delaying action until his infantry could come to his support; if, on the other hand, the Indians proved to be so badly shaken by the bold and unexpected crossing of the river that they took to their heels, he would be able to press hard on the retreating army, and the more men they lost during their withdrawal, the lighter his own task would subsequently be. . . .

Porus' son arrived on the scene with . . . 2,000 mounted troops and 120 chariots . . . but Alexander had been too quick for him and had already effected his final crossing from the island. Against this force Alexander first sent his mounted archers, while he himself moved on with the cavalry, thinking that Porus was on the way to engage him with the main strength of his army, and that this cavalry contingent, posted in the van, preceded the rest of the Indian troops. But as soon as Alexander received an accurate report of the enemies' numbers, he attacked at once, and the Indians, seeing Alexander there in person and his massed cavalry coming at them in successive charges, squadron by squadron, broke and fled. The Indians' losses in the action were some 400 mounted men, Porus' son being himself among the killed; their chariots and horses were captured as they attempted to get away—speed was impossible, and the muddy ground had rendered them useless even during the fight.

The Indians who did succeed in getting away reported to Porus that Alexander had crossed the river in force and that his son had been killed in the action. Porus was faced with a difficult choice, for the troops under Craterus, who had been left behind in Alexander's original position opposite the main Indian army, could now be seen making their way over the river. Swiftly he made up his mind; he determined to move in force against Alexander, and to fight it out with the King of Macedon himself and the flower of his men. Then, leaving behind a small force with a few elephants to spread alarm among Craterus' cavalry as they attempted to land on the river-bank, he marched to meet Alexander with all his cavalry, 4,000 strong, all of his 300 chariots, 200 elephants, and the picked contingents of his infantry, numbering some 30,000 men.

Much of the ground was deep in soft mud, so he continued his advance till he found a spot where the sandy soil offered a surface sufficiently firm and level for cavalry manœuvre, and there made his dispositions. In the van he stationed his elephants at intervals of about 100 feet, on a broad front, to form a screen for the whole body of the infantry and to spread terror among the cavalry of Alexander. He did not expect that any enemy unit would venture to force a way through the gaps in the line of elephants, either on foot or on horseback; terror would make the horses uncontrollable, and infantry units would be even less likely to make the attempt, as they would be met and checked by his own heavy infantry and then destroyed by the elephants turning upon them and trampling them down. Behind the elephants were the foot-soldiers, though not on a front of equal extent: the various units, forming a second line, were so disposed as to fill the intervals in the line of elephants. There was infantry on both wings as well, outflanking the elephants, and, finally, on both flanks of the infantry were the mounted units, each with a screen of war-chariots.

Noting that the enemy was making his dispositions for battle, Alexander checked the advance of his cavalry to allow the infantry to come up with him. Regiment by regiment they made contact, moving swiftly, until the whole force was again united. Alexander had no intention of making the fresh enemy troops a present of his own breathless and exhausted men, so he paused before advancing to the attack. Meanwhile he kept his cavalry manœuvering up and down the line, while the infantry units were allowed to rest until they were once more in good heart for battle.

ALEXANDER LAUNCHES HIS ATTACK

Observation of the Indian dispositions decided him against attempting an assault upon their centre, where the heavy infantry was massed in the intervals of the protecting screen of elephants, and his reluctance to take this course was based precisely upon Porus' own calculations; relying, instead, on his superiority in cavalry, he moved the major portion of his mounted troops towards the enemy's left wing, to make his assault in that sector. Coenus was sent over to the Indians' right with Demetrius' regiment and his own, his orders being that when the enemy moved their cavalry across to their left to counter the massed formations of the Macedonian mounted squadrons, he should hang on to their rear. The heavy infantry was put in charge of Seleucus, Antigenes, and Tauron, with orders not to engage until it was evident that the Indians, both horse and foot, had been thrown into confusion by the Macedonian cavalry.

Once the opposing armies were within range, Alexander launched his mounted archers, 1,000 strong, against the enemy's left wing, hoping to shake it by the hail of their arrows and the weight of their charge, and immediately afterwards himself advanced with the Companions against the Indian left, intent upon making his assault while they were still reeling under the attack of the mounted archers and before their cavalry could change formation from column into mass.

The Indians meanwhile withdrew all the cavalry from other sections of their line, and moved it across to meet and counter Alexander's movement towards their flank, and it was not long before Coenus' men could be seen following, according to orders, close in their rear. The Indians were thereupon compelled to split their force into two; the larger section, containing the best troops, continued to proceed against Alexander, while the remainder wheeled about in order to deal with Coenus. This, of course, was disastrous not only to the effectiveness of the Indians' dispositions, but to their whole plan of battle. Alexander saw his chance; precisely at the moment when the enemy cavalry were changing direction, he attacked. The Indians did not even wait to receive his charge, but fell back in confusion upon the elephants, their impregnable fortress—or so they hoped. The elephant-drivers forced their beasts to meet the opposing cavalry, while the Macedonian infantry, in its turn, advanced against them, shooting down the drivers, and pouring in a hail of missiles from every side upon the elephants themselves. It was an odd bit of work— quite unlike any previous battle; the monster elephants plunged this way and that among the lines of infantry, dealing destruction in the solid mass of the Macedonian phalanx, while the Indian horsemen, seeing the infantry at one another's throats, wheeled to the assault of the Macedonian cavalry. Once again, however, the strength and experience of Alexander's mounted troops were too much for them, and they were forced back a second time on the elephants.

During the action all the Macedonian cavalry units had, by the exigencies of the fighting rather than deliberate orders, concentrated into a single body; and now its successive charges upon this sector or that inflicted heavy losses on the enemy. By this time the elephants were boxed up, with no room to manœuvre, by troops all round them, and as they blundered about, wheeling and shoving this way and that, they trampled to death as many of their friends as of their enemies. The result was that the Indian cavalry, jammed in around the elephants and with no more space to manœuvre than they had, suffered severely; most of the elephant-drivers had been shot; many of the animals had themselves been wounded, while others, riderless and bewildered, ceased altogether to play their expected part, and, maddened by pain and fear, set indiscriminately upon friend and foe, thrusting, trampling, and spreading death before them. The

Macedonians could deal with these maddened creatures comfortably enough; having room to manœuvre, they were able to use their judgement, giving ground when they charged, and going for them with their javelins when they turned and lumbered back, whereas the unfortunate Indians, jammed up close among them as they attempted to get away, found them a more dangerous enemy even than the Macedonians.

In time the elephants tired and their charges grew feebler; they began to back away, slowly, like ships going astern, and with nothing worse than trumpetings. Taking his chance, Alexander surrounded the lot of them—elephants, horsemen, and all—and then signalled his infantry to lock shields and move up in a solid mass. Most of the Indian cavalry was cut down in the ensuing action; their infantry, too, hard pressed by the Macedonians, suffered terrible losses. The survivors, finding a gap in Alexander's ring of cavalry, all turned and fled. Craterus and the other officers who had been left on the bank of the river began to cross as soon as they saw Alexander's triumphant success, and their fresh troops, taking over the pursuit from Alexander's weary men, inflicted upon the vanquished Indians further losses no less severe.

Nearly 20,000 of the Indian infantry were killed in this battle, and about 3,000 of their cavalry. All their war-chariots were destroyed. Among the dead were two sons of Porus, Spitaces the local Indian governor, all the officers in command of the elephants and chariots, and all the cavalry officers and other commanders of high rank. The surviving elephants were captured. Out of Alexander's original 6,000 infantry, some eighty were killed; in addition to these he lost ten of the mounted archers, who were the first unit to engage, about twenty of the Companions, and 200 of the other cavalry.

THE TWO KINGS MEET

Throughout the action Porus had proved himself a man indeed, not only as a commander but as a soldier of the truest courage. When he saw his cavalry cut to pieces, most of his infantry dead, and his elephants killed or roaming riderless and bewildered about the field, his behaviour was very different from that of the Persian King Darius: unlike Darius, he did not lead the scramble to save his own skin, but so long as a single unit of his men held together, fought bravely on. It was only when he was himself wounded that he turned the elephant on which he rode and began to withdraw. The wound was in his right shoulder, the only unprotected part of his body; no missile, as he moved here and there in the thick of the fighting, could touch him anywhere else because of the corselet [chest armor] which he wore—a corselet exceedingly tough and closely fitting, as all who subsequently saw him could observe.

Alexander, anxious to save the life of this great and gallant soldier, sent Taxiles the Indian to him. Taxiles rode up as near as he dared and requested him to stop his elephant and hear what message Alexander sent him, as escape was no longer possible. But Taxiles was an old enemy of the Indian King, and Porus turned his elephant and drove at him, to kill him with his lance; and he might indeed have killed him, if he had not spurred his horse out of the way in the nick of time. Alexander, however, far from resenting this treatment of his messenger, sent a number of others, the last of whom was an Indian named Meroes, a man he had been told had long been Porus' friend. Porus listened to Meroes' message, stopped his elephant, and dismounted; he was much distressed by thirst, so when he had revived himself by drinking, he told Meroes to conduct him with all speed to Alexander.

Alexander, informed of his approach, rode out to meet him, accompanied by a small party of his Companions. When they met, he reined in his horse, and looked at his adversary with admiration: he was a magnificent figure of a man, over seven feet high and of great personal beauty; his bearing had lost none of its pride; his air was of one brave man meeting another, of a king in the presence of a king, with whom he had fought honourably for his kingdom.

Alexander was the first to speak. 'What,' he said, 'do you wish that I should do with you?'

'Treat me as a king ought,' Porus is said to have replied.

'For my part,' said Alexander, pleased by his answer, 'your request shall be granted. But is there not something you would wish for yourself? Ask it.'

'Everything,' said Porus, 'is contained in this one request.'

The dignity of these words gave Alexander even more pleasure, and he restored to Porus his sovereignty over his subjects, adding to his realm other territory of even greater extent. Thus he did indeed use a brave man as a king ought, and from that time forward found him in every way a loyal friend. Such was the result of the battle with Porus and the Indians beyond the Hydapses. . . .

A MAN MORE THAN HUMAN?

Alexander died in the 114th Olympiad, in the archonship of Hegesias at Athens [June 10, 323 B.C.]. He lived, as Aristobulus tells us, thirty-two years and eight months, and reigned twelve years and eight months [or more probably he was thirty-two years and eleven months old and had reigned for thirteen years when he died]. He had great personal beauty, invincible power of en-

In this drawing by German artist Max Henze, Alexander and his troops visit the Great Sphinx at Giza after liberating Egypt from the Persians.

durance, and a keen intellect; he was brave and adventurous, strict in the observance of his religious duties, and hungry for fame. Most temperate in the pleasures of the body, his passion was for glory only, and in that he was insatiable. He had an uncanny instinct for the right course in a difficult and complex situation, and was most happy in his deductions from observed facts. In arming and equipping troops and in his military dispositions he was always masterly. Noble indeed was his power of inspiring his men, of filling them with confidence, and, in the moment of danger, of sweeping away their fear by the spectacle of his own fearlessness. When risks had to be taken, he took them with the utmost boldness, and his ability to seize the moment for a swift blow, before his enemy had any suspicion of what was coming, was beyond praise. No cheat or liar ever caught him off his guard, and both his word and his bond were inviolable. Spending but little on his own pleasures, he poured out his money without stint for the benefit of his friends.

Doubtless, in the passion of the moment Alexander sometimes erred; it is true he took some steps towards the pomp and arrogance of the Asiatic kings: but I, at least, cannot feel that such errors were very heinous, if the circumstances are taken fairly into consideration. For, after all, he was young; the chain of his successes was unbroken, and, like all kings, past, present, and to come, he was surrounded by courtiers who spoke to please, regardless of what evil their words might do. On the other hand, I do indeed know that Alexander, of all the monarchs of old, was the only one who had the nobility of heart to be sorry for his mistakes.

Nor do I think that Alexander's claim to a divine origin was a very serious fault—in any case, it may well have been a mere device to magnify his consequence in the eyes of his subjects. . . . Surely, too, his adoption of Persian dress was, like his claim to divine birth, a matter of policy: by it he hoped to bring the Eastern nations to feel that they had a king who was not wholly a foreigner, and to indicate to his own countrymen his desire to move away from the harsh traditional arrogance of Macedonia. That was also, no doubt, the reason why he included a proportion of Persian troops (the so-called 'Golden Apples', for instance) in Macedonian units, and made Persian noblemen officers in his crack native regiments. . . .

It is my belief that there was in those days no nation, no city, no single individual beyond the reach of Alexander's name; never in all the world was there another like him, and therefore I cannot but feel that some power more than human was concerned in his birth; indications of this were, moreover, said to be provided at the time of his death by oracles; many people saw visions and had prophetic dreams; and there is the further evidence of the extraordinary way in which he is held, as no mere man could be, in honour and remembrance. Even today, when so many years have passed, there have been oracles, all tending to his glory, delivered to the people of Macedon.

In the course of this book I have, admittedly, found fault with some of the things which Alexander did, but of the man himself I am not ashamed to express ungrudging admiration. Where I have criticized unfavourably, I have done so because I wished to tell the truth as I saw it, and to enable my readers to profit thereby. Such was the motive which led me to embark upon this History: and I, too, have had God's help in my work.

Rome Conquers and Rules the Mediterranean World

CHAPTER 2

THE ROMANS UNIFY ITALY

CHESTER G. STARR

The Greeks long controlled the eastern Mediterranean and the Carthaginians the sea's western sphere. But in the period lasting from the early fifth to the early third centuries B.C., a new and formidable power rose in their midst—Rome, which steadily expanded its influence until it was master of the whole Italian peninsula. As explained here by Chester G. Starr, former Bentley professor of history at the University of Michigan, the members of the Latin League (a loose confederation of early Latin towns, of which Rome was a member), the Etruscans (who lived in Etruria, north of Rome), the Samnites (a hardy, warlike Apennine hill people), the Greeks (who had colonized southern Italy in recent centuries), and others fell, one by one, under Rome's control. Starr also provides an excellent analysis of the reasons for Rome's success, including its superior army organization and its lenient policies toward the peoples it conquered.

W hile the Romans culturally fell into a backwater, their political and military abilities were never more marked than from the era from 509 to 264 B.C. During this dimly lit period they . . . went on to conquer all the peninsula. Internally they hammered out, slowly and with many false starts, a reorganization of their political system which eventually produced technical democracy.

Down to 340 B.C. the wars of the Early Republic took place in a narrow strip of western Italy, 30 miles from the sea to the central mountains and 90 miles from the Ciminian hills of south

Etruria to the jutting promontory of Tarracina at the edge of the Latin districts. The main opponents were initially the expanding hill tribes of the Aequi and Volsci, who pressed on both the Latins and the Romans. After the Latin league had secured its indepen-dence from Rome at the battle of Lake Regillus (c. 496 B.C.) the two powers nonetheless found themselves forced to join in a treaty of equal alliance to oppose the hillsmen. . . . The critical battle appears to have been that of Mt. Algidus in 431, after which the tide turned in favor of the plainsmen.

The Romans were also at odds on their own with the neigh-boring Etruscan center of Veii, which traded southward across the Tiber via Praeneste. The direct route was cut by Roman ad-vance up the Tiber in 426–25, but reduction of Veii itself was a bit-ter struggle. In the end Veii was taken in 396 and was utterly de-stroyed by the general M. Furius Camillus after a continuous siege over several years. During the last stage the Roman state had to institute regular payment for the soldiers thus kept away from their farms.

Then came the worst blow Rome was ever to suffer until its final collapse in the fifth century after Christ. Uncivilized Celts, called Gauls, had been moving down into the Po valley from central Europe and launched a series of great raids into central Italy. In 390, according to conventional Roman chronology, the Roman army marched out to meet the Gauls north of Rome at the Allia river, but was wiped out. The city itself was almost to-tally destroyed.

The dogged Romans, however, rose nobly to the threat. They appointed Camillus dictator and raised a new army. In 378–57 they built a stone wall five and one-half miles long about the city, far larger than that of any Etruscan city. As defenders of central Italy Rome gained extensive support and by 350 was virtually master of the neighborhood.

MASTERS OF THE PENINSULA

To lay a solid basis for further expansion had required almost two centuries, but now the Romans blazed forth. During the pe-riod 340 to 264 they conquered all the rest of the Italian penin-sula. The initial stimulus came from a revolt of the Latin league, which chafed at its increasingly dependent position; in a brief war, 340–38, the Romans defeated and dissolved the league. Dur-ing the hostilities with the Latins, their southern neighbors, the wealthy Oscans who had become civilized in Campania [the fer-tile region south of Latium] appealed again for assistance against their Samnite kinsmen of the central mountains. Capua, Cumae, and other cities were accordingly added to Roman control.

This latter step brought the Romans by 326 into serious conflict with the Samnites, who were far more numerous but less well unified. Although the first phase ended in 321 when the Samnites trapped a Roman army at the Caudine forks, the wars flared up again and again. It was probably in this long-protracted struggle that the Romans reorganized their basic military unit, the legion, into a more supple structure. During the Samnite wars they had also to face from time to time Etruscan and Gallic foes; but they skillfully divided and conquered their enemies, while their own subjects generally remained loyal. The Roman victory at Sentinum in 295 delivered the crucial blow to an army of Samnites and Gauls; final settlement, however, scarcely came until 282.

There remained southern Italy, where the Greek cities of the coast were barely maintaining themselves against inland Lucanian tribes. In 282 Rome sent an army south at the request of Thurii and dispatched a few ships to the gulf off Tarentum, in violation of an old agreement with that state. The Tarentines sank the ships and invited into Italy the king of [the Greek Kingdom of] Epirus, Pyrrhus (319–272). This skilled Hellenistic general defeated the Romans at Heraclea (280) and Asculum (279), partly through using the new tactical weapon of elephants.

Pyrrhus then essayed to make peace. The Senate almost approved his terms; but the Carthaginians hastily offered Rome naval and financial aid, and an aged Roman leader, Appius Claudius, had himself carried into the Senate House to speak against compromise. Since Pyrrhus could not hope to conquer all central Italy from the Romans, he turned to Sicily upon the invitation of the Greeks in the islands and fought the Carthaginians. When he returned to Italy in 275, the Romans checked him at Beneventum; Pyrrhus withdrew to Epirus; and the Greek cities of the south had to admit Roman garrisons. Thenceforth the Romans were masters of the Italian peninsula.

SUCCESS FATED BY THE GODS?

The Roman conquest of Italy was not a process the Romans deliberately planned, for it took over two centuries of almost haphazard actions. If the Romans fought so continuously, the reasons lie partly in the ill-stabilized conditions. In Italy at this time strife between plainsmen and hillsmen was unending and opened the way for the Gauls; the Greeks quarreled among themselves and tempted intervention by their Italic neighbors. The Roman system of alliances, which made Rome responsible for protecting each ally, also involved Rome in an ever-widening circle of external entanglements.

Potent forces of expansion existed within Rome itself. The Romans remembered their days of greatness in the kingdom; their leaders sought military glory, which would enhance the honor of their families and bring them booty; and the population of Rome seems to have increased at a rapid rate. Beside looting their victims of movable property, the Romans commonly took about a third of conquered lands on which they settled colonies of Roman and Latin farmers.

To explain their victories, the Romans had one fundamental answer: "We have overcome all the nations of the world, because we have realized that the world is directed and governed by the gods" [Cicero, *On the Responses of the Haruspices* 9]. Divine support was gained by scrupulous attention to religious vows by the leaders and by rewards of booty to the temples; the Romans, too, had a ceremony conducted by the *fetiales* [state priests] which ensured that their wars were just defenses of the Romans and their allies. This religious machinery undoubtedly had a considerable effect in heartening the troops and generals to their tasks, but more earthly factors also had a potent role both in bringing victory and in aiding the maintenance of Roman rule.

A FLEXIBLE MILITARY SYSTEM

Tactically and strategically the Romans hammered out ever more supple principles of organization and operations. Most of their enemies, who were not civilized, could be divided and met in detail by Roman forces, which were kept concentrated and had a central geographical position. Even skilled opponents like Pyrrhus could win only battles, not wars, against the abundance of Roman manpower and the dogged persistence of Roman leadership. Initially the Romans organized their legions into phalanxes, but during the Samnite wars they developed a more articulated division of the legion into blocs or *maniples*, grouped in three lines which operated independently; most soldiers were now armed with short swords and javelins.

As far as possible, the Romans fought only on ground of their own choosing and at the time when they were ready. To aid them in refusing battle under unfavorable circumstances they picked up from Pyrrhus the habit of fortifying their camp every night. Roman commanders were mostly experienced veterans, and since they were also the chief officials of the state they normally could decide on their own judgment when and how to give battle.

Holding down the conquered called for skills of a more political nature. The establishment of colonies provided bases and points of control over conquered areas, and by the late fourth century the Romans had begun to build all-weather roads to link the capital with other districts. Appius Claudius laid out the first great Roman road, the *via Appia*, to Capua in 312. More important, however, was the treatment of the defeated. A Roman conquest was not in itself a gentle matter, and a considerable part of conquered lands was taken for Roman settlers. Yet the Romans generally were fighting peoples of similar culture and language, and after the destruction of Veii they commonly spared the vanquished from utter destruction.

INCORPORATING CONQUERED PEOPLES

Across the fourth century the Romans developed a very deftly arranged set of varying positions for their subjects. Most defeated states became "allies" (*socii*), who paid no tribute and retained local self-government; they furnished a set number of troops upon call and surrendered foreign policy to Rome. After the Latin league was dissolved in 338, many Latin states received "Latin status," holders of which could gain citizenship if they settled in Rome; most colonies also received this status. Dating from the annexation of Tusculum in 381, however, some Latin communities were absorbed down the years into the Roman citizen territory but retained their legal existence as local *"municipia."* Yet a fourth status, that of Roman citizenship without the right to vote, was given to areas in Campania and elsewhere. By 225 B.C., as we know from a list of [the second-century B.C. Greek historian] Polybius, about 1,000,000 male inhabitants of Italy were Roman citizens (either full citizens, full citizens having a local center in their *municipium,* or citizens without a vote), 500,000 were Latins, and 1,500,000 were allies, grouped in some 120 to 150 small states.

Thereby the Romans bound particularly the upper classes in the subject territories to their rule and divided Italy so that it could not feel a sense of common opposition to a tyrannical master. Unwittingly the Romans began thus to enlarge the concept of Rome and so took great steps toward solving the problem of welding conquered to home territories, a problem which had shattered the Athenian empire. One of Rome's opponents [Macedonia's King Philip V] was later to praise this liberality in granting citizenship. . . . Eventually in A.D. 212 Roman citizenship was to be given to virtually all free men of the entire Mediterranean basin.

The Punic Wars Make Rome a World Power

Antony Kamm

Having recently become masters of the Italian peninsula, in the second half of the third century B.C. the Romans continued their expansion and became a Mediterranean and world power. Clearly, their first two hard-won victories over the maritime empire of Carthage (264–241 and 218–201 B.C.) did not bode well for Carthage's future (nor for the Greek realms in the sea's eastern sphere, which would be the next to face Roman might). And sure enough, in the second century B.C., Rome crushed the life out of what was left of Carthage in the Third Punic War (249–246 B.C.). The following concise overview of these conflicts, the first two of which were the largest ever fought on earth up to that time, is by Antony Kamm, a lecturer at the University of Stirling.

The spark which ignited the metamorphosis of Rome from an Italian to a Mediterranean power was a small enough incident. The Greek city of Messana, on the north-eastern tip of Sicily, had in 289 BC been seized and occupied by a notorious gang of retired Campanian mercenaries. They were still there in 264 BC, when the king of Syracuse, the famous Greek stronghold lower down the coast, decided to winkle [force] them out. The mercenaries asked the Carthaginians, who occupied parts of the west coast of Sicily, to send a fleet and raise the siege. The Carthaginians duly obliged, but their fleet stayed on in the harbour. The mercenaries then appealed to Rome to rid them of the Carthaginians, on the somewhat specious grounds that their Campanian blood entitled them to the same protection as the Campanian allies of Rome on the mainland. The senate havered and passed the buck to the *comitia tributa* [tribal assembly], which voted if not actually for war, then at least for the dispatch of an expedition against the interfering Carthaginians to restore Messana to its criminal element. The arrival of the expedition so surprised or unnerved the Carthaginian commander at Messana that he embarked and took his ships home. The Carthaginian government, however, humiliated by what they saw as a defeat, resolved to recapture Messana. Thus was started, by accident, the first world war in history to be contested on principles. It was fought to the finish, and to the death. It lasted, in three 'bites' totalling forty-two years, for well over a century. When it ended, Carthage, which at one time had, according to the Greek geographer Strabo (*c.* 64 BC–AD 19), '300 cities in Libya and 700 thousand people in its own city' (*Geography*, XVII. 3), was a smoking heap of rubble.

CARTHAGE AND THE FIRST WAR

Carthage was originally a Phoenician colony: hence the Latin name for a Carthaginian, *Poenus*, from which comes the adjective 'Punic'. The language of the Carthaginians was Semitic, and their gods, too, were those of the Phoenicians, notably Ba'al-Hammon, god of the sky and of fertility, and Tanit, the moon-goddess. Its literature has not come down to us. The Punic Wars went on for so long and were fought with such intensity on both sides that within a hundred years the word *punicus* had an accepted literary meaning of 'treacherous', though, while hostilities were conducted with the utmost passion and brutality, there is no evidence that either side acted more dishonestly than the other.

The Carthaginians can justly be called one of the most successful peoples of the ancient world. Virgil refers to their city as 'opposite Italy and the mouths of the Tiber, rich in resources and especially severe in the pursuit of war' (*Aeneid*, I. 13–14). It was this key strategic position in the Mediterranean which governed their military tactics and, in turn, their economic policy. Carthage was a sea-going nation, using its fleet, which was manned by its citizens, virtually to close the western Mediterranean to other nations, to wage war, and to trade in goods all round the Mediterranean and down the west coast of Africa as far as Guinea—gold, ivory, bronze, tin, pottery, grain, perfume, dyes, and, of course, slaves. It founded colonies along the North African coast as far as Cyrenaica, in southern Spain, in Corsica, Sardinia, and on the

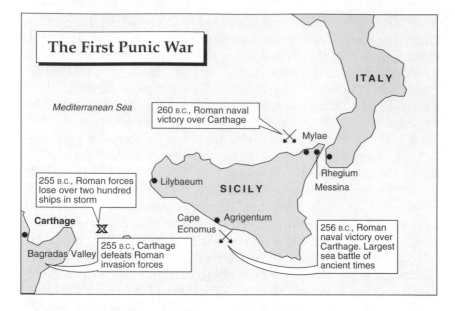

western tip of Sicily. Carthaginian citizens did not normally fight in the army, which was composed mainly of African conscripts and mercenaries from all parts of the Mediterranean—and Carthage could afford to employ the best. This multi-racial army still had to be forged into a coherent fighting force, which was the responsibility of its commanders, who were Carthaginians and professional career soldiers.

The First Punic War (264–241 BC) was largely fought at sea. The Romans purpose-built a series of fleets to match the Carthaginian numbers and manned them with marine commandos trained in hand-to-hand fighting—in an age of rudimentary artillery, the standard naval tactic was to attach grapples to an enemy ship and then overwhelm its crew by superior numbers. The losses on both sides were enormous, but the Romans were better at unearthing and deploying ever more resources, and finally the Carthaginians sued for peace and agreed to withdraw all claims to Sicily. Shortly after hostilities ceased, however, the Romans took advantage of the temporary preoccupation of the Carthaginians with a revolt of their mercenaries to annex Corsica and Sardinia, an act which was undeniably foul play.

HANNIBAL AND THE SECOND WAR

Carthage retaliated by increasing its empire in another quarter: the whole of southern Spain, with its potential wealth and manpower, was overrun. This Spanish campaign was led successively by a brilliant family trio of generals: Hamilcar (d. 229 BC), his son-in-law Hasdrubal (d. 221 BC), and Hamilcar's son Hannibal

(247–182 BC). It was so successful that in order to prevent Carthage extending its influence still farther north, the Romans were forced into a diplomatic manoeuvre. The river Ebro was to be regarded as the boundary between the interests of the two sides, but the town of Saguntum on the east coast would remain nominally under Roman protection. When in 221 BC Hasdrubal was murdered by a slave whose master he had put to death, Hannibal succeeded to the command. He started the Second Punic War (218–202 BC) by attacking and capturing Saguntum. This was clearly a deliberate ploy. The Carthaginians were motivated to set up this new confrontation by a desire for revenge and by their fear of Roman incursions into their newly-won territory.

The Romans began by assuming that tactically this war would be a continuation of the first, and prepared a fleet in which they could cross to Carthage and this time take the city itself. Hannibal confounded them (and the rest of the world then and since) by doing not just the unexpected, but the impossible. He marched his army—infantry, cavalry, baggage train, and heavy tanks in the form of his famous elephants—out of Spain and across the river Rhône on a flotilla of boats and rafts, against continual opposition from native Gallic tribes. He invaded Italy by a route which took him over, and through, the Alps; at one point he had to blast away a wall of solid rock by heating it with fires and then dashing on to it quantities of raw wine. According to [the second-century BC Greek historian] Polybius, who is regarded as the most reliable authority, Hannibal entered Italy with 20,000 foot and 6,000 cavalry, having lost 18,000 infantry and 2,000 horsemen since crossing the Rhône. With these, and the surviving elephants, he soon gained control of northern Italy, having outflanked one Roman army before the river Trebia, and trapped another by Lake Trasimene. Rome itself was too tough a nut to crack, so Hannibal bypassed the city and went on into the south, where at Cannae he outmanoeuvred a numerically much stronger Roman force and virtually annihilated it. Then for fourteen years he and his army rampaged around southern Italy before being lured back to Carthage, and to defeat at Zama in 202 BC, by a splendid African campaign conducted by Cornelius Scipio (234–183 BC), who had already driven the Carthaginians out of Spain and was afterwards awarded the honorific surname of Africanus. In particular, he managed at Zama to neutralize Hannibal's tactics of opening the battle with a frontal charge of his eighty elephants. Hannibal survived the battle, only to end his life in exile in Asia, having failed in his attempt to rebuild his country's fortunes by political means. . . .

Cato and the Third War

After the Second Punic War, Rome confiscated Spain, leaving Carthage with just its north African colonies, and promptly waded into local Spanish conflicts to keep the tribes there in order, besides being involved in full-scale wars in Macedonia, Asia Minor, and Syria. In spite of the sanctions and conditions of peace that had been imposed on Carthage at the end of the war, there was the possibility that it might rise again and try to take revenge on its conquerors. Old Cato [the Elder, a noted, very conservative Roman Senator], who in 157 BC had been a member of a diplomatic mission to Africa to mediate between Carthage and neighbouring Numidia, saw this more clearly than anyone else.

> It is said that he even contrived to drop a Libyan fig on the floor of the senate as he rearranged his toga. Then, as the rest admired its size and lusciousness, he warned them that the land where it grew was only three days away from Rome by sea. In another respect, he was even more uncompromising. Whatever question was being addressed in the senate, he incorporated into his speech the words, 'In my opinion, Carthage must be destroyed.'

> (Plutarch, *Lives: Cato*, XXVII)

The Carthaginians were finally manoeuvred into the position of having to defend themselves against Numidian invasions of their territory. This was technically a breach of the treaty of 201 BC, under which they were forbidden to take up arms without Rome's permission. The senate, which, egged on by Cato, had made plans for just such an eventuality, voted for war once again. They sent out a trained army comprising, according to the Alexandrian Greek historian Appian (*c.* AD 95–*c.* 165), 80,000 infantry and 4,000 cavalry, under the command of the consuls, 'to whom they gave secret orders not to discontinue the war until Carthage had been razed to the ground' (*Punic Wars*, VIII. 11). The Third Punic War lasted for just three years (149–146 BC). That it continued so long was due to a heroic Carthaginian defence of their city. It was hastily mounted, since the messenger who brought the news of the senate's declaration of war also carried the announcement that the expeditionary force had sailed. It was, too, frenziedly maintained, since as part of the conditions of the surrender of the city at the end of the previous war the Carthaginians had handed over '200,000 full suits of armour and 3,000 anti-siege engines as sureties against their going to war again' (Strabo, *Geography*, XVII. 3). Carthage was duly destroyed. The 50,000 survivors of the siege were sold into slavery.

THE MILITARY SYSTEMS OF GREECE AND ROME COMPARED

POLYBIUS

A Greek statesman and important historian, Polybius (ca.200–ca.117 B.C.) was taken to Rome as a hostage in 168 B.C. There, he became a friend of the Roman general Scipio Aemilianus. Later, Polybius wrote a forty-volume history of Rome (the *Histories*) covering the period 220–146 B.C., part of which has survived. In the portion of the work titled "On the Phalanx," presented here, he compares the two chief military systems of the day—the Greek and Roman. The Greek system relied on the Macedonian phalanx, a huge unit of soldiers standing in rows, one behind another, and carrying battle pikes of increasing length (the points of which protruded lethally from the front of the formation). Though formidable under certain conditions, the historian explains, the phalanx had its weaknesses; and these proved fatal in the face of Rome's battle formations (small units called maniples, which could move around and form units of varying size and shape), which were more flexible and efficient. This analysis is vital, for it was the superiority of Rome's military system (along with Greek disunity) that ensured the coming fall of the Greek states to the Roman juggernaut.

I n the past the Macedonian formation was proved by operational experience to be superior to the others which were in use in Asia and Greece, while the Roman system overcame those employed in Africa and among all the peoples of Western

From *The Rise and Fall of the Roman Empire*, by Polybius, translated by Ian Scott-Kilvert (Penguin Classics, 1979). Translation copyright © Ian Scott-Kilvert, 1979. Reprinted by permission of Penguin Books Ltd.

Europe. In our own times we have seen both the two formations and the soldiers of the two nations matched against one another, not just once but on many occasions. It should prove a useful exercise, and one well worth the trouble, to study the differences between them, and to discover the reason why on the battlefield the Romans have always proved the victors and carried off the prize. If we examine the matter in this way we shall not, like the ignorant majority of mankind, speak merely in terms of chance, and congratulate the victors without giving the reasons, but shall be able to pay them the praise and admiration they deserve because we have come to understand the causes of their success. . . .

There are a number of factors which make it easy to understand that so long as the phalanx retains its characteristic form and strength nothing can withstand its charge or resist it face to face. When the phalanx is closed up for action, each man with his arms occupies a space of three feet. The pike he carries was earlier designed to be twenty-four feet long, but as adapted to current practice was shortened to twenty-one, and from this we must subtract the space between the bearer's hands and the rear portion of the pike which keeps it balanced and couched. This amounts to six feet in all, from which it is clear that the pike will project fifteen feet in front of the body of each hoplite when he advances against the enemy grasping it with both hands. This also means that while the pikes of the men in the second, third, and fourth ranks naturally extend further than those of the fifth rank, yet even the latter will still project three feet in front of the men in the first rank. I am assuming of course that the phalanx keeps its characteristic order, and is closed up both from the rear and on the flanks. . . .

At any rate if my description is true and exact, it follows that each man in the front rank will have the points of five pikes extending in front of him, each point being three feet ahead of the one behind.

From these facts we can easily picture the nature and the tremendous power of a charge by the whole phalanx, when it advances sixteen deep with levelled pikes. Of these sixteen ranks those who are stationed further back than the fifth cannot use their pikes to take an active part in the battle. They therefore do not level them man against man, but hold them with the points tilted upwards over the shoulders of the men in front. In this way they give protection to the whole phalanx from above, for the pikes are massed so closely that they can keep off any missiles which might clear the heads of the front ranks and strike those immediately behind them. Once the charge is launched, these rear ranks by the sheer pressure of their bodily weight greatly in-

The extraordinary cohesiveness and power of the Greek phalanx is clearly illustrated in this modern drawing of a battle between Greeks and non-Greek tribesmen.

crease its momentum and make it impossible for the foremost ranks to face about.

I have described both in general terms and in detail the composition of the phalanx. I must now for purposes of comparison explain the special features of Roman equipment and tactical formation, and the differences which distinguish the two. With the Romans each soldier in full armour also occupies a space three feet wide. However, according to the Roman methods of fighting each man makes his movements individually: not only does he defend his body with his long shield, constantly moving it to meet a threatened blow, but he uses his sword both for cutting and for thrusting. Obviously these tactics require a more open order and an interval between the men, and in practice each soldier needs to be at least three feet from those in the same rank and from those in front of and behind him if he is to perform his function efficiently. The result of these dispositions is that each Roman soldier has to face two men in the front rank of the phalanx, and so has to encounter and fight against ten spear points. It is impossible for one man to cut through all of these once the battle lines are engaged, nor is it easy to force the points away; moreover, in the Roman formation the rear ranks do not support the front, either in forcing the spears away or in the use of their swords. It is easy to understand then, as I mentioned at the beginning, how nothing can withstand the frontal assault of the phalanx so long as it retains its characteristic formation and strength.

What then is the factor which enables the Romans to win the battle and causes those who use the phalanx to fail? The answer is that in war the times and places for action are unlimited, whereas the phalanx requires one time and one type of ground only in order to produce its peculiar effect. Now if the enemy were compelled to position themselves according to the times and places demanded by the phalanx whenever an important battle was imminent, no doubt those who employ the phalanx would always carry off the victory for the reasons I have given above. But if it is quite possible, even easy, to evade its irresistible charge, how can the phalanx any longer be considered formidable? Again, it is generally admitted that its use requires flat and level ground which is unencumbered by any obstacles such as ditches, gullies, depressions, ridges and watercourses, all of which are sufficient to hinder and dislocate such a formation. There is general agreement that it is almost impossible, or at any rate exceedingly rare, to find a stretch of country of say two or three miles or more which contains no obstacles of this kind. But even assuming that such an arena could be found, if the enemy refuses to come down into it, but prefers to traverse the country sacking the towns and devastating the territories of our allies, what purpose can the phalanx serve? If it remains on the ground which suits it best, not only is it unable to assist its allies, but it cannot even ensure its own safety, for the transport of its supplies will easily be stopped by the enemy when they have undisputed command of the open country. On the other hand, if it leaves the terrain which favours it and attempts an action elsewhere, it will easily be defeated. Or again, supposing that the enemy does decide to descend into the plain and fight there, but, instead of committing his entire force to the battle when the phalanx has its one opportunity to charge, keeps even a small part of it in reserve at the moment when the main action takes place, it is easy to forecast what will happen from the tactics which the Romans are now putting into practice.

The outcome indeed does not need to be demonstrated by argument: we need only refer to accomplished facts. The Romans do not attempt to make their line numerically equal to the enemy's, nor do they expose the whole strength of the legions to a frontal attack by the phalanx. Instead they keep part of the forces in reserve while the rest engage the enemy. Later in the battle, whether the phalanx in its charge drives back the troops opposed to it or is driven back by them, in either event it loses its own peculiar formation. For either in pursuing a retreating enemy or falling back before an oncoming one, the phalanx leaves behind the other units of its own army; at this point the enemy's reserves can occupy the space the phalanx has vacated, and are no longer obliged to attack from the front, but can fall upon it from flank and rear. When it is thus easy to deny the phalanx the opportunities it needs and to minimize the advantages it enjoys, and also impossible to prevent the enemy from acting against it, does it not follow that the difference between these two systems is enormous?

Besides this, those who rely on the phalanx are obliged to march across and encamp on ground of every description; they must occupy favourable positions in advance, besiege others and be besieged themselves and deal with unexpected appearances of the enemy. All these eventualities are part and parcel of war, and may have an important or a decisive effect on the final victory. In all these situations the Macedonian formation is sometimes of little use, and sometimes of none at all, because the phalanx soldier cannot operate either in smaller units or singly, whereas the Roman formation is highly flexible. Every Roman soldier, once he is armed and goes into action, can adapt himself equally well to any place or time and meet an attack from any quarter. He is likewise equally well-prepared and needs to make no change whether he has to fight with the main body or with a detachment, in maniples or singly. Accordingly, since the effective use of the parts of the Roman army is so much superior, their plans are much more likely to achieve success than those of others. I have felt obliged to deal with this subject at some length, because so many Greeks on those occasions when the Macedonians suffered defeat regarded such an event as almost incredible, and many will still be at a loss to understand why and how the phalanx proves inferior by comparison with the Roman method of arming their troops.

Rome Subdues Greece

Arthur E.R. Boak and William G. Sinnigen

Eager to punish Macedonia's king, Philip V for helping Carthage during the Second Punic War, late in 200 B.C. the Romans crossed the Adriatic Sea into Illyria (Illyricum), the Balkan region bordering Macedonia in the west. Soon afterward they entered Greece, and within only a few years managed to defeat not only Philip, but the able and energetic Seleucid ruler Antiochus III, the feisty Aetolian and Achaean Confederacies (or Leagues), and other Greeks as well. This well-informed synopsis of Rome's seizure of control over Greek lands and affairs is by former University of Michigan professor Arthur E.R. Boak and former Hunter College professor William G. Sinnigen.

During the thirty-five years which followed the battle of Zama, Rome attained the same dominant position in the eastern Mediterranean that she had won in the West as a result of the First and Second Punic Wars. The explanation of Roman interference in the East and the rapid extension of her authority there lies in the political situation of the Hellenistic world at the close of the third century, one which Rome exploited by virtue of her increasingly important role as patron to states east of the Adriatic. . . .

Down to the year 201 Rome can hardly be said to have had any definite eastern policy. Diplomatic intercourse with Egypt had followed the visit of an Egyptian embassy to Rome as early as 273, but this had had no political consequences. Since that date she had come into conflict with the Illyrians and with Macedo-

From *A History of Rome to A.D. 565*, by Arthur E.R. Boak and William G. Sinnigen (New York: Macmillan, 1921).

nia and had established a small protectorate across the Adriatic, but in so doing her actions had been spasmodic and had been brought about by the attacks of the Illyrians and Macedonians upon her allies or herself and were not the result of any aggressive policy of her own. The interest and outlook of Rome's agrarian oligarchy did not include Hellas [Greece] as a whole or the Greek East. This may be seen in the favorable peace terms granted Philip V of Macedonia in 205, by which Rome abandoned her formal alliances with Philip's enemies, especially the Aetolians. This is the first known instance in which Rome failed to fulfill to the letter her written agreements with her friends, and marks an important stage in the growing sophistication of her foreign policy. These actions made her very unpopular in most of Greece. Her erstwhile allies, especially the Aetolians, protested that they had been left in the lurch, while other Greek states felt antagonistic because Rome had permitted the Aetolians to treat them brutally during the recent war. Rome still found it possible to maintain friendly relations, albeit without formal and possibly entangling treaties, with Pergamon, the Illyrians, some city-states of the Peloponnesus, and possibly Athens. Rome's general attitude toward the Greek world in the period 205–201 was watchful rather than disinterested; she had no vital or definite commitments in the area except the defense of her Illyrian clients.

THE ROMANS TURN EASTWARD

A combination of circumstances involving Illyria brought about the Second Macedonian War. After the peace of 205 Philip apparently misread the Roman attitude toward Greece as one of total disinterest and attempted by diplomacy to seduce the Illyrians from their connection with Rome. Just as Rome was observing the Illyrian situation with increasing disquiet in 202, the envoys of Rhodes and of Attalus I, King of Pergamon, arrived to inform the Senate of Philip's Aggressions in the East and of his alleged pact with Antiochus to partition the Egyptian Empire. They requested Roman help. The Senate, basically unconcerned with what was going on in the Aegean and undisturbed by the unlikely prospect of the "alliance" between Philip and Antiochus being directed against Italy at some future date, was interested, however, in humbling the king who had stabbed her in the back during the recent war with Hannibal and who was now tampering with her Illyrian clients. It seized upon Philip's aggressions against Attalus as a possible *casus belli* [justification for war]. Roman ambassadors were sent to Greece in 201/200 to proclaim a basic change in Roman policy—protection of all Greeks against future Macedonian aggression—and to mobilize Greece under the Roman aegis against Philip. They also carried an ultimatum for Philip which they delivered to one of his generals, a demand that he refrain from war with any Greek state and that he submit his differences with Attalus to arbitration. The ultimatum revealed Rome's new aims: the reduction of Philip to the status of a client prince and the consequent conversion of Greece into a Roman protectorate. Although the Senate was apparently committed to war when these demands were not met, the Roman people as a whole shrank from embarking upon another war so soon after the close of the desperate conflict with Carthage. At first the Centuriate Assembly voted against the proposal, and at a second meeting was induced to sanction it only when the people were told they would have to face another invasion of Italy if they did not anticipate Philip's action. When the Assembly finally gave its approval, one of the Roman ambassadors whom the Senate had already sent to Greece to threaten Philip and encourage his opponents presented the formal declaration of war to the king, who was at that time engaged in the siege of Abydos on the Hellespont, whereupon the conflict began. In accordance with their instructions the ambassadors then visited Antiochus in Syria, perhaps to intercede on behalf of Egypt or to assure him of the good will of Rome so that he might not abandon his Syrian campaign and unite his forces with those of Philip in Macedonia. Roman diplomacy leading up to the war shows that at this stage of her history Rome took states unilaterally under her protection without the formality of a treaty and tended to regard her friends not as equals but as clients.

THE SECOND MACEDONIAN WAR

Late in 200 a Roman army under the consul Sulpicius Galba crossed into Illyricum and tried to penetrate into Macedonia. Both in this and in the succeeding year, however, the Romans, although aided by the Aetolian Confederacy, Pergamon, Rhodes, and Athens, were unable to inflict any decisive defeat upon Philip or to invade his kingdom.

With the arrival of one of the consuls of 198, Titus Flamininus, the situation speedily changed. The Achaean Confederacy was won over to the side of Rome, and Flamininus succeeded in forcing Philip to evacuate Epirus and to withdraw into Thessaly. In the following winter negotiations for peace were opened. At the insistence of her Greek allies, Rome now demanded not merely a guarantee that Philip would refrain from attacking the Hellenes but also the evacuation of Corinth, Chalcis, and Demetrias, three fortresses known as "the fetters of Greece." Philip refused to make this concession.

The next year military operations were resumed with both armies in Thessaly. Early in the summer a battle was fought on a ridge of hills called Cynoscephalae (the Dogs' Heads), where the Romans won a complete victory. Although the Aetolians rendered valuable assistance in this engagement, the Macedonian defeat was due primarily to the superior flexibility of the Roman legionary formation over the phalanx. Philip fled to Macedonia and sued for peace. The Aetolians and his enemies in Greece sought his destruction, but Flamininus realized the importance of Macedonia to the Greek world as a bulwark against the Celtic peoples of the lower Danube and would not support their demands. The terms fixed by the Roman Senate were: autonomy of the Hellenes, in Greece and Asia; evacuation of the Macedonian possessions in Greece, in the Aegean, and in Illyricum; an indemnity of 1,000 talents ($1,200,000); and the surrender of nearly all his warships. These conditions Philip was obliged to accept (196). Soon afterwards he became a Roman ally. . . .

ANTIOCHUS AND THE AETOLIANS PROVE TROUBLESOME

Even before Flamininus and his army had withdrawn from Greece, the activities of Antiochus had awakened the mistrust of the Roman Senate and threatened hostilities. The Syrian king had completed the conquest of Lower Syria in 198. Profiting by the difficulties in which Philip of Macedon was involved, he had then turned his attention toward Asia Minor and Thrace with the hope of recovering the possessions once held by his ancestor, Seleucus I. The Romans were at the time too much occupied to oppose him. Outwardly he professed to be a friend of Rome and to be limiting his activities to the reestablishment of his empire's former extent. Eventually, in 196 he crossed over into Europe and took Thrace. The Romans tried to induce him to withdraw but were unsuccessful. Two years later Antiochus himself opened negotiations with the Senate to secure Roman recognition of his claims to Thrace and to certain cities in Asia Minor which, relying upon Roman support, refused to acknowledge his overlordship. The Roman government, cynically enough, was willing to abandon its self-proclaimed status as protector of the Greeks in Asia if Antiochus would evacuate Thrace. Since Antiochus, although harboring no designs against Rome, refused to be forced out of his European possessions, he decided to support the anti-Roman elements in Greece to force Rome to yield the points at issue. Accordingly, he willingly received deputations from the Aetolians, who were the leading opponents of Rome among the Greeks

The Aetolians, Rome's allies in the war just concluded and

greatly exaggerating the importance of their services, were disgruntled because Macedonia had not been entirely dismembered and they had been restrained from enlarging the territory of the Confederacy at the expense of their neighbors. In short, they wished to replace Macedonia as the leading Greek state. Accustomed to regard war as a legitimate source of revenue, they did not easily reconcile themselves to Rome's imposition of peace in Hellas. Ever since the battle of Cynoscephalae they had striven to undermine Roman influence among the Greeks, and now they sought to draw Antiochus into conflict with Rome.

In 192 they brought matters to a head by unexpectedly attacking some of Rome's supporters in Greece and seizing the fortress of Demetrias, which they offered to the king, to whom they also made an unauthorized promise of aid from Macedonia. Trusting in the support promised by the Aetolians, Antiochus sailed to Greece with an advance force of 10,000 men. Upon his arrival the Aetolians elected him their commander in chief. . . .

THE ROMANS DEFEAT ANTIOCHUS AND THE AETOLIANS

In 191 a Roman army under the consul Acilius Glabrio appeared in Greece and defeated the forces of Antiochus at Thermopylae. The king fled to Asia. Contrary to his hopes he had found little support in Greece. Philip of Macedon and the Achaean Confederacy adhered to the Romans, and the Aetolians were made helpless by an invasion of their own country. The Rhodians and Eumenes, the new king of Pergamon, joined their navies to the Roman fleet.

As Antiochus would not listen to the peace terms laid down by the Romans, the latter resolved to invade Asia Minor. Two naval victories, won with the aid of Rhodes and Pergamon, secured control of the Aegean, and in 190 a Roman force crossed the Hellespont. For commander the Senate had wished to designate Scipio Africanus, the greatest Roman general. As he had recently been consul he was now ineligible for that office. The law was circumvented by election of his brother Lucius to the consulate and his assignment to the command, and by the appointment of Publius to accompany him, apparently as a legate. This arrangement permitted Publius to assume practical direction of the campaign.

One decisive victory over Antiochus at Magnesia [in western Asia Minor] in the autumn of 190 brought him to terms. He agreed to surrender all territory north of the Taurus mountains and west of Pamphylia, to give up his war elephants, to surrender all but ten of his ships of war, to pay an indemnity of 15,000 talents ($18,000,000) in twelve annual instalments, and to abstain from attacking the allies of Rome. Unlike Carthage, he was still at liberty to defend himself if attacked. Peace upon these conditions was formally ratified in 188. This time Rome did not "free" all the Greeks as she had done in 196, since such an action would have produced too many petty states and future imbroglios [entanglements]. Some of the Greek city-states did receive their freedom, but Rhodes and Pergamon were the principal beneficiaries of the peace, which brought them an accession of territory at the expense of neighboring Greeks and non-Greeks alike. . . .

The Roman campaign of 191 against the Aetolians had caused the latter, who were also attacked by Philip of Macedon, to seek terms. The Romans demanded unconditional surrender, and the Aetolians decided to continue the struggle. No energetic measures were taken against them at once, but in 189 the consul Fulvius Nobilior pressed the war vigorously and besieged their chief stronghold, Ambracia. Since the obstinate resistance of its defenders defied all his efforts and since the Athenians were trying to act as mediators in ending the war, the Romans abandoned their demand for unconditional surrender. The Aetolians proved that they had not understood the meaning of clientship, and the Romans were determined that any peace treaty with them should express their dependent status. Peace was finally made on the following conditions: the Aetolian Confederacy was granted a permanent alliance with Rome on an unequal footing, with the obligation to support Rome against all her enemies; the Confederacy gave up all territory captured by its enemies during the war; Ambracia was surrendered and sacked. . . .

MACEDONIA DISMANTLED

Although by her alliance with the Aetolians Rome had planted herself permanently on Greek soil and in the war with Antiochus had claimed to exercise a protectorate over the Greek world, the Senate as yet gave no indication of reversing the policy of Flamininus, and the Greek states remained friends of Rome in the enjoyment of political "independence." It was not long, however, before these friendly relations became seriously strained and Rome was induced to embark upon a policy of political and then military interference in Greek affairs, which ultimately put an end to the apparent freedom of Hellas. The fundamental cause of the change was that, while Rome interpreted Greek freedom to mean liberty of action provided that the wishes and arrangements of Rome were respected, the Greeks understood it to mean the perfect freedom of sovereign communities and resented bitterly any infringement of their supposed rights. Keeping in mind these conflicting points of view, it is easy to see how difficulties were bound to arise, inevitably to be settled according to the wishes of the stronger power. . . .

Philip V of Macedon considered that the assistance he had furnished to Rome in the Syrian War was proof of his loyalty and warranted the annexation of the territory he had overrun in that conflict. The Senate was not inclined to allow the power of Macedonia to attain dangerous proportions, and he was forced to forego his claims. Henceforth he was bitter toward Rome. He devoted himself to the development of the military resources of his kingdom with the ultimate view of challenging once again Rome's authority. At his death in 179 he left an army of from 30,000 to 40,000 men and a treasure of 6,000 talents ($7,200,000). His son and successor Perseus inherited his father's anti-Roman policy and entered into relations with the enemies of Rome everywhere in Greece.

The Senate was kept well aware of his schemes by his enemies in Greece. . . . Therefore it determined to forestall his plans and force him into war. In 172 a Roman commission visited Perseus and required of him concessions which meant loss of liberty. Upon his refusal to comply with their demands the commissioners returned home, and Rome declared war. When success depended upon energetic action, Perseus sought to avoid the issue and tried vainly to placate the Romans. In 171 a Roman force landed in Greece and made its way to Thessaly. In the campaigns of this and the following year the Roman commanders were too incapable and their troops too undisciplined to make any headway, but Perseus showed no ability to take advantage of his opportunities. . . . Finally, in 168, the Romans found an able general in the consul Aemilius Paullus, who restored the morale of the Roman soldiers and won a complete victory over Perseus in the battle of Pydna. Perseus took flight but soon was obliged to give himself up. He was taken to Rome, where he was treated with ignominy and died in captivity. The Macedonian kingdom was at an end. Its territory was divided into four autonomous republics. . . . A yearly tribute of 100 talents was imposed upon them; the royal mines and domains became the property of Rome, and for a time the gold and silver mines were shut down.

ROME DEFEATS THE REST OF GREECE

Having disposed of Macedonia, the Romans turned their attention to the other Greek states with the intention of rewarding their friends and punishing their enemies. During the recent war the Greeks had realized that Perseus' defeat would make Roman power unchallengeable, and consequently anti-Roman parties had arisen in many parts of Greece. The situation was worsened, especially in the Peloponnese, by social disorder which added to the strife from political causes. Death or exile awaited the leaders of the anti-Roman parties, many of whose names became known from the papers of Perseus. Although the Achaeans had given no positive proof of disloyalty, 1,000 of their leading men, among them the historian Polybius, were carried off to Italy, nominally to be given the chance of clearing themselves before the Senate but really to be kept as hostages in Italy for the future conduct of the Confederacy.

The Rhodians, because they had endeavored to secure a peaceful settlement between Rome and Perseus, were forced to surrender their possessions in Asia Minor. . . . Their commercial prosperity was crippled by the establishment of a free port at the island of Delos. Eumenes of Pergamon, whose actions had made him suspect to Rome, was subjected to humiliating treatment, although he kept his kingdom. Far worse was the fate of Epirus, seventy of whose towns were sacked and 150,000 of the inhabitants carried off into slavery.

Henceforth it was clear that Rome was sovereign in the eastern Mediterranean and that her friends and allies enjoyed only local autonomy, while expected to be obedient to the orders of Rome. This is well illustrated by the anecdote of the circle of Popilius. During the Third Macedonian War, Antiochus IV, Epiphanes, King of Syria and former Roman hostage, invaded Egypt. After the battle of Pydna a Roman ambassador, Gaius Popilius, was sent to request his withdrawal. Popilius met Antiochus before Alexandria and delivered the Senate's message. The king asked for time to consider, but the Roman, drawing a circle around him in the sand, bade him answer before he left the spot. Antiochus yielded and evacuated Egypt. . . .

The mutual rivalries among the Greek states, which frequently evoked senatorial intervention, and the ill will occasioned by the harshness of the Romans toward the anti-Roman party everywhere caused a large faction among the Hellenes to look for the first favorable opportunity for freeing Greece from Roman suzerainty. . . .

The Achaean Confederacy was one especially anti-Roman state. There the irksomeness of the Roman protectorate was heightened by the return of the 300 survivors of the political exiles of 167. The anti-Roman party, supported by the extreme democratic elements in the cities, was in control of the Confederacy when border difficulties with Sparta broke out afresh in 149. The matter was referred to the Senate for settlement, but the Achaeans did not await its decision. They attacked and defeated Sparta, confident that the Romans were preoccupied by the wars in Spain, Africa, and Macedonia.

The Senate determined to punish the Confederacy by detaching certain important cities from its membership. In 147 the Achaean assembly tempestuously refused to carry out the orders of the Roman ambassadors, although the Macedonian revolt had been crushed. Their leaders, expecting no mercy from Rome, prepared for war, and they were joined by the Boeotians and other peoples of central Greece. Everywhere they were supported by the poorer classes in the cities, who saw hope for economic betterment in a social revolution. The next year the Achaeans again refused to comply with Roman advice, whereupon the Romans sent a fleet and an army against them under the consul Lucius Mummius. Metellus, the conqueror of Macedonia, subdued central Greece, and Mummius routed the forces of the Confederacy at Leucopetra on the Isthmus (146). Corinth was sacked and burnt, its treasures were carried off to Rome, and its inhabitants sold into slavery. Its land, like that of Carthage, was added to the Roman public domain. . . . This was a warning which the other cities of Greece could not misinterpret. A senatorial commission dissolved the Achaean Confederacy as well as the similar political combinations of the Boeotians and Phocians. The cities of Greece entered into individual relations with Rome. Those which had stood on the side of Rome, as Athens and Sparta, retained their previous status as Roman allies; the rest were made subject and tributary.

CAESAR'S CONQUEST OF GAUL

JOHN WARRY

The Conquest of Gaul (the area now encompassed by France and Belgium) by the Roman statesman-general Julius Caesar in the 50s B.C. had momentous consequences. It opened up a large portion of western Europe to Roman settlement; and Roman customs, language, and ideas survived there well past Rome's fall, helping in profound ways to shape the emerging European character. This synopsis of Caesar's Gallic conquests, beginning with his defeat of the Helvetii, a tribal people who had recently entered the region from western Switzerland, is by noted ancient military historian John Warry. (He mentions "Italian Gaul"; the Romans called this section of northern Italy Cisalpine Gaul. They called the region beyond the Alps, which Caesar conquered, Transalpine Gaul. Warry also cites Caesar's commentaries; these were the personal journals he kept of some of his campaigns, works that have fortunately survived.)

Editor's Note: Circumvallation was an ancient siege technique in which a town or fortress was completely encircled by walls, guard towers, ditches, and/or booby traps.

It may be asked whether Caesar's conquest of Gaul was in fact a great achievement in the Roman national interest or whether it was simply a means to personal prestige and political power at home. The same question may be asked of many Roman military exploits in the first century BC. . . .

Caesar's command as proconsul in 59 BC was at first limited to

From *Warfare in the Classical World*, by John Warry (Norman: University of Oklahoma Press, 1995). Copyright © 1980 Salamander Books Ltd. Reprinted by permission of the University of Oklahoma Press.

Italian Gaul and Illyricum. It was then extended to Gaul beyond the Alps. There was good reason for posting Roman forces in this area. German and Gallic tribes were once more on the move and Roman memories of the Cimbric war [in which the Cimbri, a large German Tribe, threatened Gaul and Italy] were only half-a-century old. The Helvetian Gauls had, at the time of Caesar's proconsulate, already been forced southwards into north Switzerland by pressure from the Germanic Suebi. When the Suebi, intervening in Gallic tribal disputes, infiltrated west of the Rhine, the Helvetii, now in danger of being isolated from the rest of Gaul, decided to migrate westwards, and asked in 58 BC permission to move peacefully through the Roman Province (southern France). Caesar, as he explains, unable to see where such a movement might end and remembering that the Helvetii, in alliance with the Cimbri, had once inflicted humiliating defeat on a Roman army, refused his permission and built an elaborate 19-mile (28 km) earthwork, complete with forts and command posts, between Lake Geneva and the Jura mountains, to block the migrants' southward exodus. The extent of this fortification and the speed with which it was constructed are further testimony to the growing part played by military engineering in Roman strategy during this period of their history.

Caesar had already gained time by a rather disingenuous protraction of negotiations with the Gauls, and he was able to collect five legions in north Italy before the Helvetii, frustrated by his Geneva line of fortifications, had made their way with difficulty across the Jura mountains and the valley of the Saône. He attacked the Helvetii and inflicted a defeat on the clan that formed their rearguard as it waited to follow the main body across the Arar river (Saône). Very swiftly bridging the river, Caesar followed in their tracks for some two weeks until, encouraged by difficulties which he had with his corn supply, they unwisely took the offensive. After a battle which lasted into the night, the Helvetii were defeated. As a result, other tribes, fearing reprisals from Caesar, refused to supply them with corn. Starvation forced them to surrender, and Caesar resettled them in their Swiss homeland. If his ambition had been less far sighted, it would have been simple and lucrative to sell them all as slaves. But the Helvetii, apart from their inconvenience elsewhere, were required in their original location—as a buffer state against the Germans.

DEALING WITH THE SUEBI

This move, of course, made no sense unless the German infiltration into Gaul were at the same time halted. After an uncompromising diplomatic exchange with Ariovistus, king of the Suebi,

Caesar found himself committed to a new war—which indeed he must have expected. The generation of Roman soldiers which Caesar commanded . . . had not previously encountered German warriors, and the new enemy's towering physique and warlike reputation dismayed them. At one point something like a panic occurred. But Caesar's charismatic leadership and the fearlessness which he communicated especially to the Tenth Legion, his *corps d'élite*, soon rallied officers and men alike. . . . The Romans defeated Ariovistus in a major battle in the plain of Alsace and drove him back across the Rhine—which he never recrossed. In this action, Publius Crassus . . . was in charge of Caesar's cavalry, and at a difficult moment his initiative swung the Roman reserve line into action on the hard-pressed left wing, turning a doubtful issue into a certain victory.

After the victory over Ariovistus, Caesar travelled south to perform his judicial functions as governor in Italian Gaul. Meanwhile, he left his army, under command of a deputy, encamped for the winter west of the Jura mountains. But the Belgic Gauls to the north, who were of mixed Celtic and Germanic extraction, were preparing for war.

THE BELGIC TRIBES SUBDUED

In the following summer, after arranging for some diversionary operations by the Aedui, a friendly Gallic tribe, Caesar met a combined force of Belgic tribes, some 40,000 strong, in a battle on the Axona river (Aisne). Caesar's camp had been fortified on a low hill, with the bend of the river embracing it. The corn supply was again in question and the position was chosen not only for tactical defence but to prevent an enemy encircling movement which might cut the Romans off from friendly country in their rear—the source of their provisions. Anticipating battle on level ground in front of the camp and being heavily outnumbered, Caesar protected his flanks on either side by digging trenches; these extended from the Roman camp at one end to terminal forts in which artillery engines were installed. A battlefield was thus prepared, as in a kind of arena.

However, despite skirmishing in which Caesar's cavalry had the advantage, neither army would risk attacking across the intervening marsh. The Belgians then found fords on the river, and attempted to cross in order to cut Roman communications in the rear. This plan was defeated by Caesar's prompt use of cavalry and light-armed troops which, attacking the enemy in the water, inflicted heavy losses. The Belgians had already, in the course of their march, failed to capture a Gallic town to which, as an ally, Caesar had sent timely aid; now, finding themselves short of provisions, they became disheartened. It was decided that the tribes should disperse, each to its own territory, on the understanding that all should reassemble for the defence of any one that was attacked. Their retreat, however, was so disorderly and unplanned that the Romans were able to fall upon the various contingents separately and massacre them amid scenes of confusion.

Most of the Belgic tribes were now glad to make peace with Caesar, but the strongest of them, the Nervii, still defied him. Having gained intelligence of the normal Roman order of march, they decided on a surprise attack. Mainly an infantry force, they issued from a wooded hilltop, driving Caesar's cavalry vanguard before them, then swept across the Sabis river (Sambre) and uphill, to attack the Romans as they made ready to entrench their camp. Six Roman legions had marched in front of the baggage, which was guarded by two rear legions. This differed from the arrangement which the Nervii had been led to expect, for when there was no immediate likelihood of fighting, each legion was separated by its baggage from the next.

Even then, the surprise was so effective that the Romans scarcely found time to put on their helmets and remove the covers from their shields. Snatching a shield from one of his rear men, Caesar made his way to the front line, rallying his troops in person in the thick of the fight. The Romans suffered serious casualties, but were saved from disaster largely by their training and by the fact that officers and men knew what to do without being told. The Nervii, who had relied on surprise and superior numbers, found themselves fighting at a disadvantage when the Roman rear legions arrived. Many of them fell in battle, resisting with desperate courage, but the Romans now had control of the situation; on that day the Nervii were utterly destroyed as a fighting force.

Caesar completed his conquest of Belgic Gaul in a brief campaign against the Aduatuci, a Germanic tribe which had been associated with the Cimbri. They had set out to help the Nervii but, too late for the battle, found themselves isolated. Caesar demanded the surrender of their weapons, but some were secretly retained, and the Aduatuci attempted an armed sally from their town by night. For this kind of action Caesar was prepared with signal fires. He inflicted heavy losses in the fighting which followed, and sold the whole of the surviving population as slaves—350,000 persons in all.

VICTORY OVER THE ATLANTIC COASTAL TRIBES

Publius Crassus, in the same campaigning season, had been sent to force the submission of the Gallic states on the Atlantic seaboard. This submission was soon received, and it should be noted that Caesar now regarded as suspect any tribe which did not approach him with offers of peace. In the following year, however, the Veneti (of the south Brittany region) led neighbouring tribes in a resistance movement and seized Roman officers who had been sent on forage missions among them, the object being to force the release of hostages whom they themselves had previously given. Indignant at this act of treachery, Caesar prepared for war against the maritime Gauls. This demanded the use of a navy. At the mouth of the Liger river (Loire) he built ships, recruited rowers from the Province (south of France) and engaged sailors and pilots.

The south Brittany coast is indented by a series of estuaries which, even today, impedes motor traffic. The Veneti and their neighbours built their strongholds on coastal eminences, which were islands when the tide flowed and peninsulas when it ebbed. Any land attacks on these citadels would be frustrated by the incoming tide, whereas a naval force would be left on the rocks when the water receded. The Romans, with great effort, built moles and raised siegeworks to provide themselves with a base of operations. But when the defenders were seriously threatened, their navy always arrived and evacuated them, together with their possessions, and the Romans were obliged to repeat the same engineering feat elsewhere.

The destruction of the enemy's fleet thus offered the only solution. But here again the Romans were at a disadvantage. The Gallic ships were built of oak, with massive transoms fixed by iron nails of a thumb's thickness, and they relied on stout leather sails. These ships were intended to resist the Atlantic wind and waves, and they also resisted the rams of the Roman war galleys. At the same time, their greater height made them difficult to grapple and thus invulnerable to boarding parties. . . .

However, with perseverence, ingenuity and good luck, the Romans, under command of Decimus Brutus (who was destined later to be one of Caesar's assassins), were at last victorious in a decisive sea battle. . . . Once the fleet of the maritime Gauls had been thus eliminated, Caesar had no difficulty in subduing the states of the Atlantic coast, which had depended completely on their ships. He was quite merciless, for he considered that the arrest of his officers, after a negotiated submission, was a breach of international law. All the leading men of the Veneti were executed and the rest sold as slaves.

CAESAR'S FORAYS INTO BRITAIN

Caesar's campaigns in Gaul had begun as a defensive operation designed to keep the Germans out of Gaul. . . . In the north and

IVLIVS CÆSAR

A later European drawing of a triumphant Caesar in ceremonial garb and wearing a crown of laurel leaves. Hundreds of such fanciful depictions of Caesar have been produced over the centuries.

west of Gaul, however, Roman action was no longer purely defensive. It becomes clear from the tone of Caesar's commentaries that he regarded himself and his army as the agents of a civilizing mission. He also intended that the Gallic habit of tribal warfare should give way to widespread Roman law and order, and that the whole country as far as the Rhine to the east and the

Channel to the north should be accessible to Roman trade, enterprise and public works. His desire to ensure that these frontiers should remain inviolate led, in 55 BC, to campaigns (both northward and eastward) against the peoples who inhabited the lands beyond them.

In this year, German tribes, already threatening the Meuse region, crossed the Rhine under pressure from the Suebi. Caesar negotiated with the migrants, but realized that they were only playing for time. He eventually took them by surprise and defeated them with great slaughter. He then, in ten days, built a wooden bridge over the Rhine and marched his legions across, for a reconnaissance in force which lasted 18 days. He did not attempt a battle with the Suebi but retired again into Gaul, destroying his bridge, having frightened his enemies and put heart into his allies.

It was already late summer in the same year when Caesar set on foot an expedition to Britain. British help to his Gallic enemies provided a military pretext, but his motives, personal ambition apart, were partly those of an explorer. . . .

When preparations were completed, Caesar sailed with two legions in 80 transport vessels, escorted by warships, across the Channel (probably from a point near Boulogne). The British were assembled on the cliffs when he arrived, but the cliffs alone made landing impossible until he found an open beach seven miles farther up-Channel (probably between Walmer and Deal). Here the Roman legionaries landed under great difficulties, wading through water with full packs while British cavalry, chariots and infantry attacked them. Fortunately, it was discovered that the Britons had never seen oared galleys and were frightened by the Roman warships. The movement of the oars possibly suggested the legs of a sea monster. Caesar also used the warships' dinghies, together with light reconnaissance craft, to aid his men as they struggled in the surf. Landing was eventually effected and the Britons were driven back. But the Roman cavalry, embarked in a separate transport fleet, had been forced by foul weather to return to the continent, and without them Caesar's characteristically swift pursuit of a conquered enemy was made impossible.

The Romans at once fortified a camp. Caesar received a chastened embassy from the conquered Britons. . . . But the spring tide unexpectedly filled the beached Roman galleys with water and heavy storm damage rendered the whole fleet unseaworthy. In these circumstances, the Britons immediately took heart and renewed hostilities. However, with foresight Caesar had laid in corn supplies, and he now repaired his less seriously damaged ships with wood and bronze material which he salvaged from the 12 total wrecks. He again imposed himself on the Britons and was promised that hostages would be sent to him in Gaul. He then recrossed the Channel before the autumn equinox. Only two tribes complied by sending hostages.

In the following year, despite turbulence among the Gauls, Caesar made an expedition with five legions, 2,000 horse and a correspondingly larger fleet, to his previous point of landing in Britain. On this occasion he penetrated inland, forded the Thames, and subdued the British king Cassivellaunus, who ruled over the Hertford area. Caesar again returned to the continent before winter, having once more been obliged to repair a fleet damaged by storms. The two expeditions to Britain amounted to extended raids rather than invasions. It is surprising that no British ships attempted to interfere with the Roman landing on either occasion. No doubt they would have been heavily outnumbered. Perhaps the Britons had lost ships helping the Veneti, or perhaps they were warned by the example of that unhappy people. . . .

GAUL RISES IN REBELLION

Caesar's initial conquest of Gaul had been deceptively simple. The Gauls did not remain docile, and Gallic uprisings alternating with Roman reprisals soon assumed the aspect of a vicious circle. Not long after Caesar's British campaign, the Belgic tribes revolted. Two of Caesar's senior officers were lured out of their camp and killed with almost their entire force, while another Roman camp was relieved by Caesar's arrival in the nick of time. The Germans once more intervened and a new retaliatory expedition across the Rhine became necessary. Caesar built a bridge even more quickly than he had done on the previous occasion. But when he had subdued the Gauls in the north-east, he had one of their leaders flogged to death. The resentment and apprehension which this execution caused was a stimulus to further revolt.

During the period of the Gallic Wars, Caesar spent every winter in north Italy where, apart from all other considerations, he was able to keep in touch with Roman politics. Returning to Transalpine Gaul in 52 BC, he found the whole country in a state bordering on general rebellion. At Cenabum (Orleans), a massacre of the Roman trading community had taken place. The situation was so dangerous that when Caesar reached the Roman Province in south France, he dared not summon his legions to him from their stations farther north, lest they should be attacked while he was not present to command them in person. Nor dared he travel through Gallic territory unattended by his army.

However, he gathered some troops in the Province, marched up into the Cevennes amid winter snows, and then left his force to occupy the enemy's attention, while he himself travelled so swiftly north-eastwards, through once friendly areas, that his old Gallic allies had no time to organize treachery, even if they would have wished it. Thus rejoining his legions, Caesar captured several rebel strongholds and avenged the massacre at Cenabum, but he now faced an enemy leader of great courage and skill in the person of Vercingetorix, chief of the Arverni tribe in central Gaul. At the siege of Avaricum (Bourges), both Romans and Gauls suffered intense hardship, for Vercingetorix' scorched-earth strategy inflicted terrible privations on enemies and friends alike. Meanwhile, the Gauls had learnt to counter Roman siege techniques. The defenders set fire to Caesar's assault towers and undermined the ramp which he had raised against their walls; many Gauls were by occupation iron-miners. But the Romans took Avaricum at last. Caesar says that only 800 out of 40,000 persons escaped to join Vercingetorix in his impregnable camp amid the marshes. Vercingetorix now retreated to another impregnable position, this time deploying the tribes under his command on a mountainous plateau before the town of Gergovia in Arverni territory. Caesar managed to occupy a hilly eminence opposite the town and established here a small garrison, which he connected with the main camp by means of a double ditch and rampart. The result was to impede the enemy's supplies of food and water, but the move was not decisive, and while Caesar faced Vercingetorix at Gergovia he was not available for operations elsewhere. Once, when his departure was temporarily necessary to deal with a threatened revolt among the Aedui, the enemy launched a sortie against the force which he had left behind him and the Roman camp was defended only with difficulty.

In these operations, Vercingetorix used archers and other missile-troops in great numbers and with devastating effect. The Romans retaliated vigorously with catapult artillery. Finally, a Roman assault on the fortified plateau miscarried, although it had been carefully planned by Caesar. Legionaries who broke through the defending wall and tried to push their attack into the town itself were repulsed with heavy loss. . . .

THE SIEGE OF ALESIA

The action at Gergovia amounted to the most serious reverse that Caesar faced in the whole of the Gallic Wars. He had for some time been contemplating withdrawal, to deal with threats elsewhere in Gaul. But the mere fact of his withdrawal encouraged revolt and led to the defection of the Aedui, whose old allegiance to him had been wavering as a result of Vercingetorix' continued success. . . . Vercingetorix had now collected a vast force of cavalry and launched an offensive against the Gallic peoples on the frontiers of the Roman Province. Caesar, however, had enlisted the help of German cavalry from Rhine tribes with whom he had previously come to terms. Vercingetorix was seriously repulsed and retired to Alesia in a territory subject to the Aedui (almost certainly at Alise-Sainte-Reine).

The Gallic leader hoped to repeat the experience of Gergovia, but he now saw that Caesar was bent on a massive blockade. Before the Roman circumvallations could close round him, he sent out his cavalry contingents each to its own tribe, to organize relief forces from every direction. Caesar had soon to deal with these relief forces. But his double circumvallation was so effective that he was able to hold off all attacks from outside and from within, until Vercingetorix and his force were starved into surrender. Vercingetorix was held captive for six years, for exhibition in Caesar's triumph in Rome. He was then executed, according to the usual custom, when the celebrations were over. . . .

In Caesar's commentaries, engineering operations around Alesia are described in great detail. The Roman entrenchments linked an encircling chain of camps and forts. The inner ditch was 20 feet (6m) wide, with sheer sides (ie, not tapering at the bottom), and the main circumvallation was constructed 400 paces [2,000 feet] behind this ditch. Here, there were two trenches each 15 feet (4.4m) wide and 8 feet (2.4m) deep; the river was diverted to carry water into the inner trench wherever possible. Behind the trenches was a 12-foot (3.6m) earthwork and palisade, with antlered prongs projecting from it. Breastworks and battlements were overlooked by turrets at intervals of 80 feet (23.6m). Caesar also sowed the ground beyond his fortifications with prongs and pitfalls of various patterns, illustratively or humorously termed "lilies" and "stingers" (*stimuli*). A parallel line of fortifications was then provided as an outer circumvallation against the inevitable relief force. The inner perimeter was 11 Roman miles (10.1 miles/16.3 km) long; the outer 14 Roman miles (12.9 miles/20.7 km).

Caesar writes that the Gallic relief force, when it came, amounted to 250,000 infantry and 8,000 cavalry. . . .

When the Romans were attacked simultaneously by the huge relief force and the desperate men from Alesia, the issue remained for some time uncertain, but Caesar had apparently held his German cavalry in reserve and his use of it late in the day routed the enemy cavalry and exposed to massacre the archers and light-armed troops who had accompanied them. . . .

The final assault on the Roman circumvallation, which was made simultaneously from within and without, was again decided by cavalry action. Caesar had unostentatiously sent out a cavalry force, which took the outer enemy in the rear, just at the moment when they were heavily engaged on the ramparts. At this moment, in particular, the situation at Alesia must have been that of a nest of boxes. In the centre was the town. Vercingetorix had fortified the surrounding plateau with a six-foot (1.8m) wall, to protect his camps in the enclosure. Outside this was the Roman double circumvallation, now attacked by the Gallic relief forces from beyond. But these finally had been surprised by the appearance of Caesar's cavalry behind their backs.

After this action, which forced the surrender of Alesia, many Gallic leaders fell into Caesar's hands.

CREATION OF THE ROMAN EMPIRE

MICHAEL GRANT

The creation of the Roman Empire was largely the work of Augustus (originally Octavian), the first emperor. After defeating his rivals in the last of a long series of devastating civil wars, he set about consolidating a wide range of autocratic powers, though he shrewdly cloaked them in the trappings of the old republican institutions, such as the Senate and the tribunes of the people. In another wise move, he did not call himself emperor, choosing instead the less intimidating title of *princeps,* meaning "first citizen." Consequently, his new form of government, and the Empire itself, became known as the Principate. Augustus eventually summarized his considerable achievements in a document known as the *Res gestae* (also called the *Monumentum Ancyranum*). The prolific scholar Michael Grant, of Edinburgh University, provides this informative overview of the Empire's birth.

AUGUSTUS (Gaius Octavius) (31 BC–AD 14) was the first Roman *princeps* or emperor. He was born Gaius Octavius, and changed his name to Gaius Julius Caesar after Caesar's death, but is generally described as Octavian until he was granted the designation of Augustus in 27 BC.

Born in 63 BC, he came of a prosperous family of knights (*equites*) from Velitrae, south-east of Rome. His father Gaius Octavius had been the first of the family to become a senator, rising to the rank of praetor. After his death in 59 BC, his widow Atia was left in charge of the child's upbringing. She was the niece of Julius Caesar, and it was Caesar who launched the future em-

Reprinted with the permission of Scribner, a division of Simon & Schuster, and of Weidenfeld & Nicolson, an imprint of the Orion Group, from *The Roman Emperors*, by Michael Grant. Copyright © 1985 by Michael Grant Publications Ltd.

peror into a Roman public career. When he was twelve, he delivered the funeral speech in honour of his grandmother Julia. At fifteen or sixteen he was appointed a priest (*pontifex*). After accompanying Caesar, now dictator (that is to say absolute ruler, though he is never thought of as the first of the emperors), at his Triumph in 46 BC, the young man, despite delicate health, joined him in his Spanish campaign of the following year. Then, with his friends Marcus Agrippa and Marcus Salvidienus Rufus, he was sent to Apollonia in Epirus to complete his academic and military studies; and it was there, in 44 BC, that he learnt of Caesar's assassination by Brutus and Cassius (who subsequently left for the east).

OCTAVIAN'S RISE TO PROMINENCE

The publication of the dead man's will disclosed that he had been posthumously adopted as the dictator's son and made his chief heir. Therefore despite his youthful years (he was only eighteen), he decided—against the advice of his stepfather and others—to take up this perilous inheritance and avenge his adoptive father's death. Proceeding to Rome, he tried but failed to persuade Caesar's principal supporter Marcus Antonius (Antony) to hand over the late dictator's assets and documents. Octavius was thus compelled to distribute Caesar's legacies to the Roman public from whatever funds he was able to raise from other sources. At the same time, though, he felt obliged to assert himself against this contemptuous attitude of Antonius. His first step was to celebrate the Games of the Victory of Caesar to win public support. Then, on the initiative of the elder statesman and orator Cicero (who however did not realize the young man's formidable potentialities), the senate granted him, although he was not yet twenty, the status of senator and propraetor; and they enlisted his support in a campaign against Antonius, who was duly defeated at Mutina in northern Italy and forced to retreat into Gaul in 43 BC. Since the consuls who commanded the senatorial forces had both been killed in the battle, Octavian's legionaries compelled the senate, reluctant though it was, to award him one of these vacant posts. It was now that his posthumous adoption by the dictator received official recognition, enabling him to employ the name of Gaius Julius Caesar.

However, because the attitude of the senate remained grudging, he soon came to an understanding with Antonius, and reached agreement, too, with another of Caesar's principal adherents, Lepidus, who had succeeded to his high-priesthood. On 27 November 43 BC, the three men were officially allocated a five-year appointment as 'triumvirs for the constitution of the state', the Second Triumvirate (the first, seventeen years earlier, had been an unofficial arrangement between Pompey, Crassus and Caesar); this endowed them, jointly, with thoroughgoing autocratic powers. When Julius Caesar was recognized as a god of the Roman state (*divus*) at the beginning of 42 BC, Octavian became 'son of a god', but in the subsequent campaign against Brutus and Cassius, which brought about their defeat and death at Philippi in Macedonia, his ill-health obliged him to play a subordinate role to Antonius.

In the division of the Empire that followed, Antonius was allocated the east (and initially Gaul) while Octavian went back to Italy. There, problems arising from the settlement of his demobilized troops involved him in a campaign against Antonius' brother Lucius Antonius and Lucius' vigorous wife Fulvia. The conflict became known as the Perusine War because it culminated in the terrible siege of Perusia of 41 BC. With the aim of conciliating another potential foe, Sextus Pompeius, son of Pompey the Great, who was in control of Sicily and Sardinia, Octavian married Sextus' relative Scribonia. Not long afterwards, however—in October, 40 BC—he reached agreement with Antonius in the Treaty of Brundusium, which jettisoned Sextus, encouraging Octavian to divorce Scribonia and instead to forge a link with the aristocracy by marrying Livia Drusilla, who remained his life-long partner.

Through the Treaty Antonius retained the eastern imperial territories; Octavian, while keeping control over Italy, was allotted all the western provinces except Africa, which was occupied by Lepidus. The alliance was sealed by the marriage of Octavian's sister Octavia to Antonius. Soon afterwards, however, Antonius abandoned her to return to Cleopatra VII, Queen of Egypt, with whom he had earlier begun a liaison; but Octavian—plunged into hostilities with Sextus Pompeius—nevertheless confirmed his agreement with Antonius at Tarentum in 37 BC, whereby the triumvirs would remain in power for a further period of more than four years.

CIVIL WAR LOOMS

In 36 BC Octavian's brilliant admiral Agrippa overwhelmed the fleet of Sextus Pompeius off Cape Naulochus in Sicily. At the same time Lepidus endeavoured to oppose Octavian's authority in the west by military confrontation. But he was disarmed by Octavian, stripped of his triumviral powers and compelled to go into lasting retirement. It soon became clear, however, that Octavian, who was busy founding colonies for his loyal ex-soldiers, would soon be locked in a struggle with Antonius for control of the whole Roman world. Meanwhile, he began to employ the designation 'Imperator' in front of his name, to indicate that he was the unrivalled commander; and between 35 and 33 BC he fought three successive campaigns in Illyricum and Dalmatia which, although laborious and not entirely successful, made the north-eastern borders of Italy much safer than they had ever been before.

With Agrippa's assistance, Octavian spent massive sums on the architectural adornment of Rome. He also did everything he could to stimulate public protest against Antonius' gifts of imperial territory to Cleopatra. Amid ferocious public exchanges, the rift between the two men rapidly widened. By 32 BC the triumvirate had officially come to an end, and Octavian disingenuously denied that he was any longer exercising its powers. Antonius for his part divorced his rival's sister Octavia, whereupon her brother seized Antonius' will and published damaging concessions to Cleopatra that he claimed to have found among its contents. Each of the two leaders administered oaths of allegiance to the populations he controlled. . . . Finally Octavian declared war—not against his compatriot Antonius, since the idea of civil strife was so unpopular, but against the foreign woman Cleopatra who, according to him, had violated her status as a client of Rome.

Antonius, accompanied by Cleopatra, lined the west coast of Greece with his navy and troops. But early in 31 BC, before winter was over, Octavian surprised him by sending Agrippa across the Ionian Sea to capture Methone [in Greece]; then he himself followed, leaving his Etruscan associate Maecenas to look after Italy. Before long, Antony's fleet was trapped inside the Gulf of Ambracia, and when in September he attempted to break out, the battle of Actium ensued. He and Cleopatra, together with a quarter of their ships, forced their way into the open sea and escaped to Egypt, where they committed suicide when Octavian invaded the country the following year.

Octavian's next act was to put to death Cleopatra's son Caesarion, whose fatherhood the Queen had attributed to Julius Caesar. He then annexed Egypt, and preserved direct rule over the country through his personal representatives. The capture of Cleopatra's financial resources also made it possible for him to pay off many of his soldiers and decree their settlement in a large number of colonies throughout the Roman world which now lay wholly in his hands. He gradually reduced his sixty legions to twenty-eight, comprising a hundred and fifty thousand soldiers (mostly Italians, though some were from other Romanized areas), and this force was augmented by approximately the same number of auxiliaries drawn from the provinces (that is to say from regions of the Roman Empire outside Italy). . . . The fleet was also reorganized, with its principal bases at Misenum and Ravenna; and Octavian replaced his former Spanish bodyguard by a German unit. However, this was only supplementary to his principal guard of praetorians which, derived from the bodyguards maintained by earlier generals, was mainly composed of soldiers possessing Roman citizenship, divided into nine cohorts of five hundred infantrymen and ninety horsemen each. The praetorians, whose first joint prefects—of knightly, not senatorial, rank—Augustus appointed in 2 BC, were stationed at Rome and other Italian towns. He also created three city cohorts of a thousand men each (later increased) to serve as the police force of the capital, under the command of the city prefect (*praefectus urbi*).

CONSOLIDATING DIVERSE POWERS

These measures relating to military and security forces formed just one part, although an essential part, of a prolonged series of tentative and patient steps that created the Roman Principate. Although this was a system over which the ruler himself in effect kept full control, ample lip-service was given to the dignity of the senate, which he had reduced from about a thousand to eight hundred (later six hundred) members. Compliant though it was, and relieved and satisfied by his termination of the civil wars, Octavian however realized—remembering Caesar's fate—that this former ruling class would only welcome him if he ostensibly revived Republican traditions. Accordingly, while retaining continuous consulships from 31 to 23 BC, he made the claim, in 27, that he had 'transferred the State to the free disposal of the senate and people' (a somewhat misleading statement, as by the people he here referred to the Assembly, which now lacked political power). At the same time he was officially awarded, for a period of ten years, the government and command of a province comprising Spain, Gaul and Syria, the regions which contained the bulk of the army, and which he thenceforward governed through his subordinates (*legati*). The remaining areas of the Empire, outside Italy, were to be administered by proconsuls appointed by the senate as of old; for the *princeps* believed that his supreme prestige would ensure that his will was not crossed by these officials, whose selection, by more or less indirect means, he continued to influence.

The emperor's prestige was summed up by the solemn term *auctoritas*, resonant with traditional and religious significance. And linked etymologically with this word . . . was the designation of 'Augustus' now conferred on him, which astutely conveyed, without recourse to the constitution, his superiority over other human beings. Aided by the outstanding writers of this literary Golden Age—the historian Livy, and Maecenas' poetical protégés Virgil and Horace, whose endeavours were supplemented by some patriotic verses of Propertius and Ovid—he displayed his veneration of the old Italian religion by resuscitating many of its antique ceremonials, and repairing and reconstructing its broken-down temples. In pursuit of the same aim he celebrated the antique ritual of the Secular Games (Ludi Saeculares) in 17 BC, which marked the transition from one century or epoch to another. He also set up the Altar of Peace (Ara Pacis), adorning it with fine reliefs in the classicizing Augustan style—and very many other important buildings too, religious and secular alike, were erected throughout the Empire. Then on the death of Lepidus in 12 BC Augustus succeeded him as the official chief priest (*pontifex maximus*) of the State religion.

His constitutional settlement of 27 BC had been followed by forceful steps to extend and pacify the imperial frontiers: turbulent Alpine tribes were reduced, Galatia (central Asia Minor) was annexed, and Augustus himself directed part of a campaign to complete the subjugation of Spain. But his health suffered a serious collapse. In 23 BC he seemed at the point of death, and put an end to the continuous series of consulships he had held, assuming instead the *imperium majus,* a power which raised him above the proconsuls and which was separated altogether from office and its practical chores. He was also granted the power of a tribune or *tribunicia potestas*. This award, systematizing earlier, partial conferments, conveniently empowered him to summon the senate. But in particular, because it was the traditional role of the annually elected tribunes of the people (from whom the *tribunicia potestas* took its name) to defend the citizens' rights, the power enveloped him in a 'democratic' aura, all the more needed because the true foundations of his system were, in fact, provided by the support of the established classes. In 19 BC there were further adjustments of Augustus' powers to allow him to exercise authority more conveniently in Italy, and the two following years witnessed social legislation intended, though probably without much effect, to encourage marriage and curb adultery and extravagance. . . .

THE EMPIRE UNIFIED AND STRENGTHENED

Meanwhile, the entire administration of Rome and the Empire was being overhauled. This was made possible by a thoroughgoing reform of the financial structure, in which the central treasury was linked with the treasuries of the provinces, and particularly with those in Augustus' provinces, in an intricate relationship of which the exact nature escapes us. This imperial system was mainly funded by two direct taxes, a poll-tax and a land-tax: the latter was crucial because the economy of the Roman world was still founded on agriculture. The Augustan Peace also provided a marked stimulus to trade; and this was facilitated by a huge expansion and improvement of the Roman coinage, now comprising not only gold and silver pieces but novel token coins of yellow brass and red copper, produced at Rome and Lugdunum and elsewhere.

On all these issues every possible opportunity was taken to proclaim the main publicity themes of the régime; for example, great pride was taken in a triumphant agreement with the Parthians in 20 BC, under which they returned the legionary standards captured from the triumvir Crassus when he had been killed at Carrhae thirty-three years earlier, and acknowledged Rome's protectorate over Armenia. This country now became (precariously) one of the numerous client-states with which Augustus, characteristically extending earlier precedents, ringed the Empire. These client-states were authorized to issue coinages of their own, mainly of bronze, but occasionally of silver. . . . In many parts of the Empire itself, too, local urban communities were allowed to produce their own bronze money. These regions included Spain (for a time) as well as most territories of the east, where the old city-states, with their Greek institutions and culture, retained varying degrees of autonomy under the loose supervision of the provincial governors and their financial advisers or procurators.

THE PROBLEM OF THE SUCCESSION

Although the position of *princeps* was not a formal office to which a successor could be appointed, public attention had long been centred on Augustus' plans for the future. His nephew Marcellus, husband of his daughter Julia, died in 23 BC. In the same year Agrippa was dispatched to the east as Augustus' deputy, and four years later he completed the conquest of Spain. But although the widowed Julia had been given to Agrippa in marriage, the senators would never have accepted him as ruler. In 17 BC, therefore, Augustus adopted Agrippa and Julia's children, Gaius and Lucius, aged three and one respectively, as his own sons. Nevertheless, he also gave prominent employment to his adult stepsons Tiberius and Nero Drusus (Drusus the elder). . . .

After Agrippa's death in 12 BC, Augustus obliged his widow Julia to marry Tiberius, though each was reluctant. Both Tiberius and his brother Nero Drusus spent the next few years fighting in the north. But Nero Drusus, after he had advanced as far as the Elbe, died in 9 BC. Three years later Tiberius was elevated to a share in his stepfather's tribunician power, but then he retired from the scene, only to return as Augustus' adoptive son and evident successor following the deaths of Lucius and Gaius in AD 2 and 4 respectively. Tiberius was immediately sent to Boiohaemum to conquer the powerful west German tribal state of the Marcomanni and thus shorten the imperial frontiers. The task was interrupted when revolts broke out in Pannonia and Illyricum in AD 6 and then in Germany, where Arminius, chief of the west German tribe of the Cherusci, destroyed Varus and his three legions in AD 9. Augustus was appalled, and the annexation of Germany and central Europe had to be indefinitely postponed.

Although administrative reforms did not cease, the princeps had begun to recognize encroaching age, and in AD 13 Tiberius was made his equal in every constitutional respect. Then Augustus lodged his will and other documents at the House of the Vestal Virgins at Rome. They included a summary of the Empire's military and financial resources and a subtle, never inaccurate but often tendentious political testament known as the *Acts of the Divine Augustus* (or *Monumentum Ancyranum*, since its best-preserved copy is on the walls of the Temple of Rome and Augustus at Ancyra in Galatia). In the following year Tiberius, on his way to Illyricum, was recalled because his stepfather was seriously ill. Augustus died on 19 August and was subsequently deified.

Augustus was one of the most talented, energetic and skilful administrators that the world has ever known. The enormously far-reaching work of reorganization and rehabilitation which he undertook in every branch of his vast Empire created a new Roman Peace, in which all but the humblest classes benefited from improved communications and flourishing commerce. The autocratic régime which (learning from Caesar's mistakes) he substituted for the collapsing Republic—although challenged, from the outset, by a number of conspiracies—was to have a very long life. It brought stability, security and prosperity to an unprecedented proportion of the population for more than two hundred years; it ensured the survival and eventual transmission of the political, social, economic and cultural heritage of the classical world—Roman and Greek alike; and it supplied the framework within which both Judaism and Christianity were disseminated (Jesus Christ was born, and Judaea converted from a client-state into a Roman province, during this reign).

AUGUSTUS RECALLS HIS ACHIEVEMENTS

AUGUSTUS CAESAR

Augustus, Rome's first and arguably greatest emperor, not only created a new Roman state, but also managed it so well that he virtually ensured its continued expansion and longevity. Though he had risen to power by violent, ruthless means as a young man, as emperor he was a remarkably just, efficient, and constructive leader; and his many positive accomplishments rank him among the greatest national leaders of all times. Modesty was not among his strengths, however, for he ordered that a list he had compiled of his achievements be inscribed on bronze pillars following his death. Portions of this long inscription, the *Res gestae,* appear below. It should be noted that everything he states is technically true; however, he sometimes colors the facts, as when he makes it appear that all the old republican institutions are still in full force under his regime. (In reality, they had become merely window-dressing, for most of the real power was in his hands.) And he conveniently leaves out failures and defeats (such as the annihilation of one of his armies in a German forest in A.D. 9). Nevertheless, the document remains a rare and remarkable personal testament by one of the leading statesmen of the ancient world.

B elow is a copy of the accomplishments of the deified Augustus by which he brought the whole world under the empire of the Roman people, and of the moneys expended by him on the state and the Roman people, as inscribed on two bronze pillars set up in Rome.

1] At the age of nineteen, on my own initiative and my own

From *Res Gestae,* by Augustus Caesar, in *Roman Civilization: Selected Readings,* edited by Naphtali Lewis and Meyer Reinhold (New York: Columbia University Press, 1951–1955).

expense, I raised an army by means of which I liberated the Republic, which was oppressed by the tyranny of a faction. For which reason the senate, with honorific decrees, made me a member of its order in the consulship of Gaius Pansa and Aulus Hirtius [43 B.C.], giving me at the same time consular rank in voting, and granted me the *imperium* [power of command]. It ordered me as propraetor, together with the consuls, to see to it that the state suffered no harm. Moreover, in the same year, when both consuls had fallen in war, the people elected me consul and a triumvir for the settlement of the commonwealth.

2] Those who assassinated my father [his adoptive father, Julius Caesar], I drove into exile, avenging their crime by due process of law; and afterwards when they waged war against the state, I conquered them twice on the battlefield [at Philippi, in Greece, in 42 B.C.].

3] I waged many wars throughout the whole world by land and by sea, both civil and foreign, and when victorious I spared all citizens who sought pardon. Foreign peoples who could safely be pardoned I preferred to spare rather than to extirpate. About 500,000 Roman citizens were under military oath to me. Of these, when their terms of service were ended, I settled in colonies or sent back to their own municipalities a little more than 300,000 and to all of these I allotted lands or granted money as rewards for military service. I captured 600 ships, exclusive of those which were of smaller class than triremes.

VARIOUS HONORS BESTOWED ON ME

4] Twice I celebrated ovations, three times curule triumphs, and I was acclaimed *imperator* [supreme commander] twenty-one times. When the senate decreed additional triumphs to me, I declined them on four occasions. I deposited in the Capitol laurel wreaths adorning my *fasces*, after fulfilling the vows which I had made in each war. . . .

5] The dictatorship offered to me in the consulship of Marcus Marcellus and Lucius Arruntius [22 B.C.] by the people and by the senate, both in my absence and in my presence, I refused to accept. In the midst of a critical scarcity of grain I did not decline the supervision of the grain supply, which I so administered that within a few days I freed the whole people from imminent panic and danger by my expenditures and efforts. The consulship, too, which was offered to me at that time as an annual office for life, I refused to accept.

6] In the consulship of Marcus Vinicius and Quintus Lucretius [19 B.C.], and again in that of Publius Lentulus and Gnaeus Lentulus [18 B.C.], and a third time in that of Paullus Fabius Maximus and Quintus Tubero [11 B.C.], though the Roman senate and people unitedly agreed that I should be elected sole guardian of the laws and morals with supreme authority, I refused to accept any office offered me which was contrary to the traditions of our ancestors. The measures which the senate desired at that time to be taken by me I carried out by virtue of the tribunician power. In this power I five times voluntarily requested and was given a colleague by the senate.

7] I was a member of the triumvirate for the settlement of the commonwealth for ten consecutive years [43–33 B.C.]. I have been ranking senator for forty years, up to the day on which I wrote this document. I have been *pontifex maximus* [chief state priest], augur, member of the college of fifteen for performing sacrifices, member of the college of seven for conducting religious banquets [and a member of various other distinguished religious orders].

8] In my fifth consulship I increased the number of patricians, by order of the people and the senate. Three times I revised the roll of senators. And in my sixth consulship, with Marcus Agrippa as my colleague, I conducted a census of the people. I performed the *lustrum* [census] after an interval of forty-two years. At this *lustrum* 4,063,000 Roman citizens were recorded. Then a second time, acting alone, by virtue of the consular power, I completed the taking of the census in the consulship of Gaius Censorinus and Gaius Asinius. At this *lustrum* 4,233,000 Roman citizens were recorded. And a third time I completed the taking of the census in the consulship of Sextus Pompeius and Sextus Appuleius, by virtue of the consular power and with my son Tiberius Caesar as my colleague. At this *lustrum* 4,937,000 Roman citizens were recorded. By new legislation which I sponsored I restored many traditions of our ancestors which were falling into desuetude in our generation; and I myself handed down precedents in many spheres for posterity to imitate. . . .

10] My name was inserted, by decree of the senate, in the hymn of the Salian priests. And it was enacted by law that I should be sacrosanct in perpetuity and that I should possess the tribunician power as long as I live. I declined to become *pontifex maximus* in place of a colleague [the former triumvir, Marcus Lepidus] while he was still alive, when the people offered me that priesthood, which my father had held. A few years later, in the consulship of Publius Sulpicius and Gaius Valgius, I accepted this priesthood, when death removed the man who had taken possession of it at a time of civil disturbance; and from all Italy a multitude flocked to my election such as had never previously been recorded at Rome. . . .

MY GENEROSITY

13] The temple of Janus Quirinus, which our ancestors desired to be closed whenever peace with victory was secured by sea and by land throughout the entire empire of the Roman people, and which before I was born is recorded to have been closed only twice since the founding of the city, was during my principate three times ordered by the senate to be closed.

14] My sons [actually adopted grandsons] Gaius and Lucius Caesar, whom fortune took from me in their youth, were, in my honor, made consuls designate by the Roman senate and people when they were fifteen years old, with permission to enter that magistracy after a period of five years. The senate further decreed that from the day on which they were introduced into the Forum they should attend its debates. . . .

15] To the Roman plebs I paid 300 sesterces apiece in accordance with the will of my father; and in my fifth consulship I gave each 400 sesterces in my own name out of the spoils of war; and a second time in my tenth consulship I paid out of my own patrimony a largess of 400 sesterces to every individual; in my eleventh consulship I made twelve distributions of food out of grain purchased at my own expense; and in the twelfth year of my tribunician power for the third time I gave 400 sesterces to every individual. These largesses of mine reached never less than 250,000 persons. In the eighteenth year of my tribunician power and my twelfth consulship I gave sixty *denarii* to each of 320,000 persons of the urban plebs. And in my fifth consulship I gave out of the spoils of war 1,000 sesterces apiece to my soldiers settled in colonies. This largess on the occasion of my triumph was received by about 120,000 persons in the colonies. In my thirteenth consulship I gave sixty *denarii* apiece to those of the plebs who at that time were receiving public grain; the number involved was a little more than 200,000 persons. . . .

17] Four times I came to the assistance of the treasury with my own money, transferring to those in charge of the treasury 150,000,000 sesterces. And in the consulship of Marcus Lepidus and Lucius Arruntius I transferred out of my own patrimony 170,000,000 sesterces to the soldiers' bonus fund, which was established on my advice for the purpose of providing bonuses for soldiers who had completed twenty or more years of service.

18] From the year in which Gnaeus Lentulus and Publius Lentulus were consuls, whenever the provincial taxes fell short, in the case sometimes of 100,000 persons and sometimes of many more, I made up their tribute in grain and in money from my own grain stores and my own patrimony.

THE BUILDINGS I ERECTED

19] I built the following structures: the senate house and the Chalcidicum adjoining it; the temple of Apollo on the Palatine with its porticoes; the temple of the deified Julius; the Lupercal; the portico at the Circus Flaminius, which I allowed to be called Octavia after the name of the man who had built an earlier portico on the same site; the state box at the Circus Maximus; the temples of Jupiter the Smiter and Jupiter the Thunderer on the Capitoline; the temple of Quirinus; the temples of Minerva and Queen Juno and of Jupiter Freedom on the Aventine; the temple of the Lares at the head of the Sacred Way; the temple of the Penates on the Velia; the temple of Youth and the temple of the Great Mother on the Palatine.

20] I repaired the Capitol and the theater of Pompey with enormous expenditures on both works, without having my name inscribed on them. I repaired the conduits of the aqueducts which were falling into ruin in many places because of age, and I doubled the capacity of the aqueduct called Marcia by admitting a new spring into its conduit. I completed the Julian Forum and the basilica which was between the temple of Castor and the temple of Saturn, works begun and far advanced by my father, and when the same basilica was destroyed by fire, I enlarged its site and began rebuilding the structure, which is to be inscribed with the names of my sons; and in case it should not be completed while I am still alive, I left instructions that the work be completed by my heirs. In my sixth consulship I repaired eighty-two temples of the gods in the city, in accordance with a resolution of the senate, neglecting none which at that time required repair. In my seventh consulship I reconstructed the Flaminian Way from the city as far as Ariminum, and also all the bridges except the Mulvian and the Minucian.

21] On my own private land I built the temple of Mars Ultor and the Augustan Forum from spoils of war. On ground bought for the most part from private owners I built the theater adjoining the temple of Apollo which was to be inscribed with the name of my son-in-law Marcus Marcellus. In the Capitol, in the temple of the deified Julius, in the temple of Apollo, in the temple of Vesta, and in the temple of Mars Ultor I consecrated gifts from spoils of war which cost me about 100,000,000 sesterces. . . .

THE PUBLIC GAMES I STAGED

22] I gave a gladiatorial show three times in my own name, and five times in the names of my sons or grandsons; at these shows about 10,000 fought. Twice I presented to the people in my own name an exhibition of athletes invited from all parts of the world, and a third time in the name of my grandson. I presented games, in my own name four times, and in addition twenty-three times in the place of other magistrates. On behalf of the college of fifteen, as master of that college, with Marcus Agrippa as my colleague, I celebrated the Secular Games in the consulship of Gaius Furnius and Gaius Silanus. In my thirteenth consulship I was the first to celebrate the Games of Mars, which subsequently the consuls, in accordance with a decree of the senate and a law, have regularly celebrated in the succeeding years. Twenty-six times I provided for the people, in my own name or in the names of my sons or grandsons, hunting spectacles of African wild beasts in the circus or in the Forum or in the amphitheaters; in these exhibitions about 3,500 animals were killed.

23] I presented to the people an exhibition of a naval battle across the Tiber where the grove of the Caesars now is, having had the site excavated 1,800 feet in length and 1,200 feet in width. In this exhibition thirty beaked ships, triremes or biremes, and in addition a great number of smaller vessels engaged in combat. On board these fleets, exclusive of rowers, there were about 3,000 combatants. . . .

How I Expanded the Empire

26] I extended the frontiers of all the provinces of the Roman people on whose boundaries were peoples subject to our empire. I restored peace to the Gallic and Spanish provinces and likewise to Germany, that is to the entire region bounded by the Ocean from Gades to the mouth of the Elbe river. I caused peace to be restored in the Alps, from the region nearest to the Adriatic Sea as far as the Tuscan Sea, without undeservedly making war against any people. My fleet sailed the Ocean from the mouth of the Rhine eastward as far as the territory of the Cimbrians, to which no Roman previously had penetrated either by land or by sea. The Cimbrians, the Charydes, the Semnones, and other German peoples of the same region through their envoys sought my friendship and that of the Roman people. At my command and under my auspices two armies were led almost at the same time into Ethiopia and into Arabia which is called Felix [what is now Yemen]; and very large forces of the enemy belonging to both peoples were killed in battle, and many towns were captured. In Ethiopia a penetration was made as far as the town of Napata, which is next to Meroe; in Arabia the army advanced into the territory of the Sabaeans to the town of Mariba.

27] I added Egypt to the empire of the Roman people. Although I might have made Greater Armenia into a province

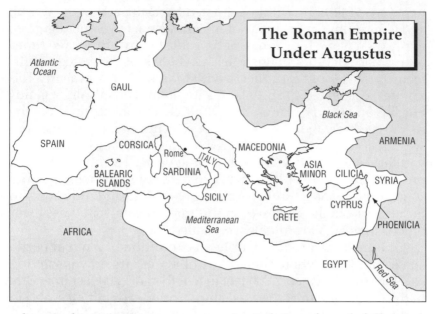

The Roman Empire Under Augustus

when its king Artaxes was assassinated, I preferred, following
the precedent of our ancestors, to hand over this kingdom, acting through Tiberius Nero, who was then my stepson, to
Tigranes, son of King Artavasdes and grandson of King Tigranes.
And afterwards, when this same people revolted and rebelled,
after I subdued it through my son Gaius, I handed it over to the
rule of King Ariobarzanes, son of Artabazus, king of the Medes,
and after his death to his son Artavasdes. When the latter was
killed, I dispatched to that kingdom Tigranes, a scion of the royal
family of Armenia. I recovered all the provinces extending beyond the Adriatic Sea eastward, and also Cyrenae, which were
for the most part already in the possession of kings, as I had previously recovered Sicily and Sardinia, which had been seized in
the slave war.

28] I established colonies of soldiers in Africa, Sicily, Macedonia, in both Spanish provinces, in Achaea, Asia, Syria, Narbonese
Gaul, and Pisidia. Italy, moreover, has twenty-eight colonies established by me, which in my lifetime have grown to be famous
and populous.

29] A number of military standards lost by other generals I recovered, after conquering the enemy, from Spain, Gaul, and the
Dalmatians. The Parthians I compelled to restore to me the spoils
and standards of three Roman armies and to seek the friendship
of the Roman people as suppliants. The standards, moreover, I
deposited in the inner shrine of the temple of Mars Ultor.

30] Through Tiberius Nero, who was then my stepson and
legate, I conquered and subjected to the empire of the Roman

people the Pannonian tribes, to which before my principate no army of the Roman people had ever penetrated; and I extended the frontier of Illyricum to the bank of the Danube River. An army of the Dacians which had crossed to our side of the river was conquered and destroyed under my auspices, and later on, my army crossed the Danube and compelled the Dacian tribes to submit to the orders of the Roman people. . . .

How I Became "Father of the Country"

34] In my sixth and seventh consulships [28 and 27 B.C.], after I had put an end to the civil wars, having attained supreme power by universal consent, I transferred the state from my own power to the control of the Roman senate and people. For this service of mine I received the title of Augustus by decree of the senate, and the doorposts of my house were publicly decked with laurels, the civic crown was affixed over my doorway, and a golden shield was set up in the Julian senate house, which, as the inscription on the shield testifies, the Roman senate and people gave me in recognition of my valor, clemency, justice, and devotion. After that time I excelled all in authority, but I possessed no more power than the others who were my colleagues in each magistracy.

35] When I held my thirteenth consulship, the senate, the equestrian order, and the entire Roman people gave me the title of "father of the country" and decreed that this title should be inscribed in the vestibule of my house, in the Julian senate house, and in the Augustan Forum on the pedestal of the chariot which was set up in my honor by decree of the senate. At the time I wrote this document I was in my seventy-sixth year.

PAX ROMANA: ROMAN RULE BRINGS PEACE AND PROSPERITY

W.G. HARDY

The period of the first century A.D. and much of the second in the Roman Empire is often referred to as the *Pax Romana,* or "Roman Peace." As former University of Alberta scholar W.G. Hardy explains here, there *were* wars and rebellions during the era, but they were largely localized and small-scale and did not disrupt the extraordinary economic freedom and prosperity enjoyed by the Mediterranean world as a whole. Rome's construction of vast numbers of roads, aqueducts, temples, theaters, and other structures, as well as its granting of citizenship to increasing numbers of people, were powerful unifying forces; and the Roman army policed the realm, making it largely safe for merchants to travel far and wide.

F or two centuries, from the battle of Actium until the death of Marcus Aurelius in 180 A.D., the Roman empire experienced a peace and prosperity such as the world has seldom seen since. True, there were frontier wars. In the last century of the republic Pompey had tightened Rome's hold on the Near East and Julius Caesar had conquered Gaul. The battle of Actium added Egypt. During the first century A.D. there was rectification of the northern frontier and Britain was conquered. The Emperor Trajan occupied Mesopotamia and what is now Roumania; Mesopotamia was soon relinquished, but Dacia, as Roumania was called, was held until Aurelian withdrew from it in 270 A.D.

From W.G. Hardy, *The Greek and Roman World* (Cambridge, MA: Schenkman, 1962). Copyright © 1962 by W.G. Hardy. Reprinted by permission of the publisher.

There was, too, more than one savage revolt of the Jews. In Rome itself, in the first century A.D., several emperors met violent deaths. But all of these happenings scarcely affected the security of the empire as a whole; and from 96 to 161 A.D. there was an era of almost uninterrupted peace. The ancient world lay cradled in the *Pax Romana*.

A VAST EMPIRE TO PROTECT

Let us take a look at that empire. From north to south, it stretched from the Great Wall in Britain, and from the Rhine, the Danube, and the Black Sea, to the Atlas Mountains, the Sahara Desert, and into the Sudan. On the west it was bounded by the Atlantic, on the east by the Arabian Desert and Mesopotamia. What is now France, Switzerland, Austria, and parts of Germany belonged to it. So did Spain, North Africa, Macedonia, Greece, and the Near East. The empire was about 2,000 miles from north to south and 3,000 from east to west. Its area was roughly two-and-a-half million square miles and its peak population is estimated at a hundred million. Thus, it was a sizeable empire for any age.

That empire was protected by the Roman fleet and the Roman army. The maximum force in the army was around 400,000 men. Under Domitian, legionaries received 1,200 *sesterces* a year . . . plus a grain allowance. In the meantime the term of service had been increased from twenty to twenty-five years. It might be pointed out here that until Marius, just before the first century B.C., the Roman army had been a citizen army. Marius and Julius Caesar between them made it into a long-service professional army of volunteers. At discharge a veteran received a bonus of 12,000 *sesterces*. . . .

THE GRANTING OF ROMAN CITIZENSHIP

Though the army was paid so poorly, it was the iron ring of the legions which kept the Roman world secure. Inside the empire there were great cities and prosperous municipalities with a large measure of local self-government. There were many Roman citizens. By the Social War of 90–88 B.C. the Romans had been forced to give the franchise to the Italians. By the end of the century all free men south of the Alps were Roman citizens. Julius Caesar granted citizenship to whole towns and tribes outside of Italy and to those who had served in the army, whatever their nationality, and he also planted colonies of citizens all over the empire. He even admitted provincials to the Roman Senate. Augustus was more conservative but there was an increase of 900,000 on the citizen roll during his reign. In this way Roman citizenship was widely extended. Thus, St. Paul, though a Jew, was proud of his Roman citizenship. Under later emperors, such as Trajan and Hadrian, the citizen franchise included the upper class of every city in the empire except in Egypt. Finally, in 212 A.D., every free man in the empire was made a citizen.

AN EXTENSIVE ROAD SYSTEM FACILITATES TRADE

Citizenship helped the romanization of the empire, particularly in the west. So did the network of roads and the trade which flowed along them. The total mileage of those roads is estimated at 47,000. The oldest of them was the Appian Way, built from Rome to Capua in 312 B.C. As the Roman power reached out, so did the roads. Along them the legions marched. And along them flowed the never-ending traffic, travellers on foot, carriages, wagons transporting goods, post-horses, and the like.

The Roman roads were the arteries of the empire. They were built to endure. Today, for example, you can still walk on patches of the Appian Way where St. Paul once trod.

Those roads were all marked at intervals with the distance from the golden milestone which stood in the Roman Forum. Quite literally, all roads led to Rome. Under the empire a passenger, freight, and express system was organized. For the imperial couriers, there were post-stations for the changing of horses. For the transport of goods, there were *mansiones*, which in English means waiting-places. These *mansiones* maintained riders, drivers, conductors, doctors, blacksmiths, wheelwrights, and about forty beasts and the appropriate amount of rolling stock. In this way the trade of the empire could be kept moving.

There was even a well-organized passenger service. By the fourth century A.D., first- and second-class tickets were being sold and from the first century A.D. the Romans had sleeping carriages in service. Free passes were issued, good for from one to five years or during the life-time of an emperor. Under the empire every Roman of any pretension at all was likely to make the 'grand tour' to Athens, Ephesus, Antioch, and down the Nile.

MERCHANTS REACH DISTANT LANDS

To the great roads must be added the seaways. To the Romans the Mediterranean was *Mare Nostrum,* which means 'our sea'. It was furrowed by countless round-bellied merchantmen, carrying passengers and freight.

The empire was, in fact, a paradise for businessmen. In foreign traffic, traders found their way to Denmark or up the old amber route from the Danube to the Baltic and across it to Sweden. Furs and slaves poured through the Brenner Pass into Italy. In the Near East Greek merchantmen worked their way to Somaliland

and beyond and Roman traders pushed by land into Abyssinia.

The most exotic trade was to Arabia Felix, India, and China. Part of this was by caravan route from Syria, either to Arabia for spices and gold-dust or to India for gems and cottons or to China for silk. The Romans called the Chinese the 'silk people' and in 97 A.D. a Chinese envoy travelled to Antioch in Syria to establish relations with the Graeco-Roman merchants. Over a century before this, however, the first tiger to be seen in Europe since the extinct sabre-tooth variety had been brought to Samos to Augustus Caesar.

The more popular route to India and the far East, however, was from Alexandria via the Red Sea and the Indian Ocean. Each year as many as 120 ships set out for India. They carried gold and silver plate, metals, tools, weapons, trinkets, luxury goods, and Roman currency. Hoards of Roman coins belonging to the first half of the first century A.D. have been dug up in southern India. After the reign of Nero, these hoards are also found in north India. Another interesting item is the discovery of a statue of the Hindu goddess of prosperity, Laksmi, at Pompeii, the town which Vesuvius buried in 79 A.D. It is known, too, that at least one Greek merchant crossed the Malay Peninsula [in south-east Asia] and sailed up the coast; while in the reign of Marcus Aurelius a group of Graeco-Roman traders reached the court of China.

A VAST MEDITERRANEAN TRADE

From India, the Romans brought back pearls, rubies, cotton-cloth, tortoise-shell, spices, teak, ebony, pepper, and Chinese silks. . . . There was no luxury the ancient world had to offer which the Romans denied themselves. But the volume of trade inside the empire was much more enormous. Where now there are a score of frontiers, there were then no barriers to free trade, no customs posts, no import dues to pay. From the Great Wall in Britain to the Sudan and to Mesopotamia there was one huge trading unit. From Britain came lead, iron, oysters, and hunting-dogs. Gaul had its own industry centering at Lugdunum, which is now Lyons. The best glass came from Egypt or from Sidon in Phoenicia. But Gaul produced glass and pottery on a large scale. From Spain, the ships and highways brought base metals, gold, silver, dyes, linen-yarns, and olive-oil. North Africa sent out slaves, gold-dust, African marble, ebony, ivory, and wild animals for the shows. Asia Minor and Syria provided woollens, purple-dyed fabrics, carpets, tapestries, leather goods, soft silken stuffs, and Damascene steel. From the Nile the merchantmen bore to Italy linens, paper, cosmetics, glass, fine jewellery, and a third of the wheat supply. Italy herself manufactured bricks, the famous Arretine pottery, and the best of steel at Puteoli, now Pozzuoli, just north of Naples—and Puteoli was the port at which St. Paul landed. The finest of wines were produced in Gaul, Italy, Greece, and Asia Minor. Apart from export and import trade, in each province there was a humming small-shop industry; while agriculture tended more and more to large estates and scientific farming. Only in Italy itself does farming seem to have declined.

From this brief sketch, I hope you will have gathered a little of the immense volume of trade and the great prosperity which was obtained in the Roman empire in the first two centuries of our era. The luxury was equal to anything the world has seen since. But there was also a solid and prosperous middle-class. Banking and credit capitalism were well advanced. Cheques were used, letters of credit were common, and Roman currency was valid anywhere. When in 154 A.D. the rhetorician, Aelius Aristides, declared 'the whole inhabited world is one city-state', he was expressing the way in which the Romans had managed to weld their whole empire into one unit.

But the colossus had feet of clay. The loss of freedom under a dictatorship brought inevitable spiritual and political repercussions. The growth of a top-heavy bureaucracy and of a benevolent paternalism went unnoticed. Most of the inhabitants of the empire did not care. The extension of Roman citizenship, the levelling influence of a world-wide trade and prosperity, and the excellent government of the provinces under the imperial administration, left them contented so long as they could make money. There was slavery, but slavery was an accepted fact. There was an idle and unemployed proletariat which had to be kept quiet by doses of 'bread and games'. But the empire was an Eden for the banker, the capitalist, and the ordinary businessman. Consequently, only a comparative few cried warnings of the dangers to come. The first two centuries of our era were, in fact, as materialistic an age as any until the present. Everywhere a man was judged not by what he was but by what he owned. As the businessman, Trimalchio, said in one of the two Latin novels left to us: 'If you have a penny, that's what you're worth.'

THE COMFORTS OF TOWN LIFE

For a brief glimpse of what life was like in the small towns of Italy during the first century A.D. fortune has left us Pompeii and Herculaneum. As you will remember, both towns were destroyed by the great eruption of Vesuvius in August, 79 A.D. Herculaneum was covered by a sea of mud which hardened to tufa rock. Consequently, it is difficult to excavate. But Pompeii was buried under a blanket of porous pumice-stone and volcanic ash;

and [many] acres of it have been uncovered.

Pompeii was a small town with only 20,000 inhabitants. Yet when we walk its long-dead streets today, we sense a comfort and even a luxuriousness of living which modern Italian towns of the present do not possess. There were fountains in the streets. The houses were roomy and comfortable. Three public baths, with facilities which included hot-air heating, have been uncovered. There was a wide rectangular forum, paved with marble, with markets opening off it. There were two theatres and an amphitheatre. This last would seat 20,000 spectators. At one end of the forum is a temple to Jupiter; at the other, the law-courts. In one house, a set of silverplate was found, of 115 pieces. Look at it in the Naples Museum and you will note the delicacy of its manufacture and chasing. In another house a set of surgical instruments was discovered and each instrument has been identified as similar to modern ones. In still another was a statue, the Dancing Faun, and that is a masterpiece for any age. The House of the Vettii has wall-paintings by unknown artists, some of which are a beauty and a delight. Most of the houses possess delightful gardens in which fountains played; and some of them still work today. There are shops with advertising, and notices for theatre shows and for municipal elections. There are fullers' establishments and dining-rooms and tavern after tavern.

It is when we realize comfort such as this in a small town that we comprehend how prosperous Roman [town and city] life was.

Beyond Europe: New Cultures, Nations, and Empires

CHAPTER 3

THE MAYANS CARVE A CIVILIZATION FROM THE JUNGLE

COTTIE BURLAND

At the same time that soldiers, merchants, religious pilgrims, and others plied the Roman roads that crisscrossed the classical Mediterranean world of the *Pax Romana*, thousands of miles to the west another high civilization was beginning to bloom in the rain forests of Central America. These were the Maya, who inhabited the region of the Yucatan Peninsula and what is now Guatemala. Influenced culturally by the Olmecs and Zapotecs, successful native peoples who flourished in southern Mexico in the first millennium B.C., the Maya erected impressive stone ceremonial centers, practiced large-scale agriculture, and developed a complex calendar. Cottie Burland, formerly a scholar at the British Museum, wrote the following summary of the rise of the Maya.

In the thickly wooded and hilly country of the Peten, and over the border between Guatemala and Mexico, there lived in ancient times a people who were simple villagers. They tilled their fields under rather difficult tropical conditions, and produced maize as their staple food-stuff wherever it was possible to grow it. As far as we know they spoke dialects of a language which we call Maya but we do not really know what title they gave to themselves.

THE RISE OF THE MAYA

At the very beginning of the Christian era there came traders and possibly warriors from the more highly civilized peoples of Mexico. In particular, at Kaminaljuyu in the Guatemalan highlands, there was a very strong influence from the Mexican city of Teotihuacan. This influence was so strong that great numbers of pottery vessels and small figures were made which are indistinguishable from those manufactured at home in the Mexican city. This settlement lasted for a considerable time, probably for four or five centuries. One can have little doubt that it influenced the Maya speaking peoples in its neighbourhood. There was very good reason for the Teotihuacanos to enter the Maya country, since the Mexican plateau produced none of the things which could be obtained in this southern region. Cocoa, vanilla, and rubber from which the balls were made for a ceremonial ball game, were all of great value in Mexico and could not be produced locally. In addition the southern lands were places where birds of gorgeous plumage could be found. There were the many coloured varieties of parrot and macaw, and also most precious of all the quetzal bird which the Maya called the kukul.

For some reason, unknown to us, the Maya villages became inspired with the idea of enlargement and improvement so that early in the second century A.D. we find a sudden outburst of a number of new towns. Each of these had a ceremonial centre; that is a large courtyard which was surrounded by temples and other courtyards in which stood large carved stone monuments called stelae. The inscriptions on them recorded calendrical dates and the period in which they were erected for the good fortune of the city where they stood. No doubt there was a preliminary stage in which buildings and monuments were constructed of wood and, probably, placed on earthen mounds. It is unlikely that the Maya came from another part of the Americas with their culture fully developed. It was a unique culture and nothing really like it has ever been discovered by archaeologists in other parts of the Central American region. It is, therefore, only reasonable to assume that it was a development from within.

It is reasonable to assume that the Maya-speaking tribes had some knowledge of the systems used by the surrounding people for recording ideas in hieroglyphic writing. It is also reasonable to assume that their particular types of buildings were basically inspired by what they had seen in the Teotihuacano settlements in the mountains and among the neighbouring Mexican tribes, such as the Zapotecs. However, it appears that the Maya were determined to produce their own type of temple, their own style of sculpture, and to use hieroglyphic writing in a way which was specially theirs. No doubt there is an echo of earlier tradition in their work, and in fact one of their earlier temples, at Uaxactun, is very like an Olmec building in many parts of its structure though it was erected some four centuries after the Olmecs themselves had ceased to make their distinctive monuments in southern Mexico.

DEVELOPMENT OF WRITING AND A CALENDAR

This spirit of individuality in art and culture marks out the Maya from other Mexican people. They developed side by side with other people but in their own way. Sometimes, apparently, they engaged in military conflict with either Teotihuacanos or people from the Totonac region of southern Mexico. Their greatest advance was the full development of the ancient systems of picture writing into a syllabary. In their script they have glyphs for something like 700 different syllables. These are strung together to make words and sentences, but the system is somewhat cumbrous, and sometimes syllables are repeated with only slight variation. This is characteristic of many early developments of human phonetic writing. It occurred early in the development of Chinese ideograms, it occurs in the Minoan scripts from Crete, and something of the kind also occurs in Egyptian hieroglyphic writing. It is apparently a necessary step in the development of writing by sound, whatever the race of people in process of inventing it. After all, this is a tremendous step forward; it is not at all natural to assume that a thing seen with the eye should represent a sound. The only way in which it could arise is from drawing part of an object and then pronouncing its name. Thus, at the origin of phonetic writing, diverse people used widely diverse symbols for given sounds. However the Maya version was sufficiently good for their needs and, although it is so far still in process of decipherment, we already realize that it can convey a great deal of information.

Unfortunately, the information which has survived has only amplified calendrical symbols and is almost entirely concerned with the passage of time and the prognostications of fate after the manner of very complicated horoscopes. So far it has been impossible to find anything which seems like history and we are still bound to rely on the archaeologist's tools for our basic historical structure of the Maya civilization. There is a sequence of regular artistic developments and alterations of style . . . and nowadays with the help of carbon 14 datings from surviving fragments of wood and bone found in Maya buildings we have an outline of dates which corresponds quite closely to the generally accepted . . . Maya calendar. Thus we are now able to read Maya dating symbols and translate them with certainty in our own calendar.

CITY-CENTERS AND AGRICULTURE

There is some evidence which leads us to think that in the Peten region a group of Maya cities in the third century A.D. were united by a common version of the calendar in which they kept the count of lunar periods exactly in conformity one with another, and do not show the minor variations characteristic of earlier times. Translated into political terms which, however, must remain rather uncertain, we would think that towards the end of the third century A.D. a number of previously independent city states had joined together into a confederation. Whether this confederation was merely to bring the magical power of their religion into a unity, or whether it marked a real political unity of the kind which might be considered to be an embryo empire we cannot say. As time went on Maya culture and the ceremonial centres, with their temples, plazas, courts for playing the sacred ball game, and inscribed calendrical monuments, greatly increased both in size and richness. Some of the Maya cities, like Tikal, are not only conglomerations of temples, but contain many simple mounds extending considerable distances round the sacred centre. These appear to have been house foundations, which indicate that some cities must have harboured a considerable urban population in ancient times. Other sites have clusters of quite beautiful monuments but no evidence of local domestic settlements.

It may be that a population cultivating comparatively small plots of land here and there throughout the forest region around the city centre came together to worship the gods only on special occasions, probably once every twenty days. This would fit in excellently with the ceremonial calendars which we know were kept by the Maya priesthood. As we have said before, the whole basis of life for the Maya depended on agriculture and in particular on maize cultivation. In their forested country they were able to practise shifting cultivation with considerable success. As a clearing became leached out by the rains and lost its fertility, it could be abandoned to the forest. Trees and creepers soon grew over the plantation and constant falling leaves and decaying vegetation rapidly enriched the soil for use again in later years. New plots were cultivated by chopping down trees with stonebladed axes and setting fire to them, so that the mixture of wood ash and vegetable humus on the ground provided a good fertile basis for a few years of cultivation.

In these circumstances the agriculturalists probably remained

in comparatively small and lightly built villages. It was only with
the development of the higher culture that it paid to have well-
built houses raised up on mounds, for the settlement of any large
section of population. Otherwise it is probable that only the
houses of members of the chiefs' families were built on mounds,
or prepared in any very special way.

We must look upon the Maya basically as a group of tribes,
speaking similar languages, and subsisting on maize cultivation
carried on in the difficult environment of the tropical forest. The
whole of their art reflects forest conditions so that we find deco-
rations composed of the growing sprouts of vines, of maize canes
growing in the fields, of tropical fruit products—particularly of
the cocoa tree—and, of course, a wonderful art of feather decora-
tions derived from the many beautiful avian species which dwelt
in the forests. The animals represented include deer, peccary, and
occasionally a creature which seems to be the tapir which lived in
that region. There were also 'terrible' creatures such as boa-
constrictors, alligators and the jaguar, which seem to have been
treated with almost religious respect. In fact they were so holy that
serpent skins, alligator masks, and beautiful jaguar skins formed
important parts of the costume of the great dignitaries of the
Maya cities. Hunting, to judge by surviving pictures, was conducted on foot with the use of darts projected from a throwing
stick, of spears and of pellet guns, in which a pellet of clay or a
round stone was blown violently from a long cane tube and was
capable of stunning birds. Spring traps, which caught up animals
which had trodden in nooses attached to them, were in common
use; and pit traps with deadfalls were used for catching dangerous creatures such as alligators. In other words, the Maya were
extremely efficient in exploiting the possibilities of their natural
habitat. It is most unlikely that they ever suffered any great shortages of food. Important accessories to this were their great flocks
of turkeys and herds of semi-domesticated peccaries.

ASPECTS OF MAYAN SOCIETY

One can have no doubt that in a well organized village society,
leisure was soon available for the construction of fine buildings
and, when the techniques reached an advanced stage, great religious monuments. Probably the first impulse was the simple one
of emulating neighbouring peoples. However, the Maya were
quite undoubtedly a nation whose cities were ruled over by a
theocracy. One finds sculptures everywhere, and occasionally
paintings, which show the priests dressed in the costumes of the
gods. Those in the enormous stone stelae stand guarding the four
directions, holding a strange double headed monster in their

arms which seems to represent the surface of the earth. From one of its heads the sun arises in the morning, and in the other head the sun is swallowed as it goes underneath the earth in the evening. These gods of the four directions are to be found on all the monuments and in some cases it is made perfectly clear that the god is actually represented by the priest.

When we come to pictures of warfare we find that the great nobles are wearing plumes of feathers, and costumes which are closely similar to those of the priesthood. In fact, in historic times when the later Maya were discovered by the Spaniards, it was still the rule that the young men of great families were educated to take alternate offices in the town government. For part of their lives they were priestly officials and for the other part civil administrators. They alternated from one phase to another as they moved up grade by grade to the final position when they would become either a chief sacrificing priest, or the Halach Uinic, the Ruler of Men or High Chief of a City State.

The status of the Mayan women seems to have been excellent. Of course, they were the people who ground the maize, who baked the bread, who bore babies, who wove the clothes, and were the centre of all the hard domestic routine. But we notice in representations of women that they often wear very fine clothes and very beautiful ornaments. Among the gods divine figures occur which are quite definitely feminine. In some of the pottery figurines we find great ladies represented in what must have been very smart dresses. These show variations in fashion through time, although the design seems to change very, very slowly compared to our modern concepts of fashion. They wore jade necklaces, fine earrings, and paint and tattoo designs on their faces, though they never quite indulged in the extent of self-mutilation adopted by the noblemen. They appear in paintings as members of the chief's court and obviously hold definite social position.

It is perfectly clear that among the Maya, great ladies were treated with a respect which approached that given to their husbands, the chiefs. The working women were so essential to their families that even in comparatively recent times the division of labour between men and women was always well defined in the family. It was considered wrong that a man should intrude into a woman's province to grind the corn or attempt to weave cloth, just as it was considered something really rather shocking for a woman to attempt to go on a military expedition or to go hunting. In recent times Maya custom has made the women the market experts of the family and it was probably the same in ancient times. They not only went out and sold things in the market, but they also selected and bought for the family. Thus,

there was full respect paid to them as skilled traders.

Children were very much loved. At birth every child was presented with a little jade bead by its relatives as a symbol of the sacredness of life. As they grew up they received education, mostly from the family and neighbours; but every child had some special teaching in temple schools, and, of course the boys learnt discipline in military schools attached to the temples. Girls probably learnt very much more from their mothers than from the priestly teachers of poetry; deportment and the use of flowers really being of importance only to women of higher social position. The mass of the ancient Maya people had, however, some kind of education which fitted them for living a fuller life than just that of primitive farmers scratching a living from the earth.

PRIESTS AND TRADERS

The present day Maya still speak a developed version of the ancient language. It is rich and complex and has poetic qualities. We know that in ancient times the Maya included poetry and the composition of hymns to the gods among the specially honoured accomplishments. There was no theatre as such but at this stage of their development the religious ceremonies enacted the legends of the gods. The great plazas in the towns, surrounded by temple pyramids, became wonderfully beautiful stages every twenty days. There the priests, dressed in magnificent coloured robes and featherwork capes, danced in impersonation of the gods and showed to the people the stories behind the ritual— probably all theatrical beginnings in this world were made in a similar way. Among the Maya the ceremonies never developed to a higher stage; at least there is no record of anything like the true dramatic performances of a secular nature which were occasionally displayed in Inca Peru.

Among the things which the Maya lacked was the potter's wheel. They used only a slow turn-table made from a block of wood which they rotated between their feet, or else a section of some large broken pottery bowl which they used to turn gently round and round as they coiled up the shape of new pottery within it. They do not appear even to have had the little wheeled toys which appear in Mexico. They had no beasts of burden whatever; we occasionally find a drawing of a dog carrying a pack on its back, but this may be more religious symbolism than real fact. There were normally only footpaths between towns; but paved roads—sometimes a few miles in length—do exist between city centres, as if for great ceremonial processions. The Maya made these causeways to allow for the proper display of the dignity and beauty of ceremonies and possibly for the conveyance of the images of the gods from one city to another. The great ceremonial courtyards were always carefully paved with stone, but in the towns built around religious centres there were no true roads, just hard-beaten earth footpaths between the buildings. There was no incentive to turn the ceremonial trackways into real roads for the transport of goods, and the comfort of porters trotting with a heavy load on their back and wearing sandals was much better assured by earthen tracks than by hard stone pavements.

A great deal of trade was carried on, by convoys of porters between the cities, and by the fleets of large canoes in the coastal towns. These were cut from ceiba or mahogany trees which could carry crews of some forty or fifty people and take bales of merchandise from one place to another. This seems to have been highly organized. In late Maya times Christopher Columbus encountered such a canoe in which the merchants commanding it sat protected from the sun under coloured cotton awnings in the centre, while rows of paddlers on either side propelled the boat towards the ports with which they intended to trade. The more ancient Maya occasionally show a canoe in a painting in one of their religious books or sometimes a canoe shape appears in sculpture, but there is no real evidence that these were very large vessels. In the painted books there are sometimes marks on these drawings as if they represented a canoe which had been made up of several pieces of wood sewn together, though this seems a rather unlikely exercise when very large tropical trees were easily available to the Maya.

WAR AND DECLINE

We know from painting and sculpture that the war leaders of Maya towns had no sinecure [easy term of service]. There was actual fighting of considerable violence sometimes, as can be seen from the painted frescoes of Bonampak. People were killed, prisoners were taken, tortured and slaughtered. We know that there was some conflict which depopulated the eastern Maya town of Palenque in the late seventh century, since there is nothing of a later date to be found there. Some of the buildings were occupied by people from southern Mexico who left weapons and carvings there and apparently erected simple stone shelters within the ancient ceremonial buildings. There is no evidence that the Maya reoccupied this town after its abandonment.

In ancient times there were a few smallish Maya towns in the Yucatan peninsula. This was a difficult region because there was little surface water and the rainfall itself rapidly soaked through the limestone and ran into channels which, over thousands of years, had been dissolved out of the underlying rock. Thus Yucatan is honeycombed with underground streams and occasionally places can be found where the roof of caves have fallen in, disclosing an underground lake or stream accessible by climbing down some thirty or forty feet. This water supply was apparently only sufficient for the needs of smaller Maya cities, though life went on in much the same way as it did in the larger and richer cities of the forest country.

Some unexplained catastrophe seems to have struck the Maya of the forests at the beginning of the tenth century. Cities were abandoned, people no longer erected time stones; occasionally an earthquake cracked the front of a temple and it was not repaired, or else it was patched up only crudely. It seems as if a great part of the Maya population either died or just went away from their cities. Whether this was the result of war, of a revolt of the peasants, or of some migration under the inspiration of the gods is by no means clear. It may be that further excavation will provide us with clues, enabling us to give shape to what is at present a mysterious and obviously unhappy page of Maya history.

EGYPT THRIVES UNDER THE RULE OF THE PTOLEMIES

MICHAEL GRANT

While Rome was consolidating its control of Italy and fighting Carthage for Mediterranean mastery, Egypt continued, as it had for thousands of years, to support a prosperous civilization along the Nile River in northeastern Africa. By this time, the country was under the rule of a Greek dynasty founded by one of Alexander the Great's successors, Ptolemy (TAH-luh-mee) I Soter; so it is often referred to by modern historians as a Hellenistic ("Greek-like") realm, like the Greek Seleucid and Macedonian kingdoms. This absorbing overview of the rise and fall of the Ptolemies and life in Egypt under their administration is by Michael Grant, author of numerous studies of ancient Greece and Rome.

U niquely shaped by the narrow but immensely fertile Nile valley, Egypt possessed formidable potential resources and strength: and Greeks had always been well aware of this. During the two centuries before Alexander, the country had been under the domination of the Achaemenid Persian empire, whose ruler Cambyses had invaded the country in 525 BC and dethroned the Egyptian Pharaoh. A native revolt in *c.* 410–404 was successful, but Artaxerxes III Ochus re-established Persian authority in 341. Nine years later, however, Alexander the Great occupied the whole of Egyptian territory without opposition, its population welcoming him as a liberator.

ALEXANDRIA: A WORLD-CLASS CITY

He left the ancient Egyptian city of Memphis as the capital of the country, but immediately set about the foundation of a new Greek colony at Alexandria. It was a mark of genius to see in the meagre fishing village of Rhacotis the immense and spectacular city of the future. Whereas most of Alexander's colonies were located and planned for a military purpose, it is probable that he founded Alexandria for commercial reasons, to take the place of Tyre in Phoenicia, which he had destroyed.

Alexandria faced both ways, and was defensible from either side: it was linked to the interior of the country by Nile canals debouching in Lake Mareotis, and to the north it had two fine harbours opening on to the Mediterranean. With the Pharos lighthouse planned by Sostratus of Cnidus under Ptolemy I Soter, and completed under his son Ptolemy II Philadelphus (c. 279), as their symbol and unfailing guide (it ranked as one of the Seven Wonders of the World), these harbours were fully able to accommodate the large ships of the epoch. Alexandria made one set of fortunes by exporting the surpluses of Egypt, and another by its maritime trading all over the near and middle east.

With dazzling speed it became the largest of all Greek cities. Dominated by a principal avenue of unprecedented width, it extended over a rectangular area measuring four miles by three-quarters of a mile, and contained, before the end of the third century, something like half a million inhabitants. These included the largest Greek (and partly Macedonian) population of any colonial foundation; the place persistently maintained its Greek customs—and for a long time preserved sentimental ties with the city-states of the homeland. The Greeks of Alexandria had their own exceptional privileges and organization (*politeuma*), but no assembly and probably no council (or had one at first, but soon lost it). The large Jewish community, too, possessed an autonomous *politeuma* of its own. But in addition, outside any civic organization, Alexandria housed tens of thousands of Egyptians and people of innumerable other races. For it was an immensely cosmopolitan centre, the first and greatest universal city, the supreme Hellenistic melting-pot. Alexandria was a place that beckoned to young and lively people of all races and creeds to come and join in its seething and infinitely varied activities.

Much of the city was magnificently constructed of stone: a Roman general later remarked that it could never be burnt down, because there was no wood to burn. Many of its buildings were world-famous—not only the Pharos, but the Museum and Library, and the temple or Sarapis. And there were also the palaces of the Ptolemies, a cluster of Greek halls and living rooms arranged round elegant parks. Remains of these buildings have now been discovered in the eastern section of the harbour area.

PTOLEMY I ESTABLISHES A DYNASTY AND EMPIRE

This was where the ruling house lived, because Ptolemy I Soter, son of a Macedonian named Lagus, moved the capital to Alexandria from Memphis. Alexander had sent Ptolemy I to Egypt as his governor, and after Alexander's death he asserted his control over the country (and Cyrenaica [the region west of Egypt]) as an independent ruler, taking the Greek title of king in 305–304 BC. His Lagid dynasty outlasted those of the other two major successor kingdoms, continuing, despite many ups and downs, until the death of Cleopatra VII in 30 BC.

Ptolemy I's brilliant administrative powers rapidly brought the country, which had not been devastated in the recent wars, into fairly full working order. [The Greek poet] Theocritus, who hoped for Ptolemaic patronage, declared that 'Lagus' son boldly achieved such grand schemes as no man but he could ever have thought of.' And then Theocritus spoke up once again, to offer more detailed flattery of Ptolemy II Philadelphus (283–246)—who made Egypt even richer.

In their dependencies in Syria and Asia Minor the Ptolemies founded colonies in the Greek style, but they decided not to do so in Egypt, where the population was already so dense (probably between six and seven millions), and thoroughly and intricately organized on traditional lines of its own.

The exceptions were Alexandria in the north and Ptolemais Hermiou in the south. Ptolemais Hermiou was intended as a centre of Hellenism in upper [i.e., southern] Egypt, as a rival to Egyptian Thebes. And on a far larger scale that was the role of Alexandria in the north, in competition with Memphis. The purpose of Alexandria was to provide the whole country with a Greek rallying point. Ptolemy I Soter himself set a seal on the city's new status by seizing the embalmed body of Alexander the Great, and, after a brief period of lodgement at Memphis, moving it to Alexandria and laying it there with great pomp. This had been the late king's foundation, and now it was to be his permanent resting-place: its presence supported Ptolemy's claim to be, in a very special sense, Alexander's successor.

Yet Alexandria was a curious capital, because, despite its links with the interior by way of the Nile, it never quite belonged to the country; the city was not so much its centre as its superstructure. People spoke of travelling from Alexandria 'to Egypt': after its role as a Greek headquarters, its other primary function was to be the chief port of the eastern Mediterranean, the capital of an empire.

For although a Ptolemy was 'king' in the eyes of the Greeks, he was not king 'of Egypt', but (like the other Successors) king in general and undefined terms—and this situation was reflected and demonstrated by his overseas dominions. They were intended to put Egypt right back into the centre of international affairs: and the monarchs made continual endeavours to keep and increase these territories. At their most, they included Cyrenaica (with the ancient city of Cyrene), Cyprus (where the old local kingships were replaced by city-states) and many other islands; and the empire extended all along the coast of Asia Minor. But the greatest efforts had to be expended on southern Syria and Lebanon. . . .

The Ptolemaic empire served very important purposes. It was designed as an advanced screen to protect Egypt from its enemies. It was also intended to bring immense commercial profit. The Ptolemies needed a positive cash balance, based on economic self-sufficiency, in order to finance their military expenditure. And by means of their foreign dominions they were able to control a massive proportion of the Aegean market, which still played a pre-eminent part in Mediterranean and near-eastern trade. In particular, these Aegean dependencies provided pitch and metals and ships' timbers, which Egypt itself did not possess. In addition, the same lands supplied the Ptolemies with the shipwrights and navigators they so greatly needed.

But the monarchs simultaneously looked towards the south and east as well, abandoning none of the old trading routes and creating many new ones. The first four Ptolemies' seamen opened up the Red Sea and went much further afield as well, and later mariners continued to explore sea-routes of Africa and India, guarding the maritime terminals of the south Arabian caravans and suppressing the pirates who threatened the passage of their merchandise. Goods came into Egypt from the south and were re-exported into the Mediterranean area, including many materials which came in raw and unworked and left the country in manufactured form. Exports were the essence of Ptolemaic policy and profit.

LARGE-SCALE, EFFICIENT POLITICAL AND ECONOMIC ORGANIZATION

In order to develop all such activities as efficiently as possible, it was necessary to raise internal organization to the highest pitch of vigorous productivity. Ptolemy I Soter began this task, but it was greatly developed and elaborated by his son Ptolemy II Philadelphus, who took excellent advantage of the country's temporary exemption from the blood-letting that was going on elsewhere. One of the remarkable features of his system was the creation of the most elaborate and far-reaching bureaucracy the world had ever known. And, at first, these Greek bureaucrats in Egypt served their state with efficient skill. A dominant figure in this process was the formidably active and versatile Apollonius, finance minister of the government from *c.* 268/7 for over twenty years, of whom we know a great deal from the archives of his trusted agent and estate administrator, Zeno of Caunus. This information comes to us from papyri; and indeed we owe most of our knowledge of what was happening in Egypt to such papyri, which its sands have so abundantly and uniquely preserved.

One of the most enlightening among these documents contains an official assertion that 'no one has the right to do what he wants to do, but everything is regulated for the best'! The governing idea was that the country belonged to the kings, who had the full right to use it for the general good. In pursuance of this doctrine, the Ptolemies tended to merge the civil and military power, so as to be able to organize the government and its pervasive police with ever greater thoroughness on the lines of military discipline.

Everything the monarchs did served the exploitation of all possible resources for their own advantage, subordinating the economy to state power; the whole structure was meant to buzz like a disciplined hive so that every conceivable form of enrichment could be extracted for the benefit of the king, at minimum expense. . . . In this task the kings were assisted by the obligatory, universal compilation of demographic and economic registers of startlingly detailed character. Through these, the government ought to have been in a position to know what most of their subjects were doing, and were worth, at any given time, although the functionaries later became swamped in their own statistics.

The system was to be seen in its most elaborate form in its application to agriculture. Spurred on by Egypt's fabulous natural resources, the first two Ptolemies were the most impressive land-improvers in Greek history. Ptolemy II Philadelphus reclaimed large tracts of desert in the Fayum, and Greek engineers introduced more scientific methods of irrigation (one of the few major technological advances of the period): so that the peasants, previously content with primitive ways of working their beneficently Nile-flooded soil, found themselves dragged sharply out of the Bronze Age into the present—that is to say, into the Iron Age, since iron tools had not been used in the country before.

A very considerable proportion of this soil was 'royal land', belonging to the kings themselves and operated by their representatives. Exactly how large this category of land may have been, we cannot say: perhaps more, proportionately, than in any other Hellenistic monarchy, since the Ptolemies were said to be able to feed half a million people from their own estates. . . . Choice pieces of real estate were assigned to Greeks and Macedonians under the name of 'cleruchies', of which the monarch himself still retained the ultimate ownership. And in particular allotments were rented out on favourable terms—indeed, often without the need for any payment at all—to senior officers and civil servants, as incentives to loyalty, for although it was the policy of the Ptolemies to take much and give little away, they showed calculated generosity in their distribution of favours to privileged persons. . . . Moreover, royal lands were also let out (on terms varying between leniency and stiffness) to a wide range of less important individuals, often of Egyptian race, as well as to institutions, including temples, or occasionally whole urban communities. . . .

The Ptolemaic system has been described as a system of monopolistic nationalization or state socialism, perhaps the most thoroughgoing until the present century. But this is not entirely accurate. For the men directly working for the kings on their royal land form only part of the picture. The numerous remaining farmers and peasants in the country were cultivating portions of land that they had leased from the monarchs, so that the latter, although they told them in such detail what to do, were not their direct employers. It was not, that is to say, so much a monopolistic state socialism as a command economy.

The results, for a century, were unprecedented and spectacular. Their most impressive manifestation was to be seen in the production of grain, especially wheat—which was Egypt's staple crop—but also barley. The grain, like other produce, had to be cultivated in every region according to an official timetable, annually adjusted to meet the king's requirements. This grain trade exceeded all others in importance, for it was Egypt's principal resource: in a society in which wheat and barley played a far larger part as foodstuffs than they do today, the Ptolemies were the greatest of all the grain merchants in the world, the greatest it had ever seen. Millions of bushels were exported by the kings' agents every year, using [the Greek islands of] Rhodes and Delos as their international distribution centres. . . .

TAXATION AND BANKING

Ptolemaic taxation was equally far-reaching. A direct, uniform land tax, on the lines adopted by some other Hellenistic states, was not levied. However, the subjects of the Ptolemies paid taxes of a size and diversity that were unprecedented in the ancient

world. Every detail of more than two hundred of these imposi-
tions is recorded, and Ptolemy II Philadelphus, in particular, extorted an abundance of taxation which could scarcely be equalled
even today. Everyone, at every level, paid heavy taxes in order
to buy from the producers, who suffered equally heavy burdens
themselves. Furthermore, in order to prevent competition from
other countries, not only did the Ptolemies maintain a separate
coin standard all their own (the light 'Phoenician' standard), but
another expedient was resorted to as well: an import tax of 50 per
cent was applied to all imported oil (notably the olive-oil of
Greece, superior to the local seed products). Moreover, if oil was
imported all the same, it had to be sold to the king at a fixed
price, cases of evasion being punished with confiscation and
heavy fines. The collection of a great deal of this revenue was entrusted, for a price, to tax-farmers, middlemen between the tax-
payers and the government. This, as the experience of the Roman
empire later showed, was a system easily liable to abuse, but the
Ptolemies—at least to begin with—controlled the tax-farmers
with exemplary strictness.

Taxation was one of the facts of life that prompted the Ptolemies
to encourage a massive development of banking. This was already an ancient institution in the Greek world: but amid the far-
flung transactions and exchange requirements of the Ptolemaic
kingdom, as elsewhere in the Hellenistic world, a new and more
professional kind of bank arose, replacing the old oral management of business by insistence upon written documents. Another
novelty of the banking system was centralization, based on the
establishment of a central state bank at Alexandria, with branches
elsewhere. It was these royal institutions that guaranteed the con-
tracts between the state and the tax-farmers; and the banks acted
as receiving agents for taxes paid either in kind or in cash. They
had many other functions as well. For example, it was their duty
to effect payments that needed to be made from the king's treasury—and, conversely, to develop every means of bringing more
wealth into its coffers. The banks also found time to look after
private funds.

GREEK VERSUS EGYPTIAN CULTURE

Banks were sometimes attached to the temples, which had been,
for millennia, the basic stable institutions of Egyptian society, and
still remained powerful economic, intellectual and artistic units.
It was only in these temple societies that the indigenous Egyptian upper class still survived; they remained the principal centres of the national civilization and script and craftsmanship, enabling the literary, . . . architectural and sculptural traditions of

Egypt to resist obliteration, and remain largely independent of the imported Greek culture. These survivals were encouraged by the Ptolemies, who reduced the temples to indirect dependence upon themselves by granting them privileges and allocating them funds. . . . The cults of Isis and Sarapis, which the Ptolemies indefatigably stimulated, were Hellenized versions of Egyptian traditions. In other respects, however, the monarchs accepted the separate existence of Egypt's religion just as it was, without attempting to convert or modify its ancient, native characteristics. The new rulers also wanted themselves to be seen not only as Greek kings but as Pharaohs of Egypt, and Ptolemy V Epiphanes (205–180) was crowned at Memphis according to Egyptian rites.

And yet, despite all these moves, Egyptian culture tended to wilt. For the relationship between Greeks (and Macedonians) on the one hand, and Egyptians on the other, remained fundamentally unsatisfactory. The trouble was that the Greeks enjoyed a markedly superior status. True, some of the ordinary Egyptians under the early Ptolemies were better off than they had been for a good many centuries past, since the monarchs felt it necessary to protect them from the worst oppressions if only out of self-interest. Nor could it be said that these rulers consciously or deliberately followed racialistic principles: their policy was not racial but royal—the pursuit of their own advantage. Nevertheless, it was the Greeks who were, to an overwhelming extent, the principal agents and supports of their régime, and this situation inevitably made itself felt and caused friction.

The Greeks, it is true, were impressed by the antiquity of Egypt. . . . Moreover, the poorer members of their community sometimes intermarried with Egyptians, at least from the time of Ptolemy II Philadelphus onwards. Yet the Greeks had brought with them into the country the conviction that every individual Egyptian was violent and dishonest, and it was a conviction that most of them persistently retained. Greek judges were grossly biased against Egyptians. Native peasants—who cheaply performed the lowest kinds of manual labour, reserved for slaves in other countries—paid much heavier taxes than Greek residents, and lived virtually in a state of profitless bondage. . . .

A STEADY DECLINE

Besides, the successes of the Ptolemaic economy did not last. For the centralized, bureaucratic system could only work adequately under men who possessed exceptional drive—and were immune from ordinary human failings. For a time the former requirement was met. But in the nature of things this could not go on for ever, and the Egyptians, under the impact of increasing

ill-treatment, inevitably became dangerously embittered, and finally desperate. The deterioration was gradual, and uneven. But
already in the reign of Ptolemy II Philadelphus . . . discrimina-
tion could be found, and was resented. 'I do not know how to
behave like a Greek (*hellenizein*)' mourns a camel-driver (perhaps an Arab). And under Ptolemy III Euergetes, a priest com-
plains that the Greek billeted in his home looks down on him
'because he is an Egyptian'. . . .

Native revolts broke out, and then proved impossible to stop.
For two decades (208/7–187/6), almost the whole of the Thebaid
in Upper Egypt, always the breeding-ground for Pharaonic na-
tionalism, fell under the independent rule of secessionist Nubian
kings, and the breakaway was only terminated by Ptolemy V
Epiphanes (205–180) amid savage repression.

This was an epoch of chaotic local uprisings, sieges and rob-
beries; and Nile transport became perilously insecure. In these
years, moreover, it was not only the Egyptians but the ruling race
who felt unsafe; for example, a recluse (named Ptolemy) is found
complaining that he has been assaulted because he is a Macedonian. Furthermore, Ptolemy V's loss of most of his imperial
possessions to the Seleucid Antiochus IV Epiphanes at the battle
of Panion (200) isolated Egypt from its eastern commerce, and
thus caused even worse impoverishment. Besides, the dynastic
quarrels and court scandals that characterized the next reigns—
in addition to new bouts of currency inflation—meant that the
welfare of the Egyptian populace declined still further.

The workers on the land had already formed the habit of reg-
istering their protests by the withdrawal of their labour—not for
better wages or conditions, because clearly these were not to be
had, but merely out of total despair: which was converted into
this sort of protest action, from time to time, by some fortuitous
irritation or hold-up. But as the second century BC continued on
its way, something much more serious began to happen as well.
For the peasants (and even tax-farmers unable to meet their
obligations) increasingly went on strike by fleeing from their jobs
and homes, usually in groups, and taking refuge in sanctuaries
or going underground. 'We are worn out,' declares a papyrus letter, 'we will run away.' And so the economic recession got worse
still, because now there were not enough people left to cultivate
the soil. Ptolemy VIII Euergetes II, who had the reputation of
favouring the native population, produced a remarkable decree
(not the first of its kind) ordering . . . amnesties, the lightening of
burdens, tax exemptions, counsels of moderation to officials. But
it was too late. Egypt continued to lurch towards collapse and
dependence on unscrupulous Romans—and on Rome itself. . . .

One of the worst problems that confronted the authorities— and these profit-seeking Roman adventurers as well—was the condition of the vast city of Alexandria. Its Graeco-Macedonian population had by now become a mixed race of exceptional live- liness, addicted to over-excitement and rioting. The palace, too, was sometimes in the hands of shady personages, notably the cunning and murderous Sosibius and his friends, who directed the régime of Ptolemy IV Philopator; and subsequently the court, although it remained Greek in culture, was dominated—like the courts of eastern states—by eunuchs, who were sometimes of sinister character. This volatile Alexandria was the power-base of Cleopatra VII Philadelphus Philopator Philopatris, who came to the throne in 51 BC and made a last determined attempt to re- vive the kingdom and empire by means of her successive asso- ciations with Julius Caesar (allegedly the father of her son, Ptolemy XV Caesar or Caesarion) and then Marcus Antonius (Antony) (by whom she had additional children). But the attempt failed . . . and after nearly three hundred years of Ptolemaic king- ship the country became a Roman province in 30 BC. In spite of all the disasters it had suffered, it was still rich enough, especially in grain, to revolutionize the Roman economy. During the rule of the Romans, however, the Egyptian people did not fare even as well as they had under the Ptolemaic house—or at least under its earlier monarchs.

The Death of Cleopatra, Last of the Ptolemies

Dio Cassius

The most famous of all the Ptolemaic rulers of Egypt was the last, Cleopatra VII, who, with her Roman lover Antony, was defeated by Octavian at Actium in 31 B.C. Her death, which marked the end of an era in the classical world (specifically the end of large-scale Greek rule and the extension of Roman power over the entire Mediterranean sphere) is described here by the Romanized Greek historian Dio Cassius (ca. A.D. 150–235). He had a distinguished political career as a Roman official, serving as a senator, twice as consul in Rome (in 205 and 229), and also as governor of the provinces of Dalmatia and Africa. The work for which he is best known is a large-scale history of Rome in eighty books (written in Greek), from which the following account is taken.

[A]fter Antony's death,] she now believed that she could place some degree of trust in Octavian and at once sent word to him of what had happened, and yet she could not feel completely confident that no harm would befall her. She therefore remained in seclusion within the building, so that even if there were no other reason for keeping her alive, she could at least trade upon Octavian's fear concerning her treasure to obtain a pardon and keep her throne. Even when she had sunk to such depths of misfortune, she remembered that she was queen and preferred to die bearing the title and majesty of a sovereign rather than live in a private station. At any rate she kept ready fire to destroy her treasure, and asps and other reptiles to end her life; she had experimented before on human beings to discover how these creatures caused death in each case.

Now Octavian was much concerned not only to make himself master of her wealth, but also to capture her alive and lead her in his triumph at Rome. However, as he had given her a pledge of a kind, he did not wish to be seen as having tricked her; rather he wanted to make her appear as his captive, who had been to some extent subdued against her will. He therefore sent Gaius Proculeius, a knight, and Epaphroditus, a freedman, to visit her, and instructed them carefully as to what they should say and do. The two accordingly obtained an audience with Cleopatra, began by discussing a number of reasonable proposals, and then, before anything had been agreed, suddenly laid hands on her. After this they removed from her any means of ending her life, and allowed her to spend some days in the monument where she was engaged in embalming Antony's body. They moved her to the palace, but did not dismiss any of her accustomed retinue or attendants: their object was that she should continue to cherish the hope of obtaining her wishes, and so do nothing to harm herself. At any rate, when she sought an audience with Octavian, her request was granted, and to further the deception he promised that he would visit her himself.

So she prepared a superbly decorated apartment and a richly ornamented couch, dressed herself with studied negligence—indeed her appearance in mourning wonderfully enhanced her beauty—and seated herself on the couch. Beside her she arranged many different portraits and busts of Julius Caesar, and in her bosom she carried all the letters Caesar had sent her. Then as Octavian entered, she sprang to her feet, blushed, and cried, 'Greetings, my lord, for now the gods have given supremacy to you and taken it from me. But now you can see with your own eyes how Caesar looked when he visited me so many times, and you have heard tell of how he honoured me and made me queen of Egypt. You should learn something of me from his own words; these are the letters which he wrote with his own hand: take them and read them.'

So saying, she went on to read many of Caesar's passionate expressions of his feelings for her. At one moment she would weep and kiss the letters, and then she would kneel and bow her head before Caesar's portraits. She kept turning her eyes towards Octavian and lamenting her fate in a plaintive musical tone. Her voice melted as she murmured, 'How can thy letters, Caesar, help me now?' and 'And yet in this man thou livest for me again,' then, 'Would that I had died before thee,' and still again, 'But if I have him, I have thee.'

Such were the subtle tones of speech and changes of expression with which she addressed Octavian, casting sweet looks towards him and murmuring tender words. Octavian understood the passion with which she was speaking and the seductive power of her gestures; however, he acted as if he were unaware of these, looked towards the ground and merely replied, 'Do not distress yourself, lady, take heart, no harm shall come to you.' But her spirits were utterly cast down, because he neither looked at her, nor made any mention of her kingdom, nor uttered so much as a word of love. She threw herself on her knees, burst out weeping, and said, 'I have no desire to live, nor can I live. But this favour I beg of you, in memory of your father, that since the gods gave me to Antony after him, I too may die with Antony. I wish that I had perished at the very instant after Caesar's death. But seeing that it was my fate to suffer that parting from him, send me to Antony. Do not grudge that I should be buried with him: as I die because of him, so may I live with him, even in Hades.'

So she spoke, in the hope of arousing his pity, but Octavian made no reply. As he was afraid that she might still end her own life, he urged her yet again to take heart. After this he did not dismiss any of her attendants, but treated her with especial care in his desire that she should make a brilliant spectacle at his triumph. She guessed that this was his plan, and since she felt such a fate to be worse than any number of deaths, she now truly longed to die. She begged Octavian time and again that her life should be ended by one means or another, and of her own accord she thought of many ways to bring this about. Finally, when she could put none of these into effect, she professed to have undergone a change of heart and to place great hopes for the future both in Octavian and in Livia [Octavian's wife]. She said that she would sail to Rome of her own free will, and prepared a number of specially treasured chosen ornaments to take as gifts. In this way she hoped to convince them that she did not intend to die, and hence that she would be less closely guarded and thus enabled to kill herself

So it came about. As soon as the others, and in particular Epaphroditus, who had been charged with her safe keeping, had become convinced that her state of mind was as she described it and so relaxed their strict surveillance, she prepared to die as painlessly as possible. First she gave a sealed paper to Epaphroditus himself to deliver, in which she begged Octavian to give orders for her to be buried beside Antony. She pretended that the letter concerned some other matter, and using this pretext to get the freedman out of the way, she set about her task. She put on her finest robes, seated herself with majestic grace, took in her hands all the emblems of royalty, and so died.

No one knows for certain by what means she perished, for the only marks that were found on her body were tiny pricks on the arm. Some say that she applied to herself an asp [poisonous snake], which had been brought to her in a water jar, or perhaps covered beneath some flowers. According to others she had smeared a pin with some poison whose composition rendered it harmless if the contact were external, but which, if even the smallest quantity entered the bloodstream, would quickly prove fatal, although also painless; according to this theory, she had previously worn the pin in her hair as usual, but now made a small scratch in her arm and caused the poison to enter the blood. In this or some similar way she had died, and her two waiting women with her. . . .

When Octavian heard of Cleopatra's death, he was astounded and not only came to see her body, but called in the aid of drugs. . . .

As for Octavian, when he found that it was impossible to revive Cleopatra, he felt both admiration and pity for her, but he was bitterly chagrined on his own account, as if all the glory of his victory had been taken away from him.

Antony and Cleopatra were the cause of many misfortunes to the Egyptians and many to the Romans. These were the circumstances in which they fought the war and met their deaths. They were both embalmed in the same manner and buried in the same tomb. The qualities of character which they possessed, and the fortunes which they experienced, may be described as follows. Antony had no superior in recognizing where his duty lay, and yet he committed many senseless acts. There were times when he excelled in courage, and yet he often failed through cowardice: he was capable equally of true greatness of spirit and of extreme baseness. He would plunder the property of others and squander his own. He showed compassion to many without cause, and punished even more without justice. Thus although he rose from most weak beginnings to a position of great power, and from the depths of poverty to the possession of great riches, yet he gained no profit from either situation. Instead, after hoping that he alone would rule the empire of the Romans, he took his own life.

Cleopatra was a woman of insatiable sexuality and insatiable avarice. She often displayed an estimable ambition, but equally often an overweening arrogance. It was by means of the power of love that she acquired the sovereignty of the Egyptians, and when she aspired to obtain dominion over the Romans in the same fashion, she failed in the attempt and lost her kingdom besides. Through her own unaided genius she captivated the two greatest Romans of her time, and because of the third, she destroyed herself.

THE PARTHIAN EMPIRE RISES IN THE NEAR EAST

JOHN CURTIS

The area of Persia (what is now Iran and Iraq) was for a short while part of the classical world. Macedonia's Alexander the Great overthrew the Persian Achaemenid dynasty in the late fourth century B.C., and soon afterward his general, Seleucis, established a large kingdom in the area. However, Asiatic influences in the form of the Parthian (or Arsacid) dynasty supplanted the Seleucid realm by the late second century B.C.; and after that, this large portion of the Near East remained on the outside fringes of the classical world. The Parthians became the Romans' chief rival in the region and the emperor Trajan (early second century A.D.) was the only Roman leader who enjoyed success against them. Scholar John Curtis, an expert on ancient Persia, provides this brief overview of Parthian history and culture.

The first serious challenge to Seleucid control of Iran came in about 238 BC, when the Parthians seized control of the satrapy [province] of Parthia, situated east of the Caspian Sea. In origin they were a nomadic Iranian tribe who migrated into the area from central Asia. Arsaces, founder of the dynasty, and his immediate successors spent the succeeding years establishing themselves and expanding at the expense of the Seleucids. Their two most important early capitals were at Nysa (ancient Mithradatkirt), now in Soviet Turkmenistan, and Shahr-i Qumis (ancient Hecatompylos) near Damghan. This Parthian expansion was not without its setbacks, but by 141 BC Mithradates I, who is often regarded as the real founder of the Parthian empire, was in a position to be crowned at Seleucia-on-the-Tigris in Mesopotamia. Perhaps at this time a winter capital was established at Ctesiphon on the opposite bank of the river. At the time of his death, in about 138 BC, the Parthians were in control of much of the Iranian plateau and Mesopotamia and part of central Asia. In spite of some further reverses, by 113 BC his successor Mithradates II had extended the western frontier of the Parthian empire to the Euphrates.

RIVALRY WITH ROME

By now Parthia was firmly straddling the Silk Route, greatly benefiting from its role as a middleman in the exchange of goods between China in the east and Rome in the west. The Parthians enjoyed cordial relations with the Chinese Han dynasty, but their expansion westwards brought them into sharp conflict with Rome. Another source of contention was Armenia, as both Rome and Parthia sought to influence the course of events there. The first major encounter between the two powers was at Carrhae (modern Harran in Turkey) in 53 BC, which resulted in a decisive defeat for [the Roman nobleman Marcus] Crassus and his Roman legions. On this occasion the Romans found their infantry no match for the mobile Parthian cavalry commanded by Suren, whose prowess in archery (the so-called 'Parthian shot') has become proverbial. Mark Antony's campaign of 36 BC was similarly abortive.

For more than a century thereafter no serious challenge was made to the territorial integrity of Parthia, but this period of comparative quiet was rudely shattered by the aggressive ambitions of Trajan. In his campaign of AD 116 this emperor succeeded in capturing Ctesiphon and marching to the shores of the Persian Gulf. Although he soon had to withdraw, from this point onwards Parthia was in decline, racked by internal dissension and threatened externally by the Kushans in the east, the nomadic Alani in the north-west and the Romans in the west. Ctesiphon was sacked twice more, and although there were periods of Parthian revival, notably under Vologases IV in the second half of the second century AD, the state was largely a spent force.

GREEK CULTURE SUPPLANTED BY PARTHIAN

For historical information about the Parthians we are largely dependent on the works of Greek and Latin authors, but generally their accounts are far from objective. Unfortunately, practically nothing the Parthians might have written about themselves has been preserved, but there are inscriptions on coins and on pot-sherds (ostraca) from sites such as Nysa; in the British Museum is a collection of nearly 200 ostraca with inscriptions in Pahlavi. . . . Parthian coins are helpful for establishing the succession of kings and their dates, and clay tablets written in cuneiform are a useful source of knowledge about local conditions in Babylonia.

Before the establishment of Parthian rule, the urban centres of Mesopotamia and Iran had been subjected to a fairly intensive period of Hellenisation [exposure to Greek customs and ideas], and naturally this influence did not suddenly disappear with the advent of a new ruling dynasty. Thus, in the early part of the Parthian period, Greek was retained as the official language. Greek cities such as Seleucia were allowed to prosper, and Mithradates I and some of his successors used the epithet 'Phil-hellene' ["friend" or "lover" of Greeks] on their coins. The art of this early period also shows marked Hellenistic influence. This can be seen on the ivory rhyta (drinking-horns) from Nysa, which are mainly decorated with Greek mythological scenes.

Towards the end of the first century BC and certainly in the first century AD, however, the situation began to change and Oriental features became more prominent in Parthian culture. A large bronze statue from a sanctuary at Shami, which can be dated to this period by comparison with images on coins, represents a man wearing a Parthian outfit of belted jacket and leggings. His hair hangs in bunches beneath a headband in a characteristic Parthian style. From the first century AD onwards some Hel-lenistic traits can still be identified, but generally the iconogra-phy and composition of works of art are characteristically Parthian. This can be clearly seen in some of the rock-reliefs in western Iran such as Bisitun, Sar-i Pul-i Zohab and Hung-i Nau-ruzi. They show scenes of investiture, combat and worship with figures dressed in the Parthian costume. Parthian elements can also be found on coins: Aramaic lettering appears for the first time in the reign of Vologases I (AD 51–78).

Evidence for art in the late Parthian period comes mainly from semi-autonomous regional centres such as Elymais in Khuzistan and Hatra in northern Mesopotamia. In Elymais we have the re-ligious centres of Masjid-i Sulaiman and Bard-i Nishandeh, dated to the late second and early third centuries AD, with many reliefs and statues showing worshipping figures. All are represented frontally and most wear the Parthian tunic and trousers. Else-where in Elymais there are rock-reliefs of this period at Tang-i Sarvak and Shimbar. At the important site of Hatra, situated on the trans-desert route linking northern Mesopotamia with sites such as Palmyra and Dura Europos in the west, many life-size statues of worshippers have been found in the complex of temples. These detailed representations provide us with much information about the elaborate costumes of this period.

OTHER ASPECTS OF PARTHIAN CULTURE

In the realm of architecture there were important developments. During the Parthian period the iwan became a widespread architectural form. This was a great hall, open on one side with a high barrel-vaulted roof, which became a distinctive feature of Parthian monumental buildings. Particularly fine examples have been found at Ashur and Hatra. In the construction of these grandiose halls, fast-setting gypsum mortar was used. Perhaps allied to the increasing use of gypsum mortar at this time is the development of gypsum stucco decoration, also attested in the Hellenistic period at Seleucia. There is particularly lavish use of stucco for wall decoration at Qaleh-i Yazdigird near Qasr-i Shirin in a palace dating from the late Parthian period, and there are some fine examples from Warka and Ashur in Mesopotamia.

Burial practices in the Parthian period were diverse, perhaps testifying to the degree of religious toleration at this time. For example, in the south-western part of the Parthian empire, bodies were often interred in so-called slipper-coffins with oval lids, sometimes elaborately decorated in blue-green glaze. Examples from Warka are decorated with figures of warriors in low relief. Associated with such coffins were a variety of grave-goods including terracotta figurines, coins, vessels in pottery and glass, gold and silver jewellery, crude bone figurines and so on—in short, all those objects which might prove useful to the deceased in the afterlife. Quite different forms of burial, on the other hand, have been attested at Nineveh. Here, bodies were placed in stone coffins, and the faces of the corpses covered with gold masks. A rich selection of jewellery was found with the burials, including a fine pair of earrings set with garnets and turquoise and a large number of small gold plaques that were sewn on to clothing. The wealth of jewellery that must have been in circulation in Parthian times is clear from coin portraits, but unfortunately there are very few examples from excavations. We do, however, have a good range of pottery from Parthian sites, and new and distinctive forms appeared at this time. In the Zagros area of western Iran 'clinky' ware, a hard red pottery which makes a clinky noise when tapped, is a hallmark of the Parthians, whereas in Mesopotamia and Syria blue-green glazed pottery was widespread.

The last Parthian king, Artabanus V, was overthrown about AD 224 by Ardashir, a local dynast in Fars whose seat was at Istakhr. He is said to have been a descendant of one Sasan, who gave his name to the Sasanian dynasty founded by Ardashir; the Sasanians were to rule Iran for more than 400 years. They saw themselves as successors to the Achaemenids, after the Hellenistic and Parthian interlude, and perceived it as their role to restore the greatness of Iran. Such ambitions inevitably brought the Sasanian monarchs into conflict with Rome and later Byzantium in the west.

THE CH'IN DYNASTY UNITES CHINA

L. CARRINGTON GOODRICH

Far to the east of the Roman, Greek, Persian, and even the Indian realms, lay China, which up until 221 B.C. consisted of a large number of small and moderate-sized warring states. In that year, the westernmost of these states, ruled by the Ch'in, a strong, authoritarian group of rulers, launched large-scale military campaigns; and in short order the Ch'in overran the other states. Under the Ch'in, for the first time in history China became a unified empire with a centralized administration. And that concept of unity and central government proved long-lived, inspiring Chinese leaders in the many centuries that followed. As L. Carrington Goodrich, a former professor of Chinese at Columbia University, points out in this essay, though the Ch'in realm did not last long, its immediate successor, ruled by the Han Dynasty, adopted and built on the Ch'in imperial model. (It is interesting to note that the Ch'in indirectly influenced the classical Romans. China's Great Wall, largely created by the Ch'in, later discouraged an invasion by the Asiatic Huns, who proceeded instead to head west and enter Europe, setting in motion the final "barbarian" incursions that destroyed the Roman Empire.)

F or a century before the final success of the Ch'in, certain princes of China were ambitious for empire or at least supremacy, and one by one they absorbed the weaker princes. . . . Scorned by the other states for their uncouthness and barbarity, the people of Ch'in absorbed some of their critics' culture and overlooked no opportunity to improve their military fitness. The teachings of a succession of statesmen . . . had made their government the best disciplined and most purposive of any east of the Gobi. In 318 the Ch'in, who dominated the northwest, moved into Szechuan and seized control of the great food-producing plain. The huge irrigation system which the governor and his son reputedly began there about 300 [B.C.] has banished serious floods and droughts for twenty-two centuries and is still in existence. A canal nearly one hundred miles long was cut across Shensi in 246 [B.C.] to enrich the alkaline soil with water laden with silt. The productivity of this region, says the annalist, promptly increased about twenty-eight pecks per square mile. Having thus assured a food supply, the authorities erected a grain station near modern Kaifeng to provision their troops. To break up the feudal system no fief was granted after 238 [B.C.]. To guard against rebellion in the rear and to provide labor there was considerable transfer of the population from one province to another during 239–235 B.C. Powerful families— 120,000 in all . . . were required to move to the capital at Hsienyang in modern Shensi. By 234 [B.C.] Chêng, who as a young boy had become head of Ch'in in 247 [B.C.], was ready to put his armies in the field and by 222 he had vanquished the last of the rival states. The combination of excellent preparation, constant pressure, and superb mastery of the newest arts of war, especially cavalry, proved too much for his enemies. He promptly created the first empire and assumed the title of First Emperor (Shih-huang-ti); his system of government lasted until the twentieth century.

MILITARY UNIFICATION AND FORTIFICATION

With the help of Li Ssǔ (280?–208), a minister of outstanding ability, the emperor set to work to establish his house for ten thousand generations. In 221 [B.C.] he decreed that the whole country should be divided into thirty-six military areas; this was shortly increased to forty-one. Each had its military governor, its civil administrator, and its supervisory official. The people were disarmed but were given rights over their property, subject to tax. Promotions and demotions were used as rewards and punishments; other punitive measures were unusually harsh. Nobility was based on gifts and services to the state rather than on birth. Customs and laws, weights and measures were unified; even the axles of wheels had to be uniform. Artisans and farmers were benefited at the expense of merchants.

In 220 [B.C.] Shih-huang-ti began a network of tree-lined roads, fifty paces broad. The sectional walls in the north were joined together to form one long barrier (known to us as the Great Wall),

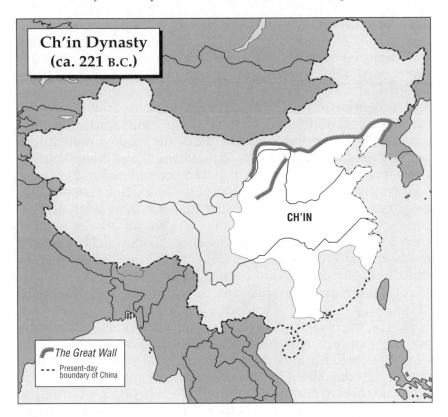

Ch'in Dynasty (ca. 221 B.C.)

CH'IN

The Great Wall
- - - Present-day boundary of China

thus for the first time indicating what was China and what barbarian. The Hsiung-nu (possibly the later Huns of the great invasions of Europe) had to be driven from the region south of the great bend of the Yellow River. Forty-four fortified encampments were built along the river (these were occupied by prisoners of war), the waterways deepened, and a long connecting highway constructed. Not content with a territory stretching from the new wall to the southern boundaries of Ch'u in modern Honan, the emperor sent his armies farther south. In a brilliant campaign during 221–214 [B.C.], they conquered the region of Fukien, Kuangtung, Kuangsi, and Tongking. This was achieved largely by the digging of a twenty-mile waterway called "the marvelous canal" which connected two streams and thus made possible water transportation all the way from the Yangtze to the West River.

A CENTRALIZED GOVERNMENT

The many styles of writing in different parts of the country Shih-huang-ti reduced to one. Because he found a large part of the literature of the past too worshipful of another way of life, he ordered it to be burned, except for the imperial archives and books on medicine, divination, farming, arboriculture, and the history

of his own house. By this means he sought to destroy sectional-
ism and any lingering support of the feudal houses, and to unify
the "hundred schools of thought." On one occasion he had 460
members of the lettered class, mainly magicians or charlatans,
put to death. The scholars whom he valued were unmolested,
and he continued the office of Learned Doctor at the court. He
himself worked indefatigably, handling "one hundred twenty
pounds" of reports each day. He frequently made investigations
in disguise, for he both feared assassination and tried to create
the impression of divinity. His palace, completed in 212 [B.C.],
was assuredly one of the wonders of the world; it measured 2500
feet from east to west and 500 feet from south to north and accommodated 10,000 people. Within a radius of some sixty miles
there were 270 lesser imperial residences "connected by covered
roads and roads bordered with walls" and furnished with "tents,
canopies, bells, drums, and beautiful women."

All of Shih-huang-ti's measures did not spring from the brains
of his own generation of leaders. Chinese pamphleteers had advocated some of them for a century and a half or so. Nor is it impossible that certain of them came in from the west. About three
centuries earlier [the Persian monarch] Darius had created an
empire that depended in large measure on provincial divisions,
arterial roads to connect the provinces, a system of imperial
posts, and personal representation. These were also features of
the empire of Chandragupta (*ca.* 321–*ca.* 297) in northern India.
. . . Whatever their source, however, such measures in China
awaited a man of the First Emperor's genius and absolute power.
Although his empire was short lived—it crumbled in the third
year of his son's reign—its founding was an event of large importance in world history. The First Empire put into practice for
the first time the idea of unity for all the peoples "within the
wall," an idea never lost to sight even during the long periods of
imperial breakdown that followed. It established a centralized
government charged with responsibility not only for law and order but also for public works, government monopolies of basic
products, coinage, and the upholding of the rights of the common man as against those of the tradesman. It made the first
sharp cleavage between the "we" group and the "they" group in
the north and northwest, and sent exiles into Korea and probably elsewhere. The first contacts with the islands of Japan reportedly date from this time, when an expedition set out from
Shantung in search of the isles of the immortals. There seems
scant doubt that the name of China is derived from the Ch'in because of the great influence of their state and empire on the peoples across Asia. The honor is well deserved.

THE END OF THE CH'IN

In spite of its absolutism, however, the empire could not wholly silence two groups—the theorists, who disliked the state whose groundwork they themselves had laid, and the descendants of the princely houses and the ministers of state for whom the empire had no place. Besides these, countless people must have suffered indescribably from the forced labor, the frontier military service, and the heavy taxation. According to a later and perhaps biased historian who wrote in the first century A.D.:

> Having united the empire, Ch'in Shih-huang made public works within, and expelled the I and Ti tribes without. He received a tax amounting to the greater half, and sent forth as soldiers (all) to the left of the village gate. The men's exertions in cultivation were insufficient for the grain taxes, and the spinning of the women was insufficient for clothing. The resources of the empire were exhausted in supplying [Shih-huang's] government, and yet were insufficient to satisfy his desires. Within the seas there was sadness and dissatisfaction, and this developed into disorder and rebellion.

When Shih-huang-ti died in 210 [B.C.] while on an expedition far from the capital, his body had to be brought back to Hsienyang in a closed carriage for fear of a revolt. The removal of his iron hand and his inept son's succession to power resulted in the overthrow of the empire by the various dissatisfied groups in 207. There followed several years of anarchy which ended when the country was reunited by a military officer who had risen from the ranks and who overcame all rival claimants to the throne.

THE AFRICAN KINGDOM OF AXUM

Harold G. Marcus

At about the time that the Roman Empire was nearing its height (in the late first century A.D.), the successful African kingdom of Axum was rising to prominence. Axum came to occupy most of what is now Ethiopia, lying along the western coast of the Red Sea south of Egypt (which had recently been ruled by the Greek Ptolemies). In fact, it was Axum's close proximity to that sea that contributed most to its prosperity; for the waterway was a liquid highway over which Greek and Roman traders made their way to Axumite ports (and vice versa). As the centuries passed, other Greek and Roman influences filtered into Axum, including the Christian faith. This fascinating tract by Harold G. Marcus, a professor of African studies at Michigan State University, shows that the African kingdom's Mediterranean connection was so vital to its prosperity that when that link was severed, Axum became isolated and fell into decline.

E thiopia early joined the Middle East and participated in the region's rich religious history. Similarly, it also shared in the evolving mercantile life of the eastern Mediterranean-Red Sea regional economy.

Trade brought the wealth that permitted the rise of elites who assumed honors and tides. Ambition and greed made for wars of aggrandizement; luck and talent brought consolidation; and success led to greater wealth, more followers, and additional pretensions. The five hundred years before the Christian era witnessed warfare that increased in scale as the stakes became greater. The winner was the inland state of Axum, comprising Akele Guzay and Agame, and dominating food-rich areas to the southwest largely inhabited by Agew-speaking farmers. The rise and then the hegemony of Axum over the coast inland into Tigray and even its subsequent expansion within and without Ethiopia appears linked to the stimulus given to regional trade by Ptolemaic Egypt (330–320 B.C.) and then by the Roman world economy.

AXUM BECOMES A PROSPEROUS TRADING STATE

When the state of Axum emerges into the wider light of history at the end of the first century A.D., it is a full-blown, if not well-integrated, trading state. The anonymous author of the *Periplus [Geography] of the Erythraean Sea* [an anonymous Greek handbook for sea captains] mentions Ethiopia's main port at Adulis, twenty miles inside the Gulf of Zula, where visiting foreign ships anchored in the channel to protect themselves against attack at night by unruly local peoples. Nevertheless, Adulis offered profit enough to receive a continuous stream of merchants who, in return for ivory, offered cloth of many types, glassware, tools, gold and silver jewelry, copper, and Indian iron and steel used to manufacture high-quality weapons. Befitting its centrality in Ethiopia's economy, Adulis was an impressive place with stone-built houses and temples, a dam, and irrigated agriculture.

Five days to the west-south-west lay the city of Axum, which dominated the ivory trade west into Sudan. The state's leaders not only monopolized the commerce but also sought to dominate trade routes and sources of supply. During the fifth century A.D., for example, Ethiopian armies campaigned northward to establish control over the commerce that flowed toward Suakin and to pacify the Beja of the Sahil, through which caravans passed en route to Adulis; south of the Tekeze to subdue the Agew-speaking agriculturists of productive but mountainous Simen; southeast-ward into the Afar desert to command the incense trade; and even across the Red Sea to force Hejaz (a province of modern Saudi Arabia) to pay tribute and to guarantee the seaborne trade.

Our information comes from an inscription copied at Adulis in 525 by the seafaring Cosmas Indicopleustes and subsequently published in his *Christian Topography* (ca. 547). The book reveals that cut pieces of brass and coins were imported in the first century A.D. to use as money in Ethiopia's markets, suggesting a commerce requiring easier exchange. Ultimately, Axum responded by issuing its own coins late in the third century. Significantly, the first mintings were rendered in Greek and were fractions of the Roman solidus, clearly indicating that the specie was used primarily in international trade. The mere existence of

Axumite money signaled Ethiopia's major role in the Middle East, where only Persia, Kushanas in India, and Rome circulated specie. The Ge'ez-speaking masses, however, continued to use traditional salt and iron bars as money and remained aloof from events that brought not only commerce but also Christianity to Axum's shores. They avoided both the coin and the cross—not so the ruling elites, whose interests came to include both.

THE INTRODUCTION OF CHRISTIANITY

From the third century, or even before, Axum's Hellenized elites had learned about the new faith from Christian traders. At court, the ideology was discussed philosophically but also, as befitted a place of power, in economic and political terms. Context was paramount: by the early fourth century, Christianity had become the established religion of the eastern Roman Empire. Since Roman trade dominated the Red Sea, it was inevitable that Christianity would penetrate Axum. Conversion was slow and occurred first in the towns and along the major trade routes. The shift was heralded, during the first third of the fourth century, by coins suddenly embossed with a cross and then by monuments carrying imperial inscriptions prefaced by Christian incantations.

According to Ethiopian church tradition, two Syrian boys, Aedisius and Frumentius, brought Christianity to Ethiopia. Shipwreck victims, they were brought to court as slaves and put to work by Emperor Ella Amida (r. ca. end of the third century A.D.). Over the years, their piety, reliability, and especially Frumentius's sagacity and wisdom as royal secretary and treasurer earned the monarch's gratitude, and his will manumitted them. His widow, as regent, asked them to remain in the palace and advise her until her infant son, Ezanas, was ready for the throne. While so engaged, Frumentius sought out Christian merchants, urged them to establish churches, and cooperated fully with them to spread the gospel.

When the young king came to power (ca. 303), Frumentius traveled to Alexandria to urge the patriarch to assign a bishop to Ethiopia to speed its conversion. He must not have been surprised—since his life had normally been astonishing—to hear the prelate nominate him. And back Frumentius went to Axum sometime around 305 (?) to begin a lifetime's work of evangelism, in so doing wresting Ezanas from his traditional beliefs. As linked to trade, Christianity proved a boon to the monarch.

CONTINUED GREEK AND CHRISTIAN INFLUENCES

Around 350, Emperor Ezanas followed his commercial star westward into the Nile valley to secure Axum's trade in ivory and other commodities. He acted because the Sudanese state of Meroë, in its decline, was unable to protect the caravan routes from raiding by the nomadic Beja. The Axumite army encountered little resistance as it made its way into Sudan (Kush), and, at the confluence of the Atbara and Nile, Ezanas raised a stela on which he described the case of his conquests and thanked the Christian God for His protection. For the next few centuries, no state is known to have challenged Axum's trading monopoly on the African side of the Red Sea.

The trade not only brought prosperity but stimulated important cultural changes. Greek remained the courtly language, but Ge'ez was increasingly the language of the people, and often royal inscriptions used the vernacular. There were Ge'ez versions of the Old and New Testaments, which tradition claims were translated from the Antioch version of the Gospels during the period of the "Nine Saints," who came from greater Syria toward the end of the fifth century. . . .

The folklore claims that the monks were good Monophysites who believed that Christ had one nature, the human subsumed in the divine, the theological view of the savior's persona championed by the see [bishop] of Alexandria and transmitted to Ethiopia by Bishop Frumentius 150 years earlier. The monks had been forced into exile after the Council of Chalcedon (451) defined Christ "as perfect God and man, consubstantial with the Father and consubstantial with Man, one sole being in two natures, without division or separation and without confusion or change." As the story goes, they found safe haven in Ethiopia, where they were warmly welcomed and then directed east of Axum into the countryside to preach the Word.

Proselytizing among people hostile to the new faith, the monks demonstrated the falseness of the old gods by establishing religious centers where they found temples and other shrines, among them the still active and rightly famous establishment at Debre Damo. They fashioned their monastic rule around communalism, hard work, discipline, and obedience, while introducing an asceticism and mysticism that attracted young idealists. After education and training, the newly ordained went into the countryside, establishing the tradition that monks would be the main purveyors of the Gospels in Ethiopia.

With the new faith came traders responding to overseas demand manifested in Adulis, the region's most important commercial center. It was the destination of choice for Byzantine and other traders who sought to transship goods to Arabia, India, and regions even farther eastward. They came to Adulis by July, to transact their business before the Ethiopian fleet, composed of sturdy vessels made from tightly roped, fitted boards, left for Asia with the summer monsoon winds. At their destinations by September, Axum's traders would sell their cargoes and purchase export goods, and when the prevailing winds changed in October, sail back to Adulis, where the awaiting foreign merchants would buy items in demand in the eastern Mediterranean and themselves return home. Commercial prosperity therefore depended on the safety of the trading lanes and access to foreign markets. Whenever these were threatened, the Axumite Empire intervened to restore security, as was the case in South Arabia in the early sixth century.

FORAYS INTO ARABIA

There Judaism was resurgent, and Christians were being persecuted, among them the Axumites involved in commerce. The victims appealed across the Red Sea for help, and Axum responded in 517 by sending forces that garrisoned strategic points in Yemen. The Jews retreated into inaccessible country, attracted converts who abhorred foreign rule, raided towns, and interrupted the import-export trade. In 523–524, Emperor Caleb (ca. 500–534; otherwise known as Ella Asbeha) requested and obtained supplies and support from the patriarch of Alexandria and from the Byzantine government—which also had a strong interest in safeguarding commerce—for a major campaign against the Jewish leader, Dhu Nuwas. Caleb immediately ordered the building of a large fleet at Adulis, rented other vessels, recruited a substantial army, and himself led the expedition to Yemen.

After hard fighting, Dhu Nuwas and his forces withdrew, as did Caleb after he had established an interim administration. With the status quo more or less restored, the Jews quickly returned to raiding government outposts and garrison towns from sanctuaries in the mountains and desert. Piecemeal pacification failed, and in 525 Caleb returned with another army that caught the rebel forces in a destructive pincer near the sea. Loath to witness the disaster, Dhu Nuwas spurred his stallion into the sea, and nothing more was seen of horse or rider. The emperor named Abreha, one of his generals, as viceroy, left him with an army of five thousand men, and returned home in triumph.

Axum was then at the apogee of its power: Christianity had developed apace with the empire's expansion, was firmly established to the south of Tigray in Wag and Lasta, and was growing in adjacent Agew areas (northern Welo), from which Axum continued to obtain export commodities. Trade from Sudan also moved through Agew, especially gold from Sasaw, today identified with the Fazughli region on the Blue Nile. Overseas, however, Axum's effort to build an empire was failing.

In 543, General Abreha rebelled and established himself as the independent ruler of South Arabia. Caleb and his successors fought back, but their limited efforts only helped consolidate and augment Abreha's authority, and he came to dominate the routes to northern Arabia and the east. His success actually advantaged many Axumites, who expanded their commercial activities internationally and locally, especially in San'a, Abreha's capital.

AXUM SLOWLY LOSES TOUCH WITH THE MEDITERRANEAN WORLD

The self-proclaimed monarch kept his options and trading connections open by paying an annual tribute to both the Axumite and Persian emperors. While Abreha ruled, South Arabia was prosperous and well governed; he improved public works and built monuments and churches, since he sought to convert his subjects. He overextended himself, however, in campaigns against Mecca, activities that disrupted the intricate web of desert trading patterns, thus helping to cause a commercial crisis. The Persians became anxious as they saw the lucrative caravan trade dissipate.

They decided to intervene when Abreha's successors proved weak and vacillating, unable to retain the support of either the people or the army. The [Persian] Sassanids reasoned that South Arabia's current rulers were Ethiopians, who paid tribute to Axum—conveniently forgetting that the same people paid them, too—and that the African power was allied to Byzantium, their bitter political and trade rival. A success in Yemen, therefore, would weaken their enemy and probably would not provoke a counterattack. In around 570, perhaps even on the day Muhammad was born, a ragtag Persian expedition of eight ships and eight hundred soldiers arrived on the South Arabian coast and proceeded systematically to destroy Ethiopian authority, helped by the people, who massacred Axumites throughout the land.

The mother country stood by, apparently impotent to intervene, thus signaling the end of Axum's political authority in Arabia. Commercial life in Adulis continued, however, and the links to South Arabia were maintained, especially with Mecca, where resident Ethiopians were important as traders and soldiers. Ships from Adulis regularly sailed to and from the Bay of Soaiba, Mecca's debouchment. The connection was destroyed, however, in the mid-seventh century as Islam triumphed in Arabia.

As Muslim power and influence grew in the eighth century, Ethiopian shipping was swept from the Red Sea-Indian Ocean, changing the nature of the Axumite state. It became isolated from the eastern Mediterranean ecumene [sphere] that for centuries had influenced its culture and sustained its economy. The coastal region lost its economic vitality as trade decreased, and Adulis and other commercial centers slowly withered. The state consequently suffered a sharp reduction in revenues and no longer could afford to maintain a large army, a complex administration, and urban amenities. The culture associated with the outside world quickly became a memory, and Ethiopia turned inward.

India Achieves Unification Under the Gupta Rulers

Percival Spear

Coinciding with the late Greco-Roman classical period was what modern historians often call India's classical period—the era of the Gupta dynasty (ca. A.D. 320–ca.540). The Guptas skillfully built on the achievements of earlier Indian dynasties. In 321 B.C., shortly after Alexander the Great briefly invaded a fragmented western India, the Maurya dynasty created the first large Indian empire. Later, in the first century A.D., a powerful group of Asian nomads, the Kushans, took control of what is now Afghanistan and northwestern India. Buddhism thrived under both the Mauryan and Kushan rulers; and though the Guptas were Hindus, they tolerated Buddhism and respected other longstanding cultural traditions. Under the enlightened Gutpas, the arts, literature, and philosophy flourished as never before in India, as explained here by Percival Spear, a noted scholar of Indian history and culture. Spear also points out how the later expansion of Indian influence in southeast Asia, which the Guptas had set in motion, contributed to the rise of numerous local kingdoms, some of which have left behind impressive ruins.

T he fourth century of the Christian era, when the Roman empire became Christian under the emperor Constantine, is known in India as the imperial age of the Guptas. During this period ancient India achieved its second cultural peak. The invaders of the preceding centuries seem to have been as-

From *India: A Modern History*, by Percival Spear. Copyright © by The University of Michigan 1961. Reprinted by permission of the University of Michigan Press.

similated, and a number of cultural developments seem to have come to completion. It was an age of fruition, like the fullness of late summer, and resembles in this respect the . . . Augustan age in Europe. This does not mean that there were not hints of further developments, as there were in eighteenth-century Europe, but rather that completion of effort and rounding off of achievement were the keynotes of the period.

THE GUPTAS'S OBSCURE ORIGINS

Very little is known of the rise of the Gupta dynasty, as very little is known of the fall of the Kushan empire, and between the two events lies about a century of almost total obscurity. We know that the Kushan empire dissolved sometime after 200 A.D. Kanishka introduced a new era, beginning, according to majority scholarly opinion, about 120 A.D. No coin of this era has been found with a date later than the year 99. We can only guess the exact causes of the Kushan collapse, but certain possibilities can be established by inference. It should first be remembered that the Kushan empire was really only semi-Indian. Its central core was Afghanistan and the Panjab, its capital at Peshawar on the borders of the modern Afghan and Pakistani states. Its control of central and northern India was more that of overlordship than direct rule. Saka "satrapies" continued to exist as subordinate states. As so often in north Indian history, the impulse of change seems to have come from outside India itself. In 226 A.D. the Arsacid [or Parthian] dynasty of Persia was replaced by the more vigorous Sassanids. The new dynasty encroached on the Kushan hold of Afghanistan and perhaps blocked the supply of adventurer recruits to the Kushan dominions upon which foreign rulers in India have always relied for the retention of their vigor. Such a crisis in the affairs of an imperial power is the moment for dependent states to revolt. This is what may have happened to the Kushans and brought their empire to an end. But there was no replacement of Kushans by Persians in the imperial seat. The new Persian kings were occupied with periodic wars with the Romans until the eve of their overthrow by the Muslim Arabs in the seventh century. In these circumstances there was something of a power vacuum between the lower Ganges Valley and the borders of Persia. Kushan chiefdoms existed in the Afghan uplands until the coming of the Muslims, while in west-central India Saka "satrapies" became independent again.

This situation was the prelude to the rise of the Guptas. The new empire . . . came from the east instead of the west. We know very little of how it came to power, but it would seem that its core was again the continuing state of Magadha. It had started its career some nine centuries earlier, about 600 B.C., and had already grown into an empire under the Mauryas. After the fall of the Mauryas, Magadha survived as an independent state, beating off the attack of the Greek Menander and his Indian allies and escaping the Kushan domination. At the end of the third century the Lichchhavi tribe, from a branch of which the Buddha sprung nearly a thousand years before, came again into prominence. The first Chandragupta married princess Kumara Devi of this tribe and was able to extend his dominions from Magadha or modern Behar as far west as modern Allahabad or Prayag. The importance of the alliance is suggested by the issue of coins in the joint names of Chandragupta, his queen, and the Lichchhavi people. Now the Lichchhavis were a people of the foothills with affiliations with Nepal and Tibet. It seems likely that they were a martial race, like the modern Gurkhas. They may have been Mongolian, but more probably perhaps, they were a mixture of Mongolian and Aryan elements. Everything is mixed in India, which is perhaps the reason that there is so much emphasis upon racial purity. In this Lichchhavi-Magadhan alliance we can see a union of Indian statecraft with hillmen's martial vigor. Thus the undoubtedly Aryan Guptas may have found the spearhead they needed to recover Magadha's one-time imperial sway.

GUPTA EXPANSION

The first Gupta king died about 330 A.D., having founded a new era in 320 A.D. His son and successor reigned for over forty years, adding Bengal, the upper Jumna-Ganges Valley, and parts of central India. In fact his empire, except for the Panjab, nearly embraced the traditional limits of Hindustan—from the Indus to the Bay of Bengal, from the river Narbada to the northern mountains. A vital addition was made by the next ruler in the series with the conquest of Malwa, Gujarat, and Saurashtra. This . . . gave the new empire access to the western sea, where it took control of Barygaza or Broach in the Gulf of Cambay. This gave the empire a window looking toward Europe, where the eastern half of the Roman empire still flourished. It is this ruler, Chandragupta Vikramaditya, whose exploits are thought to be commemorated on the Iron Pillar which stands in the Qutab mosque near New Delhi. The empire continued until the mid-fifth century, when it was beset by invading Huns. By the end of the century the Gupta empire had broken down . . . though the Magadhan kingdom still lived on. The sixth century is dark in Indian annals, from which it can be presumed that there was much strife and probably further foreign invasions. . . .

For the Gupta period and for King Harsha the sources again

become comparatively copious [plentiful]. Taken together they form the second illuminated hall in the mansion of Indian history. Coins are now copious and reveal through the centuries a bewildering variety of dynasties. Inscriptions, both on stone and copper, are numerous. The copper plate is an essential ingredient of the corpus of Indian inscriptions and a tool of the specialist. . . . Then there is architectural and archeological evidence in the shape of temples and sculptures and wall paintings. Some of the hand-hewn Buddhist caves of Ajanta and some of the work at Ellora can be ascribed to this period. Then there is a wealth of Sanskrit literature which now reached its peak of achievement. Much of it is literary and philosophic, its historical material being incidental, but there is also the historical romance of Bana, which deals with the events of Harsha's reign.

SOCIAL AND RELIGIOUS TOLERANCE

Most vivid of all the records, however, are the accounts of the Chinese Buddhist pilgrims, Fa-Hien and Hieuen Tsang. Both were Buddhist monks who braved the perils of a westward journey through central Asia and across the mountains into northwest India in order to study authentic Buddhist sacred texts. Both stayed for several years in India and traveled widely. Fa-Hien set out in 399 A.D. and spent the years 401–10 in India itself, moving from monastery to monastery. He was so absorbed in holy things that no ruler's name is mentioned, but his references to the conditions of life are all the more valuable for being incidental to his main interest and so disinterested. His visit took place at the height of the Gupta empire, during the reign of Chandragupta II. Hieuen Tsang set out in 629 A.D. and spent the years 635–43 in Harsha's empire. More observant of secular life than his predecessor, his account and the work of Bana are the main sources for Harsha's reign. The work of these two Chinese monks imparts flesh and blood to the bare bones of dates, dynastic names, and formal inscriptions which are the historian's stock in trade for so much of the early period.

Judged by modern standards, these sources are not copious. But they are enough to provide a clearer picture of the age than of any period since the Mauryan. We know little of the characters of the emperors . . . but we do get a picture of the state of the north Indian countryside and its people. The administration, as Fa-Hien describes it, was milder than in the Mauryan age. The police regulations were less severe. Capital punishment was rare, punishment usually taking the form of fines or mutilation. The land revenue collections, the backbone of Indian administration until the nineteenth century, were moderate. One-sixth was the government's share of the gross produce, as compared with a quarter in the Mauryan period. . . . The countryside was peaceful and prosperous, studded with wealthy towns. Travel was evidently reasonably safe. . . . Manners were mild, with a general abstention from meat and liquor. Outcastes, however, were severely treated. In the matter of diet Fa-Hien may have been speaking mainly of Buddhists, but his evidence is good for another feature of the day, that of tolerance. The Gupta government was Hindu, but it is clear that Hindus and Buddhists were living peaceably side by side. Fa-Hien moved freely from monastery to monastery and speaks of the great monastic establishments in the Jumna Valley. There is no hint of persecution. Hieuen Tsang found Buddhism in the east even more flourishing, for Harsha was himself a patron. At his periodic religious assemblies the image of the Buddha received the highest honors, those of the sun and Siva coming second and third. The country was open to foreign influences in a way which was not to recur for centuries. There was contact with west China by the overland route, with Europe and the Near East by sea, with Persia and the Middle East, and with Indonesia.

LITERATURE, SCIENCE, AND PHILOSOPHY

Our literary sources show that the arts and sciences had reached a high state of cultivation. Sanskrit had now replaced Pali as the official and literary language. . . . The first Sanskrit inscriptions date from about 150 A.D. Sanskrit was not only used for sacred writing, but for secular literature as well. It was during this period (fifth century) that Kalidasa, "the Indian Shakespeare," flourished, along with Dandin and Bharavi in the sixth century. Kalidasa's drama *Sakuntala* was first translated into English by Sir William Jones in the late eighteenth century and has ever since been recognized as a masterpiece by the non-Indian world. That and his lyrical nature poem the *Cloud Messenger* captivated Goethe and the early European romantics. In the realm of science Indian achievement was striking. There was interchange of ideas with the Greeks. Varahamihira, who lived in the sixth century, was learned in Greek sciences and used Greek technical terms. But the Indians went beyond the Greeks. By the seventh century they had devised a sign for zero and worked out a decimal system. In algebra they were also ahead. This knowledge was taken up by the Arabs of the early caliphate, who themselves absorbed all the knowledge they could find, whether from Greek or Indian sources. From them it percolated into Europe in its Dark Age, leading to the replacement of the abacus for calculation and the beginning of modern mathematics. In the practical arts also the

Indians were far advanced. The Iron Pillar near Delhi, whose date is about 400 A.D., is of a fineness unknown to iron smelters until recent times. In thought the majestic fabric of Indian philosophy, first developed in the treatises known as the Upanishads, was reaching its full stature. Sankara, "the chief of the Vedantic philosophers" who developed the full rigor of Indian monism, flourished about 800 A.D., but the Vedantic philosophy reached maturity under the Guptas. It was an achievement of the human mind in the realm of abstract thought with which only the thousand years of Greek philosophic thought to 500 A.D., culminating in the Neoplatonic system, is to be compared.

ART AND ARCHITECTURE

The arts had also attained a high degree of development. Most of the buildings of the Gupta period have disappeared. They were the victims of the many changes which affected the area of the empire for centuries after its fall, of the commotions of the barbarian invasions, and of Muslim-Turkish destruction on religious grounds. Only in out-of-the-way places have complete buildings survived. These show signs of vigor and bold conception. In addition, the rock-hewn temple was excavated which has given to posterity some of its finest treasures at such sites as Ajanta and Ellora. Construction remained simple, centering round the sanctuary of the god. The true arch was not used, so that size involved massive construction. The merit of these buildings is to be found in their proportions and elaborate decoration. In the case of Buddhism the need for monasteries provided an opportunity for picturesque grouping. Closely linked with architecture was the art of sculpture, for it was largely used by both Hinduism and Mahayana Buddhism to adorn their temples. At Sarnath and Mathura enough has been found to enable the Gupta style to be identified and appreciated. The figures have a dignity, a grace, and a restraint of their own which distinguish them from the more florid examples of later schools. The motif of sculpture was religious, but this did not prevent the intrusion of both secular and erotic subjects. In the case of Hinduism the stories of the gods were represented in the idiom of the time, while believers in the *shakti* cults saw in the sexual act and organs symbols of the divine creative energy. This led to the voluptuousness and "indecency" of much of later Hindu sculpture. . . .

There is evidence that painting was very widely practiced and used for the adornment of palaces as well as temples and Buddhist halls. Little remains, but there is enough to attest to its excellence and to place this period in the forefront of mural artistic excellence. The most famous are the wall paintings in the Buddhist caves at Ajanta in central India and at Sigiriya in Ceylon. The paintings are notable for their freshness and vigor, their naturalistic grace, and the variety of their subjects. Though the inspiration was religious, any scene connected with the Buddhist story was legitimate. We find not only scenes of the Buddha and his followers, as a Christian artist might depict scenes of Christ and his disciples, but episodes of the court and camp, of the home and of nature. Since all the figures are depicted in the fashions of the time, as the sixteenth-century Flemish glassworker depicted Christian sacred scenes in the churches of the day, they provide a pictorial record of contemporary life.

INDIAN CULTURAL INFLUENCES SPREAD

In social life the main outline of Hindu society had now developed (as already described). But the system was not yet so rigid as it later became nor had some of its later features become pronounced. Manners, perhaps under the influence of Buddhism, were milder than before or since. . . . Women were subordinate, but they had more freedom of movement and took more part in general society than was later the case. Education was more widely diffused, perhaps another sign of Buddhist influence.

It will be convenient here to notice the extension of cultural influence beyond the Indian borders. The first few Christian centuries formed the great age of Indian expansion. We have already noticed the spread of Buddhism into the northwest and thence along the central Asian trade routes into China. But there was another movement overseas eastward. During these centuries Indian influence spread into Burma, Malaya, Indonesia, and the areas of southeast Asia known today as Siam or Thailand, Cambodia, and south Viet-Nam. The contact at first was mainly with south India and it began, as such things so often do, with trade. It is known that a trading connection with the East Indies existed by the beginning of the Christian era; in the *Jataka* stories they are referred to as "the land of gold" or "the island of gold" (probably Java). Roman sources make it clear that there was an active commerce by the second century A.D. connected with the then flourishing European trade. It is easy to imagine that merchant voyages would lead to mercantile colonies, such as the Arabs and the Europeans established later on. Because religion was an inseparable part of the lives of these merchants, Brahmins followed to perform ceremonies and Buddhist monks to spread knowledge of the Way. . . .

In some such way Indian influence, both Hindu and Buddhist, spread over Indonesia and southeast Asia during the first ten centuries of the Christian era. The influence was real and profound, but it was the influence of the mind rather than of physical colonization. The Indians charmed by their example rather than commanded by their arms. Dynasties of rulers with Sanskrit titles are found, few of whom probably had much Indian blood in their veins. According to tradition this contact began in the first Christian century; inscriptions in tolerable Sanskrit are found from the fifth century A.D. Indian influence at first flowed mainly from the peninsula, but later Buddhist Bengal also took part. Kingdoms were founded in Java, Sumatra, Malaya, Borneo, Cambodia, and Laos. Some of them became famous, like the Cambodian kingdom or the maritime empire of Srivijaya. To match the Hindu Cambodian monuments of Angkor Vat and the Bayon was the great Buddhist stupa of Borobudur in Java. In Thailand, Cambodia, and Laos Buddhism of the older form has replaced Hinduism; in Java and the islands Islam is the successor. Only in the dream island of Bali does the Hinduism of this period live on, a living cultural fossil of Indian eastward expansion. But though forms have changed elsewhere, much Hindu influence remains behind a Muslim façade. It was the Indian expansion of this age which has given this part of the world its present picturesqueness and nostalgic charm.

WORLD HISTORY BY ERA

Religious Beginnings, Struggles, and Triumphs

CHAPTER 4

BUDDHISM EMERGES IN INDIA

A.L. BASHAM

This excellent summary of the rise of Buddhism in India is by A.L. Basham, a former professor of Asian civilization at Australia's National University at Canberra. He begins with a synopsis of Buddha's life, at least as his later followers came to know it; for as Basham points out, the actual events may have long ago been superceded by legend. Then Basham traces the spread of the faith, which gained a major boost from the patronage of the great Mauryan Indian leader, Ashoka, in the mid-third century B.C. Buddhism then split into two major sects, the Greater and Lesser Vehicles, which subsequently, during the same centuries that Christianity was rising in ancient Rome, spread beyond India into southeast Asia, China, and Japan.

A t the end of the sixth and the beginning of the fifth century B.C. [an extraordinary man] established a community of yellow-robed followers, and was known by them as the *Buddha*, the Enlightened or Awakened. Even if judged only by his posthumous effects on the world at large he was certainly the greatest man to have been born in India.

The traditional story of the Buddha, like those of most saints and heroes of ancient days, has suffered much at the hands of higher criticism. The story of his birth and early life appears only in the later books of the Buddhist Scriptures, and many of the references to him in those parts of the canon which purport to give his teachings verbatim are by no means reliable. Even the "Sermon of the Turning of the Wheel of the Law", which is said to be the first sermon preached after the Buddha's enlightenment, and which is the basic teaching of all Buddhist sects, is of dubious authenticity, and in the form in which we have it is not among the earliest parts of the canon. Much doubt now exists as to the real doctrines of the historical Buddha, as distinct from those of Buddhism. . . . We here discuss, however, not the life of the Buddha, but what his later followers believed about his life, and not what he taught, but what Buddhism taught.

Certain facts about the Buddha's life are reasonably certain. He was the son of a chief of the Śākyas, a small tribe of the Himālayan foothills. He became an ascetic [monk], and propounded a new doctrine which gained the support of numerous disciples. After many years of teaching in the kingdoms of Kosala and Magadha and in the tribal lands to the north of the Gangā, he died at the age of eighty at some time between the years 486 and 473 B.C., probably nearer the former date than the latter. The story of his life as told by his followers is far more vivid and colourful than this dry outline, and it is infinitely more important, for it has influenced countless millions throughout the whole of Asia east of Afghānistān.

THE FOUR SIGNS

One night Mahāmāyā, chief queen of Śuddhodhana, king of the Śākyas, dreamt that she was carried away to the divine lake Anavatapta in the Himālayas, where she was bathed by the heavenly guardians of the four quarters of the universe. A great white elephant holding a lotus flower in his trunk approached her, and entered her side. Next day the dream was interpreted for her by wise men—she had conceived a wonderful son, who would be either a Universal Emperor or a Universal Teacher. The child was born in a grove of sāl trees called Lumbinī, near the capital of the Śākyas, Kapilavastu. . . . At birth he stood upright, took seven strides, and spoke: "This is my last birth—henceforth there is no more birth for me."

The boy was named Siddhārtha, at a great ceremony on the fifth day from his birth. His *gotra* name was Gautama . . . by which he is commonly referred to in Buddhist literature. . . . King Śuddhodhana resolved that he should never know the sorrows of the world. He was reared in delightful palaces, from whose parks every sign of death, disease and misery was removed. He learned all the arts that a prince should learn, and excelled as a student. . . .

But for all his prosperity and success he was not inwardly happy, and for all the efforts of his father he did see the four signs foretold, which were to decide his career, for the gods knew his destiny, and it was they who placed the signs before him. One day, as he was driving round the royal park with his faithful charioteer Channa, he saw an aged man, in the last stages of infirmity and decrepitude—actually a god, who had taken this disguise in order that Siddhārtha Gautama might become a Buddha. Siddhārtha asked Channa who this repulsive being was, and when he learned that all men must grow old he was even more troubled in mind. This was the first sign. The second came a little later, in the same way, in the form of a very sick man, covered with boils and shivering with fever. The third was even more terrible—a corpse, being carried to the cremation-ground, followed by weeping mourners. But the fourth sign brought hope and consolation—a wandering religious beggar, clad in a simple yellow robe, peaceful and calm, with a mien of inward joy. On seeing him Siddhārtha realized where his destiny lay, and set his heart on becoming a wanderer. . . .

THE ENLIGHTENMENT

He stripped off his jewellery and fine garments, and put on a hermit's robe, provided by an attendant demigod. With his sword he cut off his flowing hair, and sent it back to his father with his garments by the hand of Channa. . . . Thus Siddhārtha performed his "Great Going Forth" and became a wandering ascetic, owning nothing but the robe he wore.

At first he begged his food as a wanderer, but he soon gave up this life for that of a forest hermit. From a sage named Ālāra Kālāma he learned the technique of meditation . . . but he was not convinced that man could obtain liberation from sorrow by self-discipline and knowledge, so he joined forces with five ascetics who were practising the most rigorous self-mortification in the hope of wearing away their karma and obtaining final bliss.

His penances became so severe that the five quickly recognized him as their leader. For six years he tortured himself until he was nothing but a walking skeleton. One day, worn out by penance and hunger, he fainted, and his followers believed that he was dead. But after a while he recovered consciousness, and realized that his fasts and penances had been useless. He again began to beg food, and his body regained its strength. The five disciples left him in disgust at his backsliding.

One day Siddhārtha Gautama, now thirty-five years old, was seated beneath a large pīpal tree on the outskirts of the town of Gayā. . . . He made a solemn vow that, though his bones wasted away and his blood dried up, he would not leave his seat until the riddle of suffering was solved.

So for forty-nine days he sat beneath the tree. At first he was surrounded by hosts of gods and spirits, awaiting the great moment of enlightenment; but they soon fled, for Māra, the spirit of the world and of sensual pleasure, the Buddhist devil, approached. For days Gautama withstood temptations of all kinds. . . .

[Mara] called his three beautiful daughters, Desire, Pleasure and Passion, who danced and sang before him, and tried every means of seduction. Their wiles were quite ineffectual. They offered him Universal Empire; but he was unmoved.

At last the demon hosts gave up the struggle and Gautama, left alone, sank deeper and deeper into meditation At the dawning of the forty-ninth day he knew the truth. He had found the secret of sorrow, and understood at last why the world is full of suffering and unhappiness of all kinds, and what man must do to overcome them. He was fully enlightened—a Buddha. . . .

MINISTRY AND DEATH

Leaving the Tree of Wisdom, he journeyed to the Deer Park near Vārānasī (the modern Sārnāth), where his five former disciples had settled to continue their penances.

To these five ascetics the Buddha preached his first sermon, or, in Buddhist phraseology, "set in motion the Wheel of the Law". The five were so impressed with his new doctrine that they gave up their austerities and once more became his disciples. A few days later a band of sixty young ascetics became his followers, and he sent them out in all directions to preach the Buddhist Dharma. Soon his name was well known throughout the Gangā Plain, and the greatest kings of the time favoured him and his followers. He gathered together a disciplined body of monks (called bhikṣus, or in Pāli bhikkhus, literally "beggars"), knit together by a common garb, the yellow robes of the order, and a common discipline, according to tradition laid down in detail by the Buddha himself. . . .

Though according to legend his life was attended by many wonders, the earliest traditions record few miracles accomplished by the Buddha himself. Once he is said to have performed feats of levitation and other miracles at Śrāvastī, as a result of a challenge from rival teachers, but he sternly forbade the monks to imitate him, and there is no record of his healing the sick by supernatural means. . . .

For over forty years his reputation grew and the Saṅgha (literally Society, the Buddhist Order) increased in numbers and influence. . . . His ministry was a long, calm and peaceful one, in this respect very different from that of Jesus.

The end came at the age of eighty. He spent the last rainy season of his life near the city of Vaiśālī, and after the rains he and his followers journeyed northwards to the hill country which had been the home of his youth. On the way he prepared his disciples for his death. He told them that his body was now like a worn-out cart, creaking at every joint. . . .

Soon after this he was attacked by dysentery, but he insisted on moving on to the nearby town of Kuśinagara (Pāli, Kusinārā). Here, on the outskirts of the town, he lay down under a sāl tree, and that night he died. His last words were: "All composite things decay. Strive diligently!" This was his "Final Blowing-out" (*Parinirvāṇa*). His sorrowing disciples cremated his body, and his ashes were divided between the representatives of various tribal peoples and King Ajātaśatru of Magadha.

ASOKA CHAMPIONS THE FAITH

According to tradition a great gathering of monks met at the Magadhan capital of Rājagṛha soon after the Buddha's death. At this council Upāli, one of the chief disciples, recited the *Vinaya Piṭaka*, or rules of the Order, as he recalled having heard the Buddha give them. Another disciple, Ānanda, who bears a position in Buddhism similar to that of St. John in Christianity, recited the *Sutta Piṭaka*, the great collection of the Buddha's sermons on matters of doctrine and ethics. Though there may have been a council of some sort, the story as it stands is certainly untrue, for it is quite evident that the scriptures of Buddhism grew by a long process of development and accretion, perhaps over several centuries.

A second general council is said to have been held at Vaiśālī, one hundred years after the Buddha's death. Here schism raised its head, ostensibly over small points of monastic discipline, and the Order broke into two sections, the orthodox *Sthaviravādins* (Pāli *Theravādī*) or "Believers in the Teaching of the Elders", and the *Mahāsaṅghikas* or "Members of the Great Community". The tradition of the second council is as dubious as that of the first, but it at least records that schism began very early. The minor points of discipline on which the Order divided were soon followed by doctrinal differences of much greater importance.

Numerous such differences appeared at the third great council, held at Pāṭaliputra under the patronage of Aśoka, which resulted in the expulsion of many heretics and the establishment of the Sthaviravāda school as orthodox. . . .

Aśoka classified all the religions of his empire under five heads; the (Buddhist) *Saṅgha*, the Brāhmans, the Ājīvikas, the Nirgranthas (or Jainas), and "other sects". He further declared that, while he gave his chief patronage to the Buddhists, he honoured and respected them all, and called on his subjects to do likewise.

By Aśoka's time India was covered with *vihāras*, which were both monasteries and temples. In becoming a religion Buddhism borrowed and adapted much from the popular beliefs of the time. Its simple ritual was in no way based on sacrificial Brāhmaṇism, but on the cult of *caityas*, or sacred spots. These were often small groves of trees, or single sacred trees, on the outskirts of villages, and might also include tumuli, such as those in which the ashes of chiefs were buried. These caityas were the abodes of earth-spirits and genii who, to the simpler folk, were more accessible and less expensive to worship than the great gods of the Āryans. The Jaina scriptures show that unorthodox holy-men often made their homes in or near the caityas, no doubt in order to obtain alms from visitors; and the Buddha is said to have respected these local shrines, and to have encouraged his lay followers to revere them.

Soon after the Buddha's death many communities of monks gave up the practice of constant travel except in the rainy season, and settled permanently on the outskirts of towns and villages, often near the local caityas. With time many of these little monasteries grew in size and importance.

BUDDHISM SPREADS BEYOND INDIA

With the support of Aśoka Buddhism greatly expanded, spreading throughout India and to Ceylon. There is some doubt as to how far the doctrine had developed at this time, but at least a rudimentary canon existed, though perhaps not yet committed to writing. The great Buddhist holy places—the Lumbinī Grove at Kapilavastu where the Buddha was born, the Tree of Wisdom at Gayā where he gained enlightenment, the Deer Park near Vārāṇasī where he preached his first sermon, and the grove near Kuśinagara where he died—were visited by many pilgrims, including Aśoka himself. . . .

The faith continued to grow. Of all the religious remains of between 200 B.C. and A.D. 900 so far discovered in India those of Buddhism outnumber those of Brāhmaṇism, Hinduism and Jainism together. The old stūpas were enlarged and beautified with carved railings, terraces and gateways. All classes of the community, kings, princes, merchants and craftsmen, made donations to the Order, which are recorded in numerous inscriptions. Though the individual monk was bound by his vows to own no property except bare necessities, and to touch no silver or gold, the monasteries grew rich on the alms of the faithful. The revenues of whole villages were alienated to them by pious kings, and even the individual monks began to take their vows of poverty lightly, for more than one inscription records donations made to the Order by ordained members of it.

Though there is little evidence of strong sectarian animus

within the Order, sects already existed, and the scriptures had been codified in more than one recension. It is possible that much of the Pāli canon of the Sthaviravādins, in the form in which we have it, emanates from the great monastery on a hilltop near the modern village of Sānchī, the remains of which are among the finest relics of early Buddhism.

Another very important sect, the *Sarvāstivādins*, was strong in the region of Mathurā and in Kashmīr. It was in Kashmīr, according to a tradition preserved in China, that, under the patronage of Kaniṣka (1st–2nd century A.D.), a fourth great council was held, at which the Sarvāstivādin doctrines were codified in a summary, the *Mahāvibhāṣā*. It was chiefly among the Sarvāstivādins . . . that new ideas developed, which were to form the basis of the division of Buddhism into the "Great" and "Lesser Vehicles" (*Mahāyāna* and *Hīnayāna*). The brāhmaṇs and their lay supporters had by now largely turned from the older gods, whom they worshipped with animal sacrifices, towards others, who were worshipped with reverent devotion. In N.-W. India the rule of Greeks, Sakas and Kuṣāṇas in turn had thrown open the gates to the West, and ideas from Persia and beyond entered India in greater strength than before. In these conditions teachers of the early Christian centuries gave to Buddhism a wholly new outlook. They claimed to have found a new and great vehicle which would carry many souls to salvation, while the Sthaviravādins and kindred sects had but a small one. The Great Vehicle soon became popular in many parts of India, for it fitted the mood of the times and the needs of many simple people better than did the Lesser Vehicle, which then began to lose ground. In Ceylon, however, the Lesser Vehicle resisted all the attacks of the new sects and thence it was later taken to Burma, Thailand and other parts of South-East Asia, where it became the national religion.

The Great Vehicle, on the other hand, itself soon divided by various schisms, was carried by a succession of Indian monks to China and thence to Japan.

Ruling by the Tenets of Buddhism

Ashoka

India's great Mauryan ruler Ashoka (ca.268–233 B.C.) adopted Buddhism and was so moved by its pacifistic and ethical tenets that he actually attempted to rule in accordance with them. Over the course of his reign, he recorded aspects of his efforts in this vein in numerous edicts inscribed on rocks and pillars. Following are some examples (from a modern collection edited by William T. de Bary). In the first edict, Ashoka recounts his own conversion to the faith, regrets his former warlike deeds, and calls on all rulers to be as enlightened as he is. In this regard, his claim of winning over four distant Greek kings to righteous rule is probably a reference to his sending envoys to these rulers urging them to adopt his values and policies.

W hen the king, Beloved of the Gods and of Gracious Mien, had been consecrated eight years Kalinga was conquered, 150,000 people were deported, 100,000 were killed, and many times that number died. But after the conquest of Kalinga, the Beloved of the Gods began to follow Righteousness (Dharma), to love Righteousness, and to give instruction in Righteousness. Now the Beloved of the Gods regrets the conquest of Kalinga, for when an independent country is conquered people are killed, they die, or are deported, and that the Beloved of the Gods finds very painful and grievous. And this he finds even more grievous—that all the inhabitants—brāhmans, ascetics, and other sectarians, and householders who are obedient to superiors, parents, and elders, who treat friends, ac-

From the edicts of Ashoka as they appear in *Sources of Indian Tradition*, vol. 1, edited by William T. de Bary. Copyright © 1958 by Columbia University Press. Reprinted by permission of the publisher via the Copyright Clearance Center.

quaintances, companions, relatives, slaves, and servants with respect, and are firm in their faith—all suffer violence, murder, and separation from their loved ones. Even those who are fortunate enough not to have lost those near and dear to them are afflicted at the misfortunes of friends, acquaintances, companions, and relatives. The participation of all men in common suffering is grievous to the Beloved of the Gods. Moreover there is no land, except that of the Greeks, where groups of brāhmans and ascetics are not found, or where men are not members of one sect or another. So now, even if the number of those killed and captured in the conquest of Kalinga had been a hundred or a thousand times less, it would be grievous to the Beloved of the Gods. The Beloved of the Gods will forgive as far as he can, and he even conciliates the forest tribes of his dominions; but he warns them that there is power even in the remorse of the Beloved of the Gods, and he tells them to reform, lest they be killed.

For all beings the Beloved of the Gods desires security, self-control, calm of mind, and gentleness. The Beloved of the Gods considers that the greatest victory is the victory of Righteousness; and this he has won here (in India) and even five hundred leagues beyond his frontiers in the realm of the Greek king Antiochus [II of the Seleucid kingdom], and beyond Antiochus among the four kings Ptolemy [II of the Egyptian Ptolemaic Kingdom], Antigonus [Gonatas of the Macedonian Kingdom], Magas [of Cyrene, a kingdom lying west of Egypt], and Alexander [of Epirus, a kingdom of northwestern Greece]. Even where the envoys of the Beloved of the Gods have not been sent men hear of the way in which he follows and teaches Righteousness, and they too follow it and will follow it. Thus he achieves a universal conquest, and conquest always gives a feeling of pleasure; yet it is but a slight pleasure, for the Beloved of the Gods only looks on that which concerns the next life as of great importance.

I have had this inscription of Righteousness engraved that all my sons and grandsons may not seek to gain new victories, that in whatever victories they may gain they may prefer forgiveness and light punishment, that they may consider the only [valid] victory the victory of Righteousness, which is of value both in this world and the next, and that all their pleasure may be in Righteousness. . . .

[Here, Ashoka suggests that his adoption of Buddhism has persuaded the Gods to appear on earth.] Thus speaks Ashoka, the Beloved of the Gods. For two and a half years I have been an open follower of the Buddha, though at first I did not make much progress. But for more than a year now I have drawn closer to the [Buddhist] Order, and have made much progress. In

India the gods who formerly did not mix with men now do so. This is the result of effort, and may be obtained not only by the great, but even by the small, through effort—thus they may even easily win heaven.

Father and mother should be obeyed, teachers should be obeyed; pity . . . should be felt for all creatures. These virtues of Righteousness should be practiced. . . . This is an ancient rule, conducive to long life. It is good to give, but there is no gift, no service, like the gift of Righteousness. So friends, relatives, and companions should preach it on all occasions. This is duty; this is right; by this heaven may be gained—and what is more important than to gain heaven? . . .

[In the following edict, Ashoka emphasized the importance of morality.] This world and the other are hard to gain without great love of Righteousness, great self-examination, great obedience, great circumspection, great effort. Through my instruction respect and love of Righteousness daily increase and will increase. . . . For this is my rule—to govern by Righteousness, to administer by Righteousness, to please my subjects by Righteousness, and to protect them by Righteousness. . . .

[Ashoka extended the concept of righteousness to animals, whose humane treatment is described in these edicts.] Here no animal is to be killed for sacrifice, and no festivals are to be held, for the king finds much evil in festivals, except for certain festivals which he considers good.

Formerly in the Beloved of the God's kitchen several hundred thousand animals were killed daily for food; but now at the time of writing only three are killed—two peacocks and a deer, though the deer not regularly. Even these three animals will not be killed in future.

I have in many ways given the gift of clear vision. On men and animals, birds and fish I have conferred many boons, even to saving their lives; and I have done many other good deeds. . . .

[In this edict, Ashoka expresses his moral obligation to see that his subjects are happy.] I am not satisfied simply with hard work or carrying out the affairs of state, for I consider my work to be the welfare of the whole world, of which hard work and the carrying out of affairs are merely the basis. There is no better deed than to work for the welfare of the whole world, and all my efforts are made that I may clear my debt to all beings. I make them happy here and now that they may attain heaven in the life to come. . . . But it is difficult without great effort. . . .

[Ashoka here boasts that his officials are doing a satisfactory job of implementing his policies.] My governors are placed in charge of hundreds of thousands of people. Under my authority they have power to judge and to punish, that they calmly and fearlessly carry out their duties, and that they may bring welfare and happiness to the people of the provinces and be of help to them. They will know what brings joy and what brings sorrow, and, conformably to Righteousness, they will instruct the people of the provinces that they may be happy in this world and the next. . . . And as when one entrusts a child to a skilled nurse one is confident that . . . she will care for it well, so have I appointed my governors for the welfare and happiness of the people. That they may fearlessly carry out their duties I have given them power to judge and to inflict punishment on their own initiative. I wish that there should be uniformity of justice and punishment. . . .

[In the following edict, he calls for tolerance for all religious sects, even non-Buddhist ones.] The Beloved of the Gods . . . honors members of all sects, whether ascetics or householders, by gifts and various honors. But he does not consider gifts and honors as important as the furtherance of the essential message of all sects. This essential message varies from sect to sect, but it has one common basis, that one should so control one's tongue as not to honor one's own sect or disparage another's on the wrong occasions; for on certain occasions one should do so only mildly, and indeed on other occasions one should honor other men's sects. By doing this one strengthens one's own sect and helps the others, while by doing otherwise one harms one's own sect and does a disservice to the others. Whoever honors his own sect and disparages another man's, whether from blind loyalty or with the intention of showing his own sect in a favorable light, does his own sect the greatest possible harm. Concord is best, with each hearing and respecting the other's teachings. It is the wish of the Beloved of the Gods that members of all sects should be learned and should teach virtue. . . . Many officials are busied in this matter . . . and the result is the progress of my own sect and the illumination of Righteousness. . . .

[Finally, Ashoka looks back on his achievements as a righteous ruler and is apparently satisfied that he has done the right thing.] In the past kings sought to make the people progress in Righteousness, but they did not progress. . . . And I asked myself how I might uplift them through progress in Righteousness. . . . Thus I decided to have them instructed in Righteousness, and to issue ordinances of Righteousness, so that by hearing them the people might conform, advance in the progress of Righteousness, and themselves make great progress. . . . For that purpose many officials are employed among the people to instruct them in Righteousness and to explain it to them. . . .

Moreover I have had banyan trees planted on the roads to give shade to man and beast; I have planted mango groves, and I have had ponds dug and shelters erected along the roads at every eight kos. Everywhere I have had wells dug for the benefit of man and beast. But this benefit is but small, for in many ways the kings of olden time have worked for the welfare of the world; but what I have done has been done that men may conform to Righteousness.

All the good deeds that I have done have been accepted and followed by the people. And so obedience to mother and father, obedience to teachers, respect for the aged, kindliness to brāhmans and ascetics, to the poor and weak, and to slaves and servants, have increased and will continue to increase. . . . And this progress of Righteousness among men has taken place in two manners, by enforcing conformity to Righteousness, and by exhortation. I have enforced the law against killing certain animals and many others, but the greatest progress of Righteousness among men comes from exhortation in favor of noninjury to life and abstention from killing living beings.

I have done this that it may endure . . . as long as the moon and sun, and that my sons and my great-grandsons may support it; for by supporting it they will gain both this world and the next.

THE JEWS FIGHT TO RETAIN THEIR ANCIENT HOMELAND

WILL DURANT

The classical period in the Mediterranean witnessed one of the most dramatic and tragic religious struggles in history—that of the Jews to maintain their independence and control over their ancient homeland in Palestine. This excerpt from noted historian Will Durant's famous series of historical studies traces that struggle, beginning with the Maccabees, a Jewish family that led a successful revolt against the Greek Seleucid realm; the advent of the Roman occupation of Judaea after the Roman general Pompey captured Jerusalem in the 60s B.C.; the way many Jews subsequently resisted the cultural "pollution" of Hellenism (Greek customs and ideas); and the bloody rebellions of the first and second centuries A.D., which resulted in the destruction of most Jewish culture in Palestine and the scattering of Jews across the known world. Throughout his narrative, Durant relies on information from the works of the first-century A.D. Jewish historian Josephus, who helped lead Jewish resistance for a time but later collaborated with the Romans.

I n 143 B.C. Simon Maccabee, taking advantage of the struggles among the Parthians, Seleucids, Egyptians, and Romans, wrested the independence of Judea from the Seleucid king. A popular assembly named him general and high priest of the Second Jewish Commonwealth (142 B.C.–A.D. 70), and made the latter office hereditary in his Hasmonean family. Judea became again a theocracy, under the Hasmonean dynasty of priest-kings. It has been a characteristic of Semitic societies that they closely associated the spiritual and temporal powers, in the family and in the state; they would have no sovereign but God.

Recognizing the weakness of the little kingdom, the Hasmoneans spent two generations widening its borders by diplomacy and force. By 78 B.C. they had conquered and absorbed Samaria, Edom, Moab, Galilee, Idumea, Transjordania, Gadara, Pella, Gerasa, Raphia, and Gaza, and had made Palestine as extensive as under Solomon. The descendants of those brave Maccabees who had fought for religious freedom enforced Judaism and circumcision upon their new subjects at the point of the sword. At the same time the Hasmoneans lost their religious zeal and, over the bitter protests of the Pharisees, yielded more and more to the Hellenizing elements in the population. Queen Salome Alexandra (78–69 B.C.) reversed this trend and made peace with the Pharisees, but even before her death her sons Hyrcanus II and Aristobulus II began a war of succession. Both parties submitted their claims to Pompey, who now (63 B.C.) stood with his victorious legions at Damascus. When Pompey decided for Hyrcanus, Aristobulus fortified himself with his army in Jerusalem. Pompey laid siege to the capital and gained its lower sections; but the followers of Aristobulus took refuge in the walled precincts of the Temple and held out for three months. Their piety, we are told, helped Pompey to overcome them; for perceiving that they would not fight on the Sabbath, he had his men prepare unhindered on each Sabbath the mounds and battering rams for the next day's assault. Meanwhile the priests offered the usual prayers and sacrifices in the Temple. When the ramparts fell 12,000 Jews were slaughtered; few resisted, none surrendered, many leaped to death from the walls. Pompey ordered his men to leave the treasures of the Temple untouched, but he exacted an indemnity of 10,000 talents ($3,600,000) from the nation. The cities that the Hasmoneans had conquered were transferred from the Judean to the Roman power; Hyrcanus II was made high priest and nominal ruler of Judea . . . who had helped Rome. The independent monarchy was ended, and Judea became part of the Roman province of Syria. . . .

THE RULE OF HEROD THE GREAT

[Not long afterward, the Romans set up a local client king— Herod, who] auspiciously entered upon one of the most colorful reigns in history (37–4 B.C.).

His character was typical of an age that had produced so many men of intellect without morals, ability without scruple, and courage without honor. He was in his lesser way the Augustus of Judea: like Augustus he overlaid the chaos of freedom with dictatorial order, beautified his capital with Greek architecture and sculpture, enlarged his realm, made it prosper, achieved more by subtlety than by arms, married widely, was broken by the treachery of his offspring, and knew every good fortune but happiness. . . .

He was molded in part by the hatred of those whom he had defeated or whose relatives he had slain, and by the scornful hostility of a people that resented his harsh autocracy and his alien descent. He had become king by the help and money of Rome, and remained to the end of his life a friend and vassal of the power from which the people night and day plotted to regain their liberty. The modest economy of the country bent and at last broke under the taxes imposed upon it by a luxurious court and a building program out of proportion to the national wealth. Herod sought in various ways to appease his subjects, but failed. He forgave taxes in poor years, persuaded Rome to reduce the tribute it exacted, secured privileges for Jews abroad, relieved famine and other calamities promptly, maintained internal order and external security, and developed the natural resources of the land. Brigandage was ended, trade was stimulated, the markets and ports were noisy with life. At the same time the King alienated public sentiment by the looseness of his morals, the cruelty of his punishments, and the "accidental" drowning, in the bath, of Aristobulus, grandson of Hyrcanus II and therefore the legitimate heir to the throne. The priests whose power he had ended, and whose leaders he appointed, conspired against him, and the Pharisees abominated his apparent resolution to make Judea a Hellenistic state.

Ruling many cities that were more Greek than Jewish in population and culture, and impressed with the refinement and variety of Hellenic civilization, Herod . . . naturally sought a cultural unity for his realm, and an imposing façade for his rule, by encouraging Greek ways, dress, ideas, literature, and art. . . . He beautified Jerusalem with other buildings in what seemed to the people a foreign architectural style, and set up in public places Greek statuary whose nudity startled the Jews as much as the nakedness of the wrestlers in the games. He built himself a palace, doubtless on Greek models, filled it with gold and marble and costly furniture, and surrounded it with extensive gardens after the manner of his Roman friends. He shocked the people by telling them that the Temple which Zerubbabel had set up five centuries before was too small, and proposing to tear it down and erect a larger one on its site. . . .

Jewish noblemen

Noblewomen

This nineteenth-century drawing illustrates the dress of Jewish noblemen and noblewomen during the era in which the Jews fought to free themselves from Roman domination.

On Mt. Moriah an area was cleared 750 feet square. Along its boundaries cloisters were built roofed with cedar "curiously graven," and supported by multiple rows of Corinthian columns, each a marble monolith so large that three men could barely join hands around it. In this main court were the booths of the money-changers, who for the convenience of pilgrims changed foreign coins into those acceptable to the Sanctuary; here, too, were the stalls where one might buy animals to offer in sacrifice, and the rooms or porticoes where teachers and pupils met to study Hebrew and the Law. . . . From this "Outer Temple" a broad flight of steps led up to an inner walled space which non-Jews were forbidden to enter. . . . From this second enclosure the worshiper passed up another flight of steps, and through gates plated with silver and gold, into the "Court of the Priests," where stood, in the open air, the altar upon which burnt sacrifice was offered to Yahveh. Still other steps led through bronze doors seventy-five feet high and twenty-four wide, overhung with a famous golden vine, into the temple proper, open only to priests. It was built entirely of white marble, in set-back style, and its façade was plated with gold. The interior was divided crosswise by a great embroidered veil, blue and purple and scarlet. Before the veil were the golden seven-branched candlestick, the altar of incense, and the table bearing the unleavened "shewbread" that

the priests laid before Yahveh. Behind the veil was the Holy of
Holies, which in the earlier temple had contained a golden censer
and the Ark of the Covenant. . . .

The people were proud of the great shrine, which was ranked
among the marvels of the Augustan world; for its splendor they
almost forgave the Corinthian columns of the porticoes and the
golden eagle that—defying the Jewish prohibition of graven images—symbolized at the very entrance to the Temple the power
of Judea's enemy and master, Rome. . . .

THE VARIOUS GROUPS WITHIN JUDEA

[After Herod's death in 4 B.C., his] will divided his kingdom
among three remaining sons. To Philip went the eastern region
known as Batanea, containing the cities of Bethsaida, Capitolias,
Gerasa, Philadelphia, and Bostra. To Herod Antipas went Peraea
(the land beyond the Jordan) and, in the north, Galilee, where lay
Esdraela, Tiberias, and Nazareth. To Archelaus fell Samaritis,
Idumea, and Judea. In this last were many famous cities or
towns: Bethlehem, Hebron, Beersheba, Gaza, Gadara, Emmaus,
Jamnia, Joppa, Caesarea, Jericho, and Jerusalem. Some Palestinian cities were predominantly Greek, some Syrian. . . . The gentiles were in the majority in all the coast towns except Joppa and
Jamnia, and in the "Decapolis" or ten cities of the Jordan; in the
interior the villages were almost entirely Jewish. In this racial division, not unpleasing to Rome, lay the tragedy of Palestine. . . .

Religion was to the Jews the source of their law, their state, and
their hope: to let it melt away in the swelling river of Hellenism
would, they thought, be national suicide. Hence that mutual hatred of Jew and gentile which kept the little nation in a kind of
undulating fever of racial strife, political turbulence, and periodic war. Moreover, the Jews of Judea scorned the people of
Galilee as ignorant backsliders, and the Galileans scorned the
Judeans as slaves caught in the cobwebs of the Law. . . . All these
factions agreed in hating the Roman power, which made them
pay a heavy price for the unwelcome privilege of peace.

There were now in Palestine some 2,500,000 souls, of whom
perhaps 100,000 lived in Jerusalem. Most of them spoke Aramaic; priests and scholars understood Hebrew; officials and for-
eigners and most authors used Greek. The majority of the people
were peasants, tilling and irrigating the soil, tending the orchard,
the vine, and the flock. In the time of Christ Palestine grew
enough wheat to export a modest surplus: its dates, figs, grapes
and olives, wine and oil were prized and bought throughout the
Mediterranean. The old command was still obeyed to let the
land lie fallow in each sabbatical year. Handicrafts were largely

hereditary and were usually organized in guilds. Jewish opinion honored the worker, and most scholars plied their hands as well as their tongues. Slaves were fewer than in any other Mediterranean country. . . .

Within the Temple was the hall Gazith, meeting place of the Sanhedrin or Great Council of the Elders of Israel. Probably the institution arose in the period of Seleucid rule (*ca.* 200 B.C.), to replace the earlier council mentioned in Numbers (XI, 16) as advising Moses. . . . These seventy-one men, under the presidency of the high priest, claimed supreme power over all Jews everywhere, and orthodox Jews everywhere acknowledged it. . . . They could pass sentence of death upon Jews in Judea for religious offenses, but could not execute it without confirmation by the civil power.

In this assembly, as in most, two factions fought for predominance—a conservative group led by the higher priests and the Sadducees, and a liberal group led by Pharisees and Scribes. Most of the upper clergy and upper classes belonged to the Sadducees (*Zadokim*), so named after their founder Zadok; they were nationalistic in politics and orthodox in religion; they stood for the enforcement of the Torah or written Law, but rejected the additional ordinances of the oral tradition and the liberalizing interpretations of the Pharisees. They doubted immortality and were content to possess the good things of the earth.

The Pharisees (*Perushim,* separatists) were so named by the Sadducees as meaning that they separated themselves . . . from those who contracted religious impurity by neglecting the requirements of ritual cleanliness. They . . . upheld the strictest application of the Law. Josephus, himself a Pharisee, defined them as "a body of Jews who profess to be more religious than the rest, and to explain the laws more precisely.". . . They were at once rigorous and lenient, softening the Law here and there . . . but demanding the full observation of the oral tradition as well as of the Torah. Only through this full obedience, they felt, could the Jews escape assimilation and extinction. Reconciled to Roman domination, the Pharisees sought consolation in the hope of a physical and spiritual immortality. They lived simply, condemned luxury, fasted frequently, washed sedulously, and were now and then irritatingly conscious of their virtue; but they represented the moral strength of Judaism, won the middle classes to their support, and gave their followers a faith and rule that saved them from disintegration when catastrophe came. . . .

The most extreme of the Jewish sects was that of the Essenes. . . . Numbering some 4000 in Palestine, they organized themselves into a distinct order, observed both the written and the oral Law with passionate exactitude, and lived together as almost monastic celibates tilling the soil in the oasis of Engadi amid the desert west of the Dead Sea. They dwelt in homes owned by their community, had their meals in common and in silence, chose their leaders by a general vote, mingled their goods and earnings in a common treasury, and . . . avoided all sensual pleasure and sought through meditation and prayer a mystic union with God. They hoped that by piety, abstinence, and contemplation they might acquire magic powers and foresee the future. Like most people of their time they believed in angels and demons, thought of diseases as possession by evil spirits, and tried to exorcise these by magical formulas. . . .

These—Sadducees, Pharisees, Essenes—were the chief religious sects of Judea in the generation before Christ. . . .

THE GREAT REBELLION

No people in history has fought so tenaciously for liberty as the Jews, nor any people against such odds. . . . The struggle of the Jews to regain their freedom has often decimated them, but has never broken their spirit or their hope.

When Herod the Great died the nationalists . . . declared a revolt against Herod's successor Archelaus, and encamped in tents about the Temple. Archelaus' troops slew 3000 of them, many of whom had come to Jerusalem for the Passover festival (4 B.C.). At the following feast of Pentecost the rebels gathered again, and once more suffered great slaughter; the Temple cloisters were burned to the ground, the treasures of the sanctuary were plundered by the legions, and many Jews killed themselves in despair. Patriot bands took form in the countryside, and made life precarious for any supporter of Rome. . . . Varus, governor of Syria, entered Palestine with 20,000 men, razed hundreds of towns, crucified 2000 rebels, and sold 30,000 Jews into slavery. A delegation of leading Jews went to Rome and begged Augustus to abolish the kingship in Judea. Augustus removed Archelaus, and made Judea a Roman province of the second class, under a procurator responsible to the governor of Syria (A.D. 6).

Under [Augustus's successor] Tiberius the troubled land knew a moment's peace. [Then the third emperor] Caligula, wishing to make the worship of the emperor a unifying religion throughout the Empire, ordered all cults to include a sacrifice to his image, and bade the Jerusalem officials to install his statue in the Temple. The Jews . . . were so averse to setting up the graven image of a pagan in their Temple that thousands of them, we are told, went to the governor of Syria and asked to be slain in cold blood before the edict should be carried out. Caligula eased the situation by dying. . . .

[Under the next emperor, Claudius, the governors of Judaea were mostly incompetent and unjust.] Bands of "Zealots" and "Dagger-men" (*Sicarii*) were formed in protest against this misrule. Their members, pledged to kill any disloyal Jew, mingled in street gatherings, stabbed their appointed victims from behind, and disappeared in the chaos of the crowd. . . . The old or well-to-do Hebrews counseled patience, arguing that revolt against so powerful an empire would be national suicide; the young or poor accused them of connivance and cowardice. The two factions divided the city and nearly every family; one seized the upper part of Jerusalem, the other the lower, and each attacked the other with every weapon at hand. . . . A pitched battle was fought between the groups; the radicals won, and killed 12,000 Jews, including nearly all the rich; the revolt had become a revolution. A rebel force surrounded the Roman garrison at Masada, persuaded it to disarm, and then slaughtered every man of it. . . . By September of 66 the revolution had won Jerusalem and nearly all of Palestine. The peace party was discredited, and most of its members now joined in the revolt. . . .

The approach of the [Roman] legions [under the general and future emperor, Titus] brought the defenders to a belated and fanatical unity. . . . 600,000 rebels had gathered in the city. . . . Josephus, from the Roman lines, called upon the besieged to surrender; they branded him as a traitor, and fought to the last. Starving Jews made desperate sorties to forage for food; thousands of them were captured by the Romans, and were crucified; "the multitude of these was so great," Josephus reports, "that room was wanting for the crosses, and crosses were wanting for the bodies." In the later stages of the five-month siege the streets of the city were clogged with corpses; ghouls wandered about despoiling and stabbing the dead; we are told that 116,000 bodies were thrown over the walls. Some Jews swallowed gold pieces and slipped out from Jerusalem; Romans or Syrians, capturing them, slit open their bellies, or searched their offal, to find the coins. Having taken half the city, Titus offered what he thought were lenient terms to the rebels; they rejected them. The flaming brands of the Romans set fire to the Temple, and the great edifice, much of it of wood, was rapidly consumed. The surviving defenders fought bravely, proud . . . to die on Temple grounds. Some killed one another, some fell upon their own swords, some leaped into the flames. The victors gave no quarter, but slew all Jews upon whom they could lay their hands; 97,000 fugitives were caught and sold as slaves. . . . Josephus numbered at 1,197,000 the Jews killed in this siege and its aftermath. . . .

Resistance continued here and there till 73, but essentially the destruction of the Temple marked the end of the rebellion and of the Jewish state. The property of those who had shared in the revolt was confiscated and sold. Judea was almost shorn of Jews, and those that remained lived on the edge of starvation. . . . The high-priesthood and the Sanhedrin were abolished. Judaism took the form that it has kept till our own time: a religion without a central shrine, without a dominant priesthood, without a sacrificial service. The Sadducees disappeared, while the Pharisees and the rabbis became the leaders of a homeless people that had nothing left but its synagogues and its hope. . . .

THE DIASPORA

[Following the great rebellion, the surviving Jews slowly rebuilt the economic and cultural life in Palestine. But in 132, they once again revolted, this time led by Simeon Bar Cocheba; and again the Romans brutally crushed them.] The Jews did not for centuries recover from the disaster of Bar Cocheba's revolt. From this moment they entered their Middle Ages, abandoning all secular learning except medicine, renouncing every form of Hellenism, and taking comfort and unity only from their rabbis, their mystic poets, and their Law. No other people has ever known so long an exile, or so hard a fate. Shut out from their Holy City, the Jews were compelled to surrender it first to paganism, then to Christianity. Scattered into every province and beyond [a process that became known as the Diaspora], condemned to poverty and humiliation, unbefriended even by philosophers and saints, they retired from public affairs into private study and worship, passionately preserving the words of their scholars, and preparing to write them down at last in the Talmuds of Babylonia and Palestine. Judaism hid in fear and obscurity while its offspring, Christianity, went on to conquer the world.

THE LIFE OF JESUS

E.P. SANDERS

In retrospect, one of the major events of the classical Mediterranean world was the life of Jesus, who later became the focus of one of the world's great religions. E.P. Sanders, arts and sciences professor of religion at Duke University, is the author of the critically acclaimed books *Paul and Palestinian Judaism* (1977) and *Jesus and Judaism* (1985). In this brief but comprehensive sketch from his 1993 book, *The Historical Figure of Jesus,* he summarizes the life of the central figure of the Christian religion. Topics covered include the time and place of Jesus's birth, where he preached, and his relationship with John the Baptist. Sanders also discusses Jesus's move to Jerusalem, where he angered the authorities, his arrest, execution, and the account by his followers of his resurrection, which provided the basis for belief by later converts that he was a divine being.

There are no substantial doubts about the general course of Jesus' life: when and where he lived, approximately when and where he died, and the sort of thing that he did during his public activity. When we begin to probe beneath the surface, difficulties and uncertainties arise, but for the present we shall stay on the surface. I shall first offer a list of statements about Jesus that meet two standards: they are almost beyond dispute; and they belong to the framework of his life, and especially of his public career. (A list of everything that we know about Jesus would be appreciably longer.)

Jesus was born *c.* 4 BCE, near the time of the death of Herod the Great;

he spent his childhood and early adult years in Nazareth, a Galilean village [Note: Galilee was a

Palestinian region located north of Judaea];
he was baptized by John the Baptist;
he called disciples;
he taught in the towns, villages and countryside of
    Galilee (apparently not the cities);
he preached 'the kingdom of God';
about the year 30 he went to Jerusalem for Passover;
he created a disturbance in the Temple area;
he had a final meal with the disciples;
he was arrested and interrogated by Jewish
    authorities, specifically the high priest;
he was executed on the orders of the Roman prefect,
    Pontius Pilate.

We may add here a short list of equally secure facts about the aftermath of Jesus' life:

his disciples at first fled;
they saw him (in what sense is not certain) after his
    death;
as a consequence, they believed that he would return
    to found the kingdom;
they formed a community to await his return and
    sought to win others to faith in him as God's
    Messiah. . . .

WHEN WAS JESUS BORN?

Now I shall supplement the outline with a short narrative summary.

The year of Jesus' birth is not entirely certain. . . . Most scholars, I among them, think that the decisive fact is that Matthew dates Jesus' birth at about the time Herod the Great died. This was in the year 4 BCE, and so Jesus was born in that year or shortly before it; some scholars prefer 5, 6 or even 7 BCE.

That Jesus was born a few years before the beginning of the era that starts with his birth is one of the minor curiosities of history. In this work I use the letters BCE and CE to mean 'Before the Common Era' and 'Common Era'. ('Common' means 'accepted by all, including non-Christians'.) The traditional abbreviations, however, are BC and AD, 'Before Christ' and 'Anno Domini' ('in the year of the Lord'). These letters divide history into years before Jesus was born and after his birth. How, then, could he have been born 4 BC (or BCE)? In the sixth century a Scythian monk who was resident in Rome, Dionysius Exiguus, introduced a liturgical calendar that counted years 'from the incarnation' (the birth of Jesus) rather than according to the system established by

In one of the numerous later European paintings depicting Jesus and his deeds, he heals the blind and the lame, as described in the New Testament.

the pagan Roman emperor Diocletian. Dionysius' information, however, was limited. He could fix neither the death of Herod (Matt. 2) nor the census of Quirinius (Luke 2) precisely, and he seems to have made an estimate based on other information in Luke: John the Baptist, who preceded Jesus, began preaching in the fifteenth year of Tiberius (Luke 3.1); Jesus was about thirty years old when he began his ministry (Luke 3.23). The fifteenth year of Tiberius was (by modern reckoning) 29 CE; if Dionysius Exiguus allowed one year for John the Baptist's mission, he would have concluded that Jesus began his ministry in 30 CE. If Jesus was precisely thirty years old at the time, he was born in the year 1. This is probably the reasoning that led to our present calendar. Modern scholars note that Jesus' age in Luke 3.23 is a round number, and that Luke as well as Matthew sets the beginning of the story 'in the days of Herod the king' (Luke 1.5). As I just indicated, this seems to be the firmest piece of evidence regarding the time of Jesus' birth. The calendar based on Dionysius' calculation, however, which was not based on the date of Herod's death, gained general support in the sixth and subsequent centuries, with the result that scholars now date Jesus' birth a few years 'Before Christ'.

JESUS AND JOHN

Jesus lived with his parents in Nazareth, a Galilean village. One of Herod the Great's heirs, Antipas, was the ruler of Galilee for the entirety of Jesus' life (except for the very earliest period, when Herod the Great was still alive). It is a strong possibility that virtually all of Jesus' active ministry, except the last two or three weeks, was carried out in Antipas' Galilee. Jesus was not an urbanite. The cities of Galilee—Sepphoris, Tiberias and Scythopolis (Hebrew, Beth-Shean)—do not figure in the accounts of his activities. He doubtless knew Sepphoris, which was only a few miles from Nazareth, but he nevertheless seems to have regarded his mission as being best directed to the Jews in the villages and small towns of Galilee. Nazareth itself was quite a small village. It was in the hill country, away from the Sea of Galilee, but Jesus taught principally in the villages and towns on the sea. Some of his followers were fishermen. Rural images are fairly frequent in the teaching that is ascribed to him.

When Jesus was a young man, probably in his late twenties, John the Baptist began preaching in or near Galilee. He proclaimed the urgent need to repent in view of the coming judgement. Jesus heard John and felt called to accept his baptism. All four gospels point to this as an event that transformed Jesus' life. According to Mark's account, Jesus 'saw the heavens opened and the Spirit descending upon him like a dove'; he also heard a voice saying, 'You are my beloved son' (Mark 1.9–11).

Antipas arrested John because he had criticized his marriage to Herodias (the gospels) or because he feared that the Baptist's preaching would lead to insurrection (Josephus)—or both. At about that time Jesus began his public ministry. Whereas John had worked outside settled areas, Jesus went from town to town, village to village, usually preaching in synagogues on the sabbath. He called a small number of people to be his disciples, and they joined him in his travels. Unlike John, Jesus not only preached but also healed the sick. He developed a reputation, and people thronged to see him. Soon he too had to preach in open areas because of the crowds.

DEATH AND RESURRECTION

We do not know just how long this itinerant ministry continued, but apparently it lasted only one or possibly two years. After preaching and healing for this period of time in Galilee, Jesus, with his disciples and some other followers, went to Jerusalem for Passover. Jerusalem was in Judaea, which, unlike Galilee, was a Roman province. Jerusalem itself was governed by the Jewish high priest, who was responsible to a Roman prefect. Jesus rode into the city on an ass, and some people hailed him as 'son of David'. When he went to the Temple, he attacked the money-changers and dove-sellers. The high priest and his advisers determined that Jesus was dangerous and had to die. After the Passover meal with his disciples, Jesus went apart to pray. One of his followers had betrayed him, and the high priest's guards arrested him. He was tried, after a fashion, and turned over to the Roman prefect, with the recommendation that he be executed. After a brief hearing, the prefect ordered his execution. He was crucified as an insurgent, along with two others.

He died after a relatively brief period of suffering. A few of his followers placed him in a tomb. According to some reports, when they returned two days later to anoint his body, they found the tomb empty. Thereafter his followers saw him. These resurrection experiences convinced them that Jesus would return and that in Jesus' life and death God had acted to save humanity. The disciples began to persuade others to put their faith in Jesus. They gave him various titles, including 'Anointed' (which is 'Messiah' in Hebrew and 'Christ' in Greek), 'Lord' and 'Son of God'. These titles reveal that, as the decades passed, Jesus' disciples and their converts developed various views of Jesus' relation to God and of his significance in God's plan for Israel and the world. Their movement finally separated from Judaism and became the Christian church. When the gospels were written, however, Christology (theological explanations of the person and work of Jesus) was at an early stage, and the separation of Christianity from Judaism not yet complete.

PAUL'S MISSION AND THE BEGINNINGS OF CHRISTIANITY

ROBERTA L. HARRIS

In this concise, well-written essay, biblical scholar Roberta L. Harris provides an overview of the beginnings of Christianity. She first describes the state of the faith, whose members were at first called the "people of the Way," in the years directly following Jesus's death. Then she tells how Paul at first persecuted the sect but was later converted to it and went forth to win new converts, especially among the Gentiles (non-Jews), a move that initially disturbed many other early Christians. Harris also points out the importance of the apostle Peter as a leader and symbol of the early faith. (In addition, she makes reference to Stephen, an early Christian Jew whom the local Jewish council condemned to death for attempting to spread the idea that Jesus was the Jewish Messiah; most Jews did not accept this idea, which remains one of the major doctrinal differences between Judaism and Christianity.)

T he early church in Jerusalem was tiny—no more than 120 people (Acts 1, 15)—comprising mostly Jesus' original apostles (except Judas), his mother and a few other women, including Mary Magdalene, and some disciples. Jesus' mantle of leadership had fallen on Peter, who was now indeed the rock on which the group depended. His real name was Simon but his Aramaic nickname was Cephas which means 'rock'. Translated into Greek this becomes Petros or Peter. The apostles continued to preach and to heal the sick, attracting converts among the people of Jerusalem who were all practising Jews. It is usual to call them Judaeo-Christians at this time, for they observed the Jewish law while also being followers of Jesus, whose return they expected daily as the risen Christ or the Messiah for whom all Jews were waiting.

Judaism did not at that time seek to make converts. With one exception, when Peter converted Cornelius the centurion in Caesarea, no member of the original group preached to gentiles, even though they formed a large proportion of the population in Palestine. The position of the Judaeo-Christians was never secure and they were persecuted by other Jews (Acts 2–7). Stephen, who was 'full of grace and power' (Acts 6, 8) was stoned for blasphemy and was the first Christian martyr. The destruction of Jerusalem in AD 70 sealed their fate. When [the Roman emperor] Hadrian founded his city of Aelia Capitolina on the ruins of Jerusalem, in the early 2nd century AD, the church which re-emerged was made up entirely of gentiles.

THE CONVERSION OF PAUL

As a young man studying in Jerusalem, Paul witnessed the stoning of Stephen, sometime around AD 36. He subsequently took part in the persecutions in the city of the people of 'the Way'— the name for Jesus' followers before the word 'Christian' was used (Acts 9, 2). Having asked the High Priest's permission to go to Damascus to seek out more apostates, on the road there he experienced a vision of Jesus that struck him blind. In Damascus his sight was restored by Ananias, a Judaeo-Christian.

There is no zeal like that of a new convert. All the enthusiasm and energy which Paul had previously expended in persecuting Christians was now turned to spreading the teachings of Jesus as widely as possible. Paul, with his forthright style, came into conflict with most of Jesus' original followers as well as with traditional Jews and Roman sympathizers. Most people saw him as a troublemaker and his preaching in the synagogue in Damascus aroused much hostility. The disciples in Jerusalem soon despatched him back to Tarsus for his own (and their) good.

THE FIRST CHRISTIANS

What happened next was totally unforeseen by Jesus' first disciples. After Stephen's death many Judaeo-Christians had fled Jerusalem for Syria and even Cyprus. Antioch in Syria was one of the most important cities in the Roman empire, and it was there that some of them began to preach about Jesus to the Greeks (but not to Jews). News of this so alarmed the people of the Way in Jerusalem that they sent Barnabas to Antioch to investigate. Unexpectedly, he was delighted with the sincerity of the new converts. He then travelled further north to Tarsus, looking for Paul, and brought him back to help with the work in Antioch. The two of them remained there for a year and it was in Antioch that the name Christians was first used, denoting the followers of Christ, meaning 'the Anointed One'.

The notion of Christianity as a religion separate from Judaism seems to have begun in Antioch also. Paul, if not the originator of this idea, certainly accepted it with enthusiasm, and from then on he encouraged Christian belief among Jews and gentiles alike. On his many travels he first preached to the Jewish community in each city he visited, seeking out the synagogue. When rejected by the Jews, he took his message to the gentiles, among whom he was more successful. At the Council of Jerusalem in AD 49 it was agreed that gentiles did not have to undergo circumcision or obey the Jewish law in order to be Christians. This was a great relief to those communities who were ready to follow Christ but not to accept the heavy burden of the ritual law as the Judaeo-Christians did. To the ordinary Jewish communities in the cities visited by Paul this decision was anathema. In fact it was not welcomed by all the disciples in Jerusalem either, although Peter, who had converted Cornelius the centurion, and James, the brother of Jesus, seem not to have objected.

TRAVEL IN THE FIRST CENTURY AD

Paul now began to spread the word of Christianity far and wide. Travel at this time was relatively easy, as the Romans had set up a comprehensive road system throughout their empire, which was well maintained and properly policed. It was also simple to take passage on almost any ship of the many that plied the Mediterranean. Paul could also keep in touch by letter with the various churches he set up. His correspondence contains a great deal of information about the concerns of his widespread flock. Even more important is the insight gained into Paul's teachings. It should not be forgotten that he had never sat at the feet of Jesus—all his knowledge of Christ came from visions granted directly to him—and he did not always agree with Jesus' first disciples. Preaching to the gentiles was indeed the most difficult idea for those in Jerusalem to accept.

PAUL'S MISSIONARY JOURNEYS

Paul's first missionary journey, around AD 47–48, was with Barnabas to Cyprus, a natural choice as it was the latter's home. They also travelled through southern Anatolia (modern Turkey) before returning to Antioch (Acts 13–14). Paul's second journey was far more ambitious (Acts 15, 40–18, 22). This time his companion was Silas, and the trip took them across Anatolia and then by sea to Macedonia. Paul eventually reached Athens (Acts 17). There he received his greatest rebuff, for the message of Christianity meant little to people educated in the spirit of Greek philosophy. Further south, in Corinth, he was more kindly received (Acts 18, 1–11) and stayed 18 months. Eventually he returned to Palestine after a very successful trip.

Paul could never stay long in one place. Soon he was off again (Acts 18, 21–23, 16), this time to Ephesus on the Aegean coast of Asia Minor. This was the greatest port of the region, a crowded and cosmopolitan city already over a thousand years old. It was fruitful ground for Paul, who spent two years there. Just as he was planning to leave, he became embroiled in a hysterical mob threatening violence against anyone who did not respect Diana, the patron goddess of Ephesus, whose cult attracted huge numbers of pilgrims. Her great temple had stood for centuries on the edge of the city and was one of the seven wonders of the ancient world. Once extricated from the imbroglio [commotion] Paul sailed for Greece.

THE LAST YEARS OF PAUL

After much travelling Paul eventually returned to Caesarea. The Jews of Palestine were by this time in an uproar against Felix, a particularly vicious Roman procurator [governor]. False prophets abounded, brigands made life intolerable for ordinary people and unrest was everywhere. Nevertheless Paul insisted on going to Jerusalem for the Passover, even though he was *persona non grata* [unwelcome] with Jews, Judaeo-Christians and Romans.

It was always Paul's policy to be 'all things to all men, that I might by all means save some' (I Corinthians 9, 22) and it was while he was trying to appease Jews and Christians that he was recognized on the Temple Mount and set on by a mob. He was accused of bringing a gentile into the Temple area and it was only the Roman troops, spotting trouble from their vantage point of the Antonia fortress, who rescued him from certain death (Acts 21, 17–22, 24).

Once he had declared himself to be a Roman citizen he was sent under guard to Felix in Caesarea in AD 58. From there, after two years spent in prison, he appealed to the emperor for a trial in Rome as was his right. He was despatched to Rome by a new Roman governor, Festus, at the beginning of the winter when most shipping had been laid up because of the foul weather. It was therefore a voyage full of incident, ending in a shipwreck off Malta (Acts 27, 41–28, 1). Determined as ever, Paul, together with his companion, possibly Luke (who is credited with writing the Book of Acts), finally reached Italy, landing at Puteoli, near modern Naples.

They walked up the coast to Rome, where they were greeted by a Christian community that already existed in the city. Paul was apparently placed under house arrest by the Romans (Acts 28, 11–16), but was allowed to receive visitors and to preach. It is in Rome, around AD 61–62, two years after his arrival, still preaching to all who came to him and still writing to the faithful communities established by him, that we lose sight of him for the last time. No charges were ever brought against him and we simply do not have any evidence for what happened to him. Tradition has it that he was executed in AD 67. The Basilica of St Paul Without the Wall marks the spot where he is said to be buried.

PETER SEEN AS THE HEAD OF THE CHURCH

Peter reached Rome soon after Paul, and it was he not Paul who was destined to be the real head of the church in Rome and therefore throughout the Roman empire. Peter lies buried deep beneath the altar of his great church in the Vatican City where his throne is still occupied by the popes, who are his spiritual descendants.

Roman Catholicism is only one branch of Christianity. Some of the others are at least as old. Paul found well-established communities in southern Italy as well as in Rome. There were non-Pauline groups in Asia Minor and in Egypt, where the Coptic church is one of the oldest in the world. There is no documentation about the origin of these churches as there is for the church of Peter and Paul. What seems certain, however, is that even at a very early date there was no one set of beliefs nor one single creed for all Christian communities. Even so, Christianity began to spread very fast throughout all the lands around the Mediterranean and beyond. In the early 4th century AD even Rome submitted and Christianity was adopted as the official religion of the Roman empire.

DESPITE PERSECUTION, CHRISTIANITY TRIUMPHS

CHARLES FREEMAN

This informative summary of Christianity's successful rise to spiritual and political dominance in the Roman state in its last two centuries is by noted classical scholar Charles Freeman. Among the key figures he covers are the second-century Christian writer Tertullian, perhaps the greatest of the apologists (Christian leaders who explained to pagans why Christianity was no threat to society); the western emperor Constantine I and eastern emperor Licinius, who jointly issued the famous Edict of Milan, granting the Christians religious toleration in 313; the Christian emperor Theodosius I, who closed the pagan temples in the early 390s; and Augustine of Hippo, the great thinker and writer who helped to define many aspects of emerging church doctrine.

A s early as 64 Christians were used as scapegoats by the emperor Nero when seeking to allocate blame for the fire at Rome. Nero could exploit the distrust of Christians as easterners and the seclusion in which their activities took place. There was seldom, however, any concerted activity against the early Christians and no empire-wide decree against them. Those who were considered troublesome were prosecuted under the traditional powers given to governors to maintain good order but . . . Christians should not be sought out specifically and those who had lapsed were of no concern at all.

Reprinted from *Egypt, Greece, and Rome: Civilizations of the Ancient Mediterranean*, by Charles Freeman (1996), by permission of Oxford University Press. Copyright © Charles Freeman 1996.

PERSECUTION AND THE MARTYRS

The real problem was the renunciation by Christians of all other cults, including those involving worship of the emperor. Accounts of trials show that it was not so much what Christians believed that worried local governors as their refusal to honour traditional gods. The more flexible judges tried to find compromises, some gesture which could be passed off as recognition of these gods, but many Christians would refuse. In 177 the governor of Lugdunum (Lyons) asked the emperor Marcus Aurelius' advice on how to deal with the Christian community. Marcus Aurelius, who was highly conventional in his religious beliefs, believed Christianity offered a threat to the state and he was prepared to condone local persecutions. He replied that those who recanted could be set free but those who did not could be condemned to the arena or, if they were citizens, beheaded. Among the forty-eight put to death a slave girl, Blandina, stood out for her courage. It was said that her death aroused enthusiasm among other Christians, for whom a painful but sudden death seemed little price to pay for the guarantee of eternal bliss in heaven.

One of the most moving of early Christian documents is the prison diary kept by Perpetua, an early martyr who died with her slave girl, Felicity, in the arena at Carthage in 203. Perpetua's father desperately tried to persuade her to renounce her faith, especially as she was still nursing her infant daughter, but Perpetua stood firm and in prison appears to have exercised a leadership role over other Christian prisoners. She met her death with dignity, even, it was said, guiding the gladiator's sword to her throat. It could be argued the very specific context of martyrdom shaped a role for women as leaders which was denied to them in the everyday activities of the churches. There were clearly complex psychological elements of martyrdom. In north Africa in particular, there are signs of a collective willingness among communities to face death for their beliefs, with others attracted to Christianity as a result of their example. Tertullian put it succinctly, 'The blood of the martyrs is the seed of the church.'

The persecution of Christians reached its fullest extent in the third and early fourth centuries. The intensity of these persecutions reflected the tensions of the age. It was inevitable that those who refused to sacrifice to the gods would be confronted when the continuing defeats of the empire suggested that those gods were deserting Rome. The refusal of converted soldiers to honour the cult of the emperor was particularly intolerable. There was a major persecution under the emperor Decius in 250–1, with bishops as the prime targets, and another under Diocletian

Roman soldiers disrupt a religious ceremony in the catacombs, under-ground chambers where many Christians buried their dead. It is un-known how often the Romans actually entered the catacombs.

and his successor Galerius between 303 and 312. (Diocletian's policy of elevating the traditional gods of Rome intensified the confrontation between Christians and the state.) Persecution was not applied consistently. Many Christian communities escaped it completely. However, the random nature of the attacks, in which official backing was often given to the activities of lynch mobs, was frightening. Christians really were thrown to the lions in front of howling crowds. (The Christian Lactantius, writing in the early fourth century, told of the terrible punishments God would exact in retaliation for these enormities.)

CHRISTIANITY'S STEADY GROWTH

Persecution can also be seen as a response to the success of Christianity in infiltrating official institutions such as the civil service and the army. . . . In many large cities there were now so many Christians that they overflowed into public life, acting as councillors and imperial officials. Christianity was winning converts higher in the social scale so that even Diocletian's wife was rumoured to have Christian sympathies. Bishops were becoming well-known local figures, running large and well-organized com-

munities and distributing alms among their members, while
Christian communities may also have been filling gaps left by the
decay of traditional institutions.

Cohesion was also being established between the Christian
communities although it was a slow and often painful development. There was general agreement by 200 on a basic creed affirmed by all seeking baptism which included acceptance of God
as the father, Jesus Christ as the son, the Holy Spirit, and the resurrection. (The Holy Spirit refers to the activity of God shown
in the world, typically as the power of healing, casting out devils, or prophesying through the medium of ordinary human beings, but also as the instrument through which Mary conceived
Jesus.) Gradually the sacred writings of the church were gathered into a Bible of selected books of the Old and New Testament (the Greek word *biblia* means 'the books'), although the
disputes over which early Christian writings should or should
not be included took some time to resolve. Those not accepted
were gradually discarded or in some cases declared heretical.
Most have now disappeared. . . .

There was still, however, no supreme human leader of the
church. The bishops of Rome, Antioch, and Alexandria had
gained some prominence in their local areas with the right to con-
secrate the bishops of smaller cities, although they still vigorously
refused any submission to each other. This was recognized by
Cyprian, bishop of Carthage, who argued in his treatise on the
unity of the Catholic church (251) that all bishops should act in
consensus with no one bishop supreme over others. For Cyprian
the church was the only body capable of authoritative Christian
teaching and no true Christian could exist outside it. 'He no
longer has God for his father, who does not have the church for
his mother.' This definition of a church claiming exclusive authority over all Christians had immense implications for the future of Christianity.

CONSTANTINE'S SUPPORT FOR THE CHRISTIANS

So when Constantine and Licinius offered toleration for all sects
including Christianity in 313 the church, even though it still contained only a minority of the population, was in a strong position to take advantage of it. With the added support given by
Constantine, Christianity came into its own and enjoyed a political and social respectability it had always lacked. Over the
next century it was to become the only officially tolerated religion of the empire. . . .

It is certainly likely that without imperial support Christianity
would never have been more than the religion of a minority and

to this extent the toleration and active support of Christians by Constantine does mark an important turning point in the history of the western world. . . .

[However] it is . . . misleading to talk of Constantine as a Christian emperor, even though this is the picture painted in the main source for his life, the biography by the church historian Eusebius, (died 338/9). Constantine was not baptized until shortly before he died (although this was a common practice, with baptism delayed in the hope that the purified soul would be untouched by sin before death) and most of his advisers were not Christians. Towards the end of his reign he sanctioned the building of a large temple to his family on the Flaminian Way and it was to be endowed with theatrical shows and gladiatorial fights. The vast majority of his subjects were not Christians and most of them had still probably never heard of Christ. There is little indication in Constantine's legislation, which was often extremely punitive, that he had any interest in upholding Christian ideals (although he did ban animal sacrifice). In many ways he was a highly conventional Roman and his respect for traditional rank led to his widespread patronage of the senatorial class. He even created a new senate in Constantinople, the city he founded in the eastern part of the empire. . . .

Whatever may be said about Constantine's own beliefs his support for Christianity was crucial in establishing the religion's respectability and ensuring its continued spread. Not only could Christians now operate freely but in numerous ways Constantine gave them effective help. The clergy were relieved of any obligation to serve on city councils (a move which led to a mass of ordinations so onerous had these posts now become) and taxation. There was financial help for the building of churches and as bishops were now able to receive bequests some congregations became extremely wealthy. It was, however, the emperor himself and his family who funded the first great Christian buildings. Constantine donated land from the old imperial palace of the Lateran to provide a cathedral for Rome, St John Lateran, while the mother of the emperor, Helena, visited Palestine in 326 and set in hand the building of appropriate memorials to the life of Jesus at Bethlehem and on the Mount of Olives. Constantine himself was responsible for the great Church of the Holy Sepulchre at Jerusalem over the supposed burial place of Jesus. As early as 333 pilgrims were visiting these sacred sites. Parts of the diary of one of these, a well-born Spanish nun, Egeria, survive from her visit of 384 and show that, with official help, even remote sites in Judaea, Egypt, and Galilee could be visited by those determined enough to do so.

The martyrs of the great persecutions had not been forgotten.

Their anniversaries crammed the Christian calendar and now they too were honoured in buildings. The sites of their burials and their bones if recovered excited special reverence. (In some cases, recorded Augustine, their bones could be recognized by the miraculous state of their preservation.) The Vatican Hill, the traditional burial place of Peter, saw a great church rising from a site which had to be levelled for the purpose. St Peter's was another of Constantine's foundations, and one source suggests that a mosaic with the emperor presenting the church to Christ adorned the central triumphal arch. These churches borrowed the traditional Roman hall, the basilica, as a model. The first St Peter's appears to have been 119 metres long and 64 metres wide, its aisles faced with great columns of marble taken from earlier buildings. It, like St John Lateran, no longer survives but Rome still has two fine fifth-century examples of basilicas, those of Santa Maria Maggiore and Santa Sabina. The former is adorned by magnificent mosaics while the latter boasts a finely carved set of cypress-wood doors with scenes showing the links between the Old and the New Testament. These great new buildings, with their fantastic decoration and aura of sanctity around the shrines of the martyrs, brought 'a Christianization of space' (in the words of Robert Markus). In theory God might be everywhere. In practice He now seemed especially close once a worshipper entered a church. An insistence on appropriate behaviour for the occasion (hushed voices, for instance) is still with us.

Few churches enjoyed the magnificence of the basilicas of the capitals of the empire. The three rooms found at the villa at Lullingstone in Britain must have been more typical. Christians were still in a minority in every part of the empire even though the support of the emperor had led, in the words of Eusebius, 'to the hypocrisy of people who crept into the church' to win his favour. Moreover individual churches still enjoyed a large degree of independence and there was no effective way of settling doctrinal and other disputes between them. To this extent Christianity was still not a coherent force in Roman society. This was to change as successive emperors took the lead in consolidating a unified church. . . .

CHRISTIAN METHODS BECOME AGGRESSIVE

It was in Theodosius' reign that the emperor was confirmed as the upholder of Christianity, not only against the 'pagans' but also against variants of Christian belief declared heretical. (The Greek word *hairesis* originally meant simply 'choice'. It now developed the meaning of 'unacceptable choice'.) Constantine's sons, though Christian, had continued to tolerate paganism. (Historians still use the word 'paganism' as a general term for non-Christian beliefs but they do so with increasing uneasiness. The connotations attached to the word unfairly degrade a range of beliefs, many of which were highly sophisticated.) They continued to hold the traditional title of *pontifex maximus* and subsidized pagan temples. A law of 342 prohibited the destruction of temples so as to protect the traditional entertainments associated with them. It was only in the 350s that Constantius launched a determined attack on paganism. . . . However, even this campaign had its limits. When Constantius visited Rome in 357 . . . he realized the enormous strength of paganism there and refrained from upsetting the privileges of the senators and the revenues of their temples.

When the 'pagan' emperor Julian came to power it would probably not have been too late to have shifted the balance back in favour of paganism. Certainly this was Julian's aim. He banned Christians from teaching rhetoric and grammar and abolished the exemption of clergy from taxation. Revenues were restored to the temples and Julian set about the revival of animal sacrifice with some enthusiasm. . . . [However] his intellectual tastes had little in common with the mass of pagans in the small towns and countryside of the empire. In his short reign he never developed the rapport with the pagan élites which would have ensured the restoration of the traditional cults to a central place in state ceremony.

With Jovian came a restoration of Christianity and there were to be no more pagan emperors. The church was able to resume its progress. Increasingly its influence was based on the emergence of strong bishoprics headed by men of character and power. The church had acquired great wealth, mostly in land donated by the faithful, while the bishops had been given rights of jurisdiction (they could order the release of slaves, for instance) and often had an important role in the distribution of alms. Administrative expertise was essential. For this reason bishops were normally chosen from the traditional ruling classes and in some cases were appointed even before they were baptized. One such was Ambrose, bishop of Milan from 374 to 397, and perhaps the most influential bishop and preacher of his age. He had been an effective governor of north Italy and when there was some dispute over the succession to the bishopric of Milan, he was asked to be bishop. Once baptized, he quickly mastered his new role and showed he was much more than an administrator. In the twenty-four tempestuous years of his rule he waged a formidable campaign against moral laxity, heresy and paganism. Ambrose insisted that it was the church which should define orthodoxy and set the standards of morality and the duty of the state to act in support. He first worked on the young Gratian, inducing him to surrender the post of *pontifex maximus*. His *cause célèbre* was his battle with the Roman senate over the statue of Victory which adorned the senate house in Rome. Gratian was persuaded to order its removal despite the most impassioned opposition from the pagan senators.

After Gratian's death Theodosius I came under Ambrose's influence. . . . When the emperor ordered a massacre of some rioters in Thessalonica, however, Ambrose promptly excommunicated him. Theodosius learnt his lesson and became a Christian emperor of the type desired by Ambrose. It was in his reign that a wide variety of heresies were first defined and a vigorous onslaught launched against pagan cults. In Egypt bands of fanatical monks wrecked the ancient temples. The Serapeum, near Alexandria, one of the great temple complexes of the ancient world, was dismantled in 392. In north Africa Christian vigilantes raided pagan centres and ridiculed traditional beliefs. Another element of the growing intolerance was the opposition to the Jews easily inflamed by Christian preachers such as John Chrysostom. By the beginning of the fifth century Jews were banned from the civil service. The political power of the emperor had become intertwined with the spiritual power of the church. In the late fourth-century church of Santa Pudenziana in Rome, Christ is depicted as an emperor, his apostles as if they were senators. . . .

AUGUSTINE'S CONVERSION

The triumphalist nature of much Christian writing of the period tends to overshadow the continuing vitality of pagan thought. The variety of pagan belief meant that there had never been any exclusivity. Membership of one cult did not preclude membership of another and the spiritual heritage of paganism remained rich and capable of fertile development. As the senator Quintus Aurelius Symmachus, a leading protester against the removal of the statue of Victory from the senate house, put it, 'What does it matter by which wisdom each of us arrives at the truth? It is not possible that only one road leads to so sublime a mystery.'

Some of the manifestations of pagan culture in the fourth century are explained in the early chapters of St Augustine's *Confessions*. Augustine's education, in his native Numidia, in the mid fourth century, was in the purest classical tradition. Its main component was training in rhetoric. . . . Although his mother was Christian Augustine was not attracted at first by the faith and his restless nature drove him to other spiritual alternatives. . . .

His experiences are detailed in the *Confessions*, a brilliant account of a tortured mind searching for absolute peace. The central chapters of the *Confessions* are concerned with his spiritual experiences in Milan and his eventual conversion to Christianity. They were written in the late 390s after he had returned to his native Africa. Augustine presents himself as a deeply unworthy man, tormented by his sexuality and harried, although he took some time to recognize the fact, by the looming power of God.

> I broke your lawful bounds and did not escape your lash. For what man can escape it? You were always present, angry and merciful at once, strewing the pangs of bitterness over all my lawless pleasures to lead me on to look for others unallied with pain. You meant me to find them nowhere but in yourself, O Lord, for you teach us by inflicting pain, you smite so you may heal and you kill us so that we may not die away from you. (Translation: R. Pine-Coffin)

Augustine came to accept that God's love becomes available to sinners only when they make complete submission to Him. The moment of conversion came after many struggles when he heard the voice of a child asking him to take up the New Testament. He opened it at the words of Paul, 'put on the Lord Jesus Christ and make no provision for the flesh to gratify its desires'. Suddenly he had found his true haven, in the church. Once he had renounced his sexual desires for ever, he was able to be baptized.

THE DOCTRINE OF "ORIGINAL SIN"

After his conversion and baptism, Augustine returned to his native Africa and became bishop of Hippo where he remained until his death thirty years later. While he preferred the life of the monk, he cared deeply about the needs of the ordinary Christians who thronged his churches and was more sensitive than most church leaders to their earthly desires. (He was prepared, for instance, to accept sexuality as an intrinsic part of marriage.) In the remaining years of his life, he applied the brilliance and clarity of his mind to some of the major theological issues of the day. Perhaps the most famous was the dispute with Pelagius, an ascetic who may have been of British birth, over the nature of free will.

Pelagius had argued that each individual had the freedom to follow God's will or not. The hope, of course, was that he or she would choose to aim for a life of perfection, with Christ as the model. In such a case, argued Pelagius, God would support these efforts. Augustine, on the other hand developed a different approach, one that had only been dimly formulated before his time.

This was the view that as a result of Adam and Eve's transgressions in the Garden of Eden God had burdened all human beings with an 'original sin' which was passed on from generation to generation. The concept of original sin had never been mentioned by Jesus and Augustine relied on one verse from St Paul (Romans 5:12) for support. The consequences of the sin were, however, profound. Human beings, argued Augustine, were tied by original sin to the earthly pleasures of the world (the evidence was before him in his congregations) and only the grace of God could liberate them from the burden of these pleasures. This grace could be passed on through the sacraments, especially those of baptism and the Eucharist, but it was always a gift from God, not the right of any individual, however good his or her life.

Augustine's God was, therefore, selective. Only a few would be saved. This left uncomfortable questions to be resolved. Was it possible to live a good life and still be deprived of the grace of God? What would happen to those who did not receive this grace or who were never baptized? When challenged by his opponents over what would happen to the souls of babies who had died before they were baptized Augustine was forced to accept that their original sin left them unprotected and they could never be admitted to heaven. Independently Augustine also came to reject Origen's view that eternal punishment was incompatible with the goodness of God and became one of the foremost defenders of a Hell where punishment would be harsh and eternal. There would be no mercy for those to whom the grace of God was not extended.

Augustine's concept of original sin was, in the early fifth century, a minority view held only by some of his fellow bishops in north Africa. As another opponent commented, the whole idea was improbable, making it seem as if the devil, not a loving God, had created man. What was remarkable, however, was that through sheer persistence and intellectual energy Augustine managed to get his view accepted as the official doctrine of the western church after the emperor Honorius insisted the Italian bishops adopt it. The concept of original sin received no support elsewhere. It never travelled to the east (Augustine wrote only in Latin) or was adopted by any other monotheistic religion.

THE HEAVENLY CITY

Augustine attempted to define what was meant by the 'church'. Joining the church and receiving its sacraments presumably increased the chance of receiving the gift of God's grace but the logic of Augustine's views suggested that membership of the church did not guarantee salvation and that those who did not join the church were not necessarily deprived of it. The church, however, had a duty to ensure that all who wished to join and receive the benefits of its sacraments could do so. . . .

Augustine's last great work, *The City of God*, was prompted by the sack of Rome by the Visigoths in 410. Although the physical damage was not immense (and the Christian Visigoths left the city's churches untouched), the psychological shock certainly was. It seemed as if the world as all had known it was at an end. Much of the book is concerned with pointing out the failure of traditional Roman religion to save the city or provide anything more than a self-glorification of the state. Augustine argued that the true 'city' was, instead, that inhabited by the believers loved by God, a community which extended from earth into heaven. An earthly city, even one so great as Rome, was only a pale reflection of the heavenly one and it was to the heavenly city that the aspirations of men and women must be directed. The fall of Rome was thus of little significance in the eyes of God.

Augustine's influence on the church was profound. His writing and sermons had a clarity and majesty which was unrivalled. His mind penetrated every nook and cranny of Christian thought. Much of his writing, in Book Nine of *The Confessions*, for instance, where his last conversations with his mother are recorded, is deeply moving. He was not a cold intellectual but a human being acutely aware of the power of his emotional feelings. It is hard not to feel some sympathy for him in his agonizing searches for his God. Ultimately, however, his message was a chilling one. There was no salvation without divine grace and this could not necessarily be gained through living a 'good' life. The church had the right to prosecute heretics and call on the state to support it. Only those who are convinced that divine grace is theirs and who through it have liberated themselves from their body's desires can read his works with total ease.

JEROME AND THE VULGATE

Contemporary with Augustine was another great scholar of the early church, Jerome (*c*. 347–419/20). Jerome was born in the Balkans about 347 of Christian parents but by the age of 12 he was studying philosophy and rhetoric in Rome. He developed a profound love of classical authors and one of the most shattering events of his life was a dream in which God accused him of preferring Cicero to the Bible, for which failing he was flogged. He resolved never to read a pagan author again (though his letters remain full of classical allusions).

Jerome's life was restless and tormented. He travelled incessantly and underwent periods of severe asceticism. In Peter

Brown's words, 'The human body remained for Jerome a darkened forest, filled with the roaring of wild beasts, that could be controlled only by rigid codes of diet and by the strict avoidance of occasions for sexual attraction.' At the same time, however, he studied assiduously and mastered both Greek and Hebrew in addition to his native Latin. It was this breadth of knowledge which recommended him to bishop Damasus of Rome, who employed him first as his secretary (382–4) and then as the translator of the Greek and Hebrew texts of the Old and New Testaments into Latin.

A unified and authoritative translation had long been needed. There were all too many Latin translations of varying quality circulating in the western empire. Jerome faced formidable problems in achieving his task. In Rome his censorious personality and suspicion over a new translation made him so unpopular that after the death of Damasus he was forced to leave the city. The last thirty-four years of his life were spent in Bethlehem in a monastery and it was here that his translation was finally brought to a conclusion. At first it received little recognition but by the eighth century it was accepted by the church as the authoritative Latin version of the original texts. As the Vulgate (the 'common version') it lasted unchallenged in the Catholic church for centuries and remains one of the great achievements of early Christian scholarship. . . .

A TRANSFORMED SOCIETY

In 394 the emperor Theodosius had been challenged by a usurper in Gaul, Eugenius. Eugenius was a pagan and attracted the support of many leading Roman senators. Theodosius met their forces at the River Frigidus in the Alps and crushed them. The battle was seen by contemporary Christians as the confirmation of the triumph of their faith. Certainly a different world now existed, with new concepts of spiritual authority and different visions of God and morality. . . . Moreover, a growing preoccupation with the elimination of paganism and heresy meant, inevitably, that the rich diversity of Greco-Roman spiritual experience was stifled, with the result that eventually spiritual aspirations could no longer be expressed outside a specifically Christian context. Jews were increasingly isolated, and the fourth century marks for them, in the words of Nicholas de Lange, 'the beginning of a long period of desolation'. The state and church authorities initiated measures to segregate the Jews from mainstream Christian society with consequences that were, in the long term, profound.

The Greek and Roman world had seen a variety of gods whose

own relationships and conflicts had often diverted them from human affairs. The single Christian god was portrayed as if He had few other concerns than the behaviour and attitudes of individual human beings. Their sexual behaviour in particular seemed of particular concern to Him. He had supreme majesty and no Christian would have dared to have confronted Him in the confident way a Greek might have done. (Augustine's description of himself in his *Confessions* as 'a mean thing' would have been greeted with incomprehension and, probably, contempt by his Roman predecessors.) It was perhaps at this moment that intense guilt replaced public shame as a conditioner of moral behaviour. Ever more lurid descriptions of the horrors of Hell accompanied the shift. Soon consuming fires and devils with red-hot instruments of torture entered European mythology. There were other aspects of Christian society that were significant. While Christians ensured that the poor were seen as an object of concern (and hence, for the first time, something is known of them), it was also believed that God would be pleased by the magnificence of buildings constructed in His honour. This led inevitably to a tension over the way a Christian society used its resources, whether for the relief of the poor, as the gospels would seem to support, or the glorification of God in gold and mosaic. The collaboration of the state with the only authorized religion has also to be of fundamental importance. These shifts in beliefs helped determine a framework of social, economic, spiritual, and cultural life which has persisted even into the twentieth century. It is certainly arguable that, in this respect, the fourth century is one of the most influential in European history.

The Decline and Fall of Rome and the Classical World

—| CHAPTER 5 |—

Rome's Near Collapse and Temporary Recovery

A.H.M. Jones

The dire crisis of the third century A.D., sometimes referred to as the "anarchy," brought the Roman Empire nearly to its knees. And seen in retrospect, it constituted the first major phase of the realm's ultimate decline and fall. As explained here by the late distinguished Cambridge University scholar, A.H.M. Jones, the crisis had many dimensions. Among these were poor leadership, grave military threats, a faltering economy, and a break-down of law and order. Jones pays special attention to another important development contributing to decline, namely the disintegration of Rome's old social order. He then goes on to outline the far-reaching political, military, and economic reforms of the emperor Diocletian, which gave the Empire a new lease on life but also made it a more regimented, grimmer place than it had been in the happier days before the anarchy.

M any must have despaired of the future of the empire, ravaged by civil wars and barbarian invasions, exhausted by ever-increasing requisitions, and depopulated by famines and plagues. The root cause of the troubles which had for two generations overwhelmed the empire lay in the indiscipline of the army and the political ambitions of its leaders. . . . The second great civil war which followed the murder of Commodus [reigned 180–192] in 192 had . . . serious consequences. Septimius Severus [193–211], the winner in the conflict, knowing that his power depended on the goodwill of the armies, raised their pay, increased their privileges, and by freely promoting soldiers to administrative posts militarised the whole government. His last words to his sons are said to have been, "Agree with each other, enrich the soldiers and never mind all the others," and [his son] Caracalla [211–217], having murdered his brother, obeyed the other two precepts. But the troops had by now realised that they were the masters, and in 217 a military pronunciamento overthrew Caracalla. In the next thirty-six years there were twelve emperors (not counting co-regents), not one of whom died in his bed, and after the accession of Valerian in 253, it becomes impossible to keep count. In every quarter of the empire the local armies proclaimed emperors: in Gaul there were five local emperors between 257 and 273, and between 260 and 273 Odenath, a citizen of Palmyra, and his widow Zenobia, ruled the eastern provinces from Asia Minor to Egypt. With the accession of Aurelian in 270 a recovery began, and the local pretenders were one by one suppressed. But he was assassinated in 275, his successor Tacitus lasted only six months, Probus, after a vigorous reign of six years, fell victim to another mutiny in 282, and Carus reigned only two years before he, too, was assassinated.

To add to the misfortunes of the empire, the pressure of the Germans on the Rhine and Danube frontiers was increasing during this period. We now hear for the first time of two confederations of tribes, the Franks on the Lower Rhine and the Alamans on the Upper Rhine and Danube, who were to play a large part in the ultimate collapse of Roman authority in the west, and of the Goths, who occupied the Lower Danube, whence they invaded the Balkan provinces and the Crimea, which they made their base for piratical raids on Asia Minor. During this period, too, a new peril arose on the eastern frontier, when in 226 the feeble Arsacid dynasty of Parthia was overthrown by Artaxerxes, who claimed descent from the ancient Achaemenid kings of Persia, revived the national religion, Zoroastrianism and laid claim to all the territories which [the Persian King] Darius had ruled more than seven hundred years before. Distracted as they were by their perpetual civil wars, it is surprising that the emperors were as successful as they were in dealing with external enemies. But despite all their efforts, hordes of Germans constantly broke through the frontiers and ranged over Gaul, Illyricum, Thrace, and sometimes even Italy, looting and burning; while on several occasions Persian armies swept over Syria, and in 260 a Roman emperor, Valerian, was taken prisoner by the Persians.

To the horrors of war was added financial chaos. The maintenance of a standing army had always proved a strain on the primitive economy of the Roman empire, and its budgets had been balanced with difficulty. Severus and Caracalla substantially increased the rates of pay and discharge gratuities, and the army was constantly growing as fresh units were raised by the emperors, either against their rivals or to meet the increasing pressure on the frontiers. Yet almost nothing was done to increase revenue: the only substantial increase in taxation was effected by Caracalla in 212, when by granting Roman citizenship to all free inhabitants of the empire, he made everyone liable to the inheritance tax which Augustus had imposed on Roman citizens. The assessment of the tribute, the direct tax on land and other property, was so complicated and rigid that it was left unaltered. Instead of raising further taxes the emperors preferred the easier path of depreciating the currency. The result was inflation [an increase in prices accompanied by a decline in purchasing power]. In an age when the currency was produced, not by the printing press, but by the hard labour of smiths, inflation could not achieve the speed of modern times, but over the years its cumulative effect was serious. Its extent can be gauged from the fact that the denarius, which had been in the latter part of the second century a decently engraved coin of more or less pure silver, had by the end of the third century become a roughly shaped lump of bronze, thinly washed in silver. In the early third century it was tariffed [valued] at 1,250 to the pound of gold; by 301 the official rate was 50,000.

The effect of the inflation on the population is difficult to estimate, but it was probably not catastrophic. The vast majority of the inhabitants of the empire were peasants: those who owned their plots would have profited from the rise in the price of agricultural produce, and the greater number who were tenants would not have suffered, since their rents, being normally fixed by five-year leases, would tend to lag behind prices. The shopkeepers and manual workers who formed the proletariat of the towns need not have been seriously affected, for the former would naturally raise their prices, and the latter were mostly independent craftsmen who fixed their own terms with their customers. The upper and middle classes, the millionaires who formed the senatorial order, the equestrian order from which the great mass of the higher officials were drawn, and the many thousands of decurions [local officials] who filled the town councils of the empire, all had the bulk of their wealth invested in land. Some part they farmed themselves, or rather through bailiffs, employing slave labour supplemented by casual hired workers or the services of their tenants; the bulk was let to small tenants, either for a money rent or on the métayage system for a quota of the crop. Besides land, the only regular form of investment was mortgages. Mortgages would have been swallowed by the inflation, but income from directly farmed land and from rents in kind would have risen with the rise in prices, and money rents could be put up every five years. As a whole, therefore, the propertied classes would have suffered little, though no doubt some families, which had invested excessively in mortgages, or could not adjust their rents sufficiently rapidly to their rising scales of expenditure, were ruined, and the profiteers of the age, men who had made fortunes in government service, snapped up their estates.

A Cash-Poor Government

The party most severely hit by the inflation was the government itself, and its salaried and wage-earning servants, more particularly the lower civil servants and the rank and file of the army, who had no other resource than their pay. Taxes brought in only the same nominal amount: the pay therefore of civil servants and soldiers could not be raised, and they found that it bought them less and less. Soldiers could, and did, help themselves by looting, and civil servants by corruption and extortion: it was during this period that the custom grew up whereby civil servants charged fees to the public for every act they performed—even the tax collector demanded a fee from the taxpayer for the favour of granting a receipt. On its side the government, though it did not raise the regular scale of pay, distributed special bonuses, or donatives, at more and more frequent intervals. Such donatives had long been customary on the accession of an emperor, and on special occasions such as triumphs. Now that emperors succeeded one another so rapidly, donatives naturally became more frequent. Should any emperor survive five years, it became customary to celebrate the event with a donative. The money for these distributions was procured by the "freewill offerings" of the senate, and the "crown money" voted by all the town councils of the empire; these, being arbitrary exactions, could be increased in nominal value as the currancy fell, or collected in gold bullion. And in the second place the government made free issues of rations and of uniforms both to the troops and to the civil service, obtaining the necessary supplies by requisitioning them from the public. By the end of the third century, rations (*annona*) had become, apart from irregular donatives, the substantial part of a soldier's or civil servant's pay, so much so that officers and higher officials were granted double or multiple rations, the surplus from which, after maintaining their families and slaves, they could sell back to the public. Requisitions in kind [i.e., in the form of goods and services] . . . had similarly become the main part of the revenue and the heaviest burden on the taxpayer.

BRIGANDS AND FAMINE

The combined effect of frequent devastation and looting, both by Roman armies and by barbarian hordes, and of wholesale requisitioning of crops and cattle, both for meat and for transport, was disastrous to agriculture, the basic industry of the Roman empire. Peasants deserted their holdings, either drifting to the towns, where they could pick up a living in luxury trades ministering to the rich—for landlords still collected their rents—or becoming outlaws and brigands: large hordes of these ravaged Gaul in the latter years of the third century . . . and even proclaimed their own emperors. The government endeavored to supply the shortage of agriculture labour by distributing barbarian prisoners of war to landowners, but by the reign of Aurelian the problem of "abandoned lands," which was to harass the imperial government for centuries to come, was already affecting the revenue and the emperor ruled that town councils were collectively responsible for deficits in taxation arising from that cause within their territories.

Devastation, requisitions and the shrinkage in the cultivated area led inevitably to frequent famines, and epidemics ravaged the undernourished population. It is very difficult to estimate the effect of these losses, combined with war casualties, on the population, especially as we have no evidence whatsoever on the birth-rate. But it may well be that the population of the empire, which seems during the first and second centuries, and indeed in the first part of the third, to have been slowly expanding, received a setback and, temporarily at any rate, shrank during the latter part of the third century.

THE TRADITIONAL SOCIAL ORDER

Concurrently with the wars and economic dislocation, and due partly to them, partly to more deep-seated causes, there occurred a general unsettlement of the traditional order of society. This order had, in the second century, been based on a series of hereditary but not rigidly closed classes, which by tradition and custom performed certain functions in the administration, defence and economic life of the empire. At the top of the senatorial order was legally an hereditary caste. . . . It was the function of senators to hold the ancient republican offices and to govern the provinces and command the armies. The equestrian order [made up mostly of well-to-do businessman], which supplied officers to the army and officials to the civil service, was not legally hereditary, and access to it was, in fact, freely given to persons with the requisite property qualification, whether their fathers had held this rank or not; but the son of an equestrian official, unless he passed into the senate, normally succeeded to his father's rank.

Decurions, or town councillors, were again not legally an hereditary class, but, in fact, town councils were close corporations which co-opted the sons of members, and rarely admitted a commoner, even though he had acquired the necessary amount of property. The position of a town councillor was financially burdensome, since he was expected by law or custom to subscribe generously to the needs of the town, particularly when he held a municipal office. It was, in fact, largely through the munificence [generosity] of decurions that the magnificent games and festivals of the cities were celebrated and the grandiose public buildings were erected which still impress visitors to southern France, North Africa and Syria. The position also involved a heavy burden of work and responsibility, since the council not only managed municipal affairs, but carried out for the central government many functions, such as the collection of the tribute and of requisitions and the maintenance of the imperial postal service and the repair of imperial roads. Nevertheless, the old tradition of civic patriotism survived, and service on the town council was, if not coveted as a prize, loyally undertaken as an honourable duty.

In the lower orders of society the army relied upon voluntary enlistment. Many recruits were drawn from the peasantry of the frontier provinces, but a larger number were sons of veterans. In the lower grades of the civil service the officials were either soldiers, seconded for special duty, or slaves or freedmen of the emperor, who were normally succeeded by their sons, born in servitude. The peasants, though legally the majority of them were tenants on short leases, in practice cultivated the same plot from generation to generation.

THE TRADITIONAL ORDER BEGINS TO CRUMBLE

This traditional order of things was profoundly shaken by the troubles of the third century. At one end of the scale peasants began deserting their holdings, either moving to another landlord who offered better terms, or abandoning agriculture altogether for the towns or for a career of banditry. The sons of veterans tended not to enter the army, but preferred to live as gentlemen of leisure on the proceeds of their fathers' discharge gratuities, which usually took the form of land or were invested in land. At the other end of the scale, a large number of senatorial families were killed off or reduced to poverty by the executions and confiscations which often followed a change of emperor, and their places were filled by new men. Senators began to evade the traditional magistracies, which were extremely expensive, and to be excluded from the government of the more important provinces, and in particular from the command of armies, by the policy of the emperors, who preferred to entrust such responsible posts to their own friends, who they hoped would not rebel. The equestrian order was thrown open to the lower ranks of the army, who could now aspire to become officers, governors of provinces and commanders of armies, and finally be acclaimed emperors. In the middle class, both because the burdens of office had increased and the old tradition of civic loyalty was dying, decurions strove to evade municipal office, and sons of decurions election to the council. The populace still got their games, but building ceased, and the huge monuments erected by past generations began to fall into disrepair. What was more serious, the whole administrative system was threatened with breakdown, since it was by the voluntary services of the landed gentry that the imperial taxes were collected. The government insisted that offices must be filled and the council kept up to strength, and ruled that a candidate duly nominated must accept office unless he could prove a claim to exemption.

On all sides the old traditions and the old loyalties were fading. At no time had the Roman empire inspired any active devotion in the great majority of its citizens. Men were proud to be Roman citizens and not barbarians, but were not moved by loyalty to Rome to sacrifice their lives or their money. The empire was too vast and impersonal and the emperor too distant to excite any emotion except respectful fear or sometimes gratitude. The loyalties on which the empire depended were local or professional. The soldier fought for the honour of his legion or his army or his general; the decurion worked and spent his money freely for the greater glory of his town. The generals and administrators of the senatorial and equestrian orders were moved rather by the traditions of their class than by devotion to the empire. Now the sense of *noblesse oblige* [benevolent acts by people of high birth] was fading among the aristocracy, the spirit of civic patriotism was fast vanishing in the middle class, the discipline of the troops was decaying, and there was nothing to take their place.

On 20th November, 284, there was yet another pronunciamento. The emperor Numerian [283–284], who had been leading back the legions from an expedition against Persia, was found dead in his litter, and the officers elected and the troops acclaimed the commander of the bodyguard, Valerius Diocles, or, as he was henceforth called, Diocletian. In the following spring he marched westwards, and defeated Numerian's brother, Carinus.

These events doubtless created little stir at the time: the Roman world was only too used to proclamations of emperors and civil wars. But they were to prove the beginning of better days. Diocletion was to reign for over twenty years, and then to abdicate of his own free will in favour of successors of his own choosing, and during these twenty years he was to carry out a thorough reorganisation of the empire, which in its main outlines was to last for three centuries.

THE TETRARCHY

The new emperor was, if a persistent later tradition is to be believed, of even humbler origin than his predecessors. His father was reputed to have been a freedman of a senator, and to have earned his living as a clerk. Diocletian himself must have shown some military ability to have risen to the post of commander of the bodyguard. But he was not a distinguished soldier, and when he had achieved power usually preferred to delegate the command in important operations to others. His genius lay in organisation: he had a passion for order and method, which at times degenerated into a rigid insistence on uniformity, and an enormous capacity for work and an attention to detail. . . . But his true greatness lay in his willingness to delegate authority, and in the absolute loyalty which he won from the colleagues whom he selected. He must have possessed a truly dominating personality to drive his team. . . .

Only a year after his defeat of Carinus, Diocletian decided that he needed an assistant to deal with the problems of the West, in particular the peasant revolt . . . in Gaul, and on 1st March, 286, he nominated an officer of Illyrian origin and peasant birth, Maximian, as Caesar, or subordinate emperor, and at the same time adopted him as his son: he had no son of his own, a fact which simplified his problems. About six months later . . . he promoted Maximian to the rank of Augustus: henceforth Diocletian and Maximian were constitutionally co-ordinate, but Diocletian remained the senior Augustus, and in fact completely dominated his colleague. . . .

Seven years later Diocletian decided that two Augusti were not enough to control all the armies and deal with all the perils which beset the empire. On 1st March, 293, two Caesars were created, one to serve under Diocletian in the East, the other under Maximian in the West [forming a four-man partnership known as the Tetrarachy]. For the former post Diocletian selected Galerius Maximianus, the son of a Dacian father and a barbarian mother, an energetic but brutal soldier, and married him to his daughter Valeria. As the other Caesar, Maximian chose Flavius Constantius, marrying him to his stepdaughter, Theodora. . . . Constantine [Constantius's son and the future supporter of Christianity] . . . was sent off to the court of Diocletian, doubtless as a hostage for his father's good behaviour. . . .

POLITICAL AND MILITARY REFORMS

During the years that Constantine was at court, Diocletian was steadily remodelling administration, defence and finance. On the administrative side the chief weakness lay in the lowest stratum of the structure, where it was becoming more and more difficult to goad town councils into performing their functions. Diocletian did much to keep the councils up to strength, and it was probably in his reign that the doctrine became established that sons of decurions were legally bound to enter the council. Even so, every election of a magistrate or collector on the council produced a crop of appeals to the provincial governor, and arrears in requisitions had frequently to be exacted by his officials. In the larger provinces it became impossible for the governor to keep pace with the work.

To remedy this situation Diocletian reduced provinces to a manageable and more or less uniform size—some huge old provinces were subdivided into four or five—and carved Italy, hitherto officially under the senate, into provinces. In order to relieve the central government from the increasing burden of routine administrative work, he created a new unit, the diocese, between the province and the centre. The diocese was controlled by a deputy Praetorian prefect, responsible for the same services as his chief, and also had an accountant, and an intendant of imperial domains, who answered to the Masters for their respective departments. . . .

In military affairs Diocletian's chief work was to raise the strength of the army. In view of the greatly increased pressure of the barbarians this was essential if the frontier was to be held. . . . A study of the later army list of the Roman empire suggests that Diocletian may have heavily doubled [the size of the army]. . . . It is significant that voluntary recruitment ceased to provide a sufficient intake. Diocletian had to make the military service of the sons of veterans compulsory, and to introduce a new system of conscription from the rural population of all the provinces. To ensure regular supplies of arms and uniforms, Diocletian established in numerous towns armament factories and wool and linen-weaving establishments, the former manned by soldier artificers, the latter by slaves and convicts. . . .

ECONOMIC REFORMS

Diocletian attempted a reform of the currency, issuing gold coins weighing 1/60 lb. and genuine silver coins of 1/96 lb. But he continued to mint silverwashed copper and plain copper pieces in great profusion, and the inflationary movement gathered momentum. His famous edict of 301, in which he fixed prices and wages in the minutest detail, though enforced at first with ruthless severity, merely drove goods off the market, and had to be allowed to lapse. But in finance in the wider sense Diocletian carried out a reform of capital importance. The requisitions in kind *(indictiones),* which now formed the bulk of the revenue, had hitherto been levied in haphazard fashion, when and where required, and their incidence had been most inequitable. Diocletian consolidated them into one annual indiction, which was levied at a more or less uniform rate throughout the empire. His first step was to hold a series of regional censuses, which were not actually completed until after his abdication. In these the land was surveyed and assessed in units of equal taxable value. In Syria, where Diocletian himself was in charge, the assessment was very complex and accurate, the land being valued at different rates according to its agricultural use—pasture, arable, vineyard, olives—and to its quality in each category: the unit of assessment, the *iugum,* consisted of varying quantities of land which came to the same total value. . . .

Henceforth it was possible, by a simple multiplication sum, to calculate the yield from a given city, province or diocese, or from the whole empire, of a levy at any given rate on every . . . *iugum* it contained, and the Roman empire for the first time could have an annual budget, the indiction, calculated to meet estimated expenditure. The system was applied to levies of all kinds, not only money and food crops, but uniforms, horses for the cavalry, beasts for the postal system and recruits for the army. . . .

THE PRICE OF ORDER

Diocletian was gradually bringing order out of chaos, but the price was heavy. . . . "He made three partners of his realm, dividing the empire into four parts and multiplying the armies, while each of them aspired to have a far larger number of troops than earlier emperors had had when they governed alone. The numbers of those who received began to be larger than the number of those who gave, so much so that the resources of the peasants were exhausted by outrageous levies. The fields were deserted and arable turned into forest.

[He] could find no way to secure the defence of the frontiers save to increase the number of troops, and his efforts to make the creaking wheels of the administration revolve only resulted in more and more officials. There were coming to be more idle mouths than the primitive economic system of the Roman empire could feed. It is hard to remember that, despite its great achievements in law and administration, the splendid architecture of its cities and the luxurious standard of living of its aristocracy, the Roman empire was, in its methods of production, in some ways more primitive than the early Middle Ages. Agriculture followed a wasteful two-field system of alternate crop and fallow. Yam was spun by hand with a spindle, and textiles laboriously woven on clumsy hand looms. Even corn was ground in hand querns or at best in mills turned by oxen: windmills had not been invented and watermills were still rare. In these circumstances the feeding and clothing of an individual demanded a vast expenditure of human labour, and the maintenance of any substantial number of economically unproductive persons laid a heavy burden on the rest.

The result of the government's increasing demands for supplies was that the owners of land of marginal quality found that the levies exceeded the rent that they could extract from their tenants and abandoned their estates, and that the peasants who cultivated poor land had so little left after paying their taxes if they were freeholders, or the increased rents if they were tenants, that they could not feed their children. The population could not expand to meet the increased demand for soldiers and for workmen in the mills which supplied them. A chronic shortage of manpower ensued, and to safeguard essential industries, the government froze the labour employed in them, compelling the workers to remain in their jobs and their children after them. It is difficult to trace the stages whereby labour in all industries essential to the state was gradually frozen, but in the key industry, agriculture, the peasant was probably already tied to his plot by Diocletian, by the ruling that where he was entered on the census registers there he must stay.

Diocletian was by tradition and temperament a conservative. Like all the emperors of the later third century, he claimed to be the restorer of the Roman world: he was not trying to shape a new order of society, but to press the rebellious forces of the age back into the old moulds.

THE BARBARIANS OF NORTHERN EUROPE

ARTHER FERRILL

The vast majority of modern historians agree that the single most important factor in Rome's relatively rapid decline and fall in its last century was a seemingly relentless series of large-scale incursions of Germanic and other tribes into Rome's northern border provinces. At the same time, the Roman army was undergoing its own decline in discipline and effectiveness, and was therefore unable, in the long run, to repel these invasions. The crucial turning point was the defeat of a large Roman army by the Visigoths in 378 at Adrianople (in Thrace), a disaster that initiated the Empire's final downward spiral. Appropriately, therefore, this brief overview of the breakdown and character of the barbarian tribes, by noted ancient military historian Arther Ferrill, begins three years before Adrianople, in 375. In that year, the emperor Valentinian I, who was a stronger military leader than his immediate successors, died of a stroke after a fit of temper during negotiations with some insolent barbarian ambassadors. After describing the various barbarian tribes, Ferrill provides some added details about one group, the Visigoths, and concludes with the background events of the great battle in which they would prove the victors.

E arlier, in 367, Valentinian's eight-year-old son Gratian had been proclaimed co-emperor, and he had served, insofar as a mere youth served at all, with his father in the West. Upon the death of Valentinian, Gratian was sixteen, and he assumed the reins of government from Trier. In the meantime, however, troops on the Danube had proclaimed as western co-emperor the four-year-old Valentinian II, and to guarantee the support of the Danubian legions Gratian acquiesced in the choice of the child, his half-brother.

Tragically for the Empire its finest emperor-soldier since Diocletian and Constantine died on the brink of one of the greatest military crises in Roman history, perhaps in the history of the western world. In the very next year (376) began the chain of events that led to the battle of Adrianople and the triumph of Gothic over Roman arms. Whether events would have been different had Valentinian I restrained his anger in 375, no one today can say with certainty, but most historians agree that it was by far the weaker of the two imperial brothers—Valens—who survived to face the Visigoths.

The Various Subdivisions of Germans

As background to the story of Adrianople and to the barbarian invasions that followed, we must briefly examine the Germanic nations that threatened Rome's northern frontiers. Except for the Alans and the Huns, who came from Central Asia, Rome's barbarian enemies were 'Germanic', but the word covers a wide range of people north of the Rhine-Danube line from the North Sea to the Black Sea. They were by no means monolithic in culture, and those living on the North Sea coast—the Saxons, Jutes and Danes—spoke languages completely unintelligible to the Goths on the Danube, probably even to one another. Naturally, the economic structures of the western coastal tribes differed drastically from those of central, forested Germany and from the plains tribes north of the Danube and the Black Sea.

Although the linguistic classifications are controversial, scholars frequently divide the fourth- and fifth-century Germans into three broad groups—the North, East and West Germanic dialects, corresponding geographically roughly to the three different regions mentioned above. In the North Germanic group one finds Old Norse and its derivatives. The East Germanic dialects include Gothic, and the languages of the Burgundians and Vandals appear to have been closely related. Angles, Saxons, Franks, Alamanni and Frisians spoke West-German dialects. If it was rare for Germanic tribes to know one another's languages, it is nevertheless likely that Vandals spoke almost the same language as the Goths.

Romans had had some contact with the Germans at least as early as the second century BC, and the works of Caesar and Tacitus from a later period show an increasing Roman awareness of Germanic culture. In the third century AD . . . there were important Germanic invasions of the Empire, but the invaders had ultimately been beaten back or assimilated. In the last half of the fourth century, before the coming of the Huns, the Ostrogoths (literally, East Goths) inhabited the area of southern Russia north of the Black Sea. Possibly they had come originally from Scandinavia, as the sixth-century Gothic historian, Jordanes, claimed, but that is not certain. Next to them, north of the Danube in the former Roman province of Dacia, lived the Visigoths (the West Goths). The Goths had subjugated other tribes, such as the Skiri, a tribe that later produced Odovacer, who toppled the last Roman emperor in the West in 476. The Goths generally lived a rough, village, semi-agricultural existence in which hunting and food gathering were also important. The material level of their civilization was not high, and they had been economically and politically less influenced by their civilized Roman neighbours than is sometimes assumed.

THE CHRISTIAN BARBARIANS

In religion, however, Barbarian and Roman came to share a common faith—Christianity—though the Germans were Arian heretics. Arius (died 336), a priest in Alexandria, had preached the doctrine that Christ, as the Son of God, was not truly God. Though the details of his theology remain uncertain, undoubtedly Arius emphasized the human nature of Christ and the importance of Christ's sacrifice for man. In any event, he attracted a large following in the Eastern Roman Empire, and in AD 325 the Emperor Constantine assembled the bishops in the first ecumenical council at Nicaea where they rejected Arianism and affirmed in the Nicene Creed that Christ was truly God. Arians were excommunicated, anathematized [branded as religious and social outcasts], and banished from the Roman Empire.

One of the Arians, Ulfilas (c. 311–83), converted the Goths and translated the scriptures into Gothic, thereby turning the barbarian tongue into a literary language. The conversion of the Goths to Christianity before the invasions, albeit in an heretical Arian form, was an act of great significance. From the Goths Christianity spread to other barbarian tribes such as Vandals, but not to all of them. The Angles and Saxons, for example, remained Germanic heathens until long after their invasion of the British Isles. Still, many of the barbarians who invaded the Roman Empire were Christians, and the shared religion ameliorated [lessened the negative effects of], to a certain extent, the impact of Rome's fall.

To continue the survey of Rome's northern frontier, Vandals, Burgundians, Suebi and Alamanni threatened the Upper Danube and the Upper Rhine while Franks were on the lower Rhine, and

Angles, Saxons, Jutes, and Danes faced Britain across the North Sea. This then was the 'line-up' of barbarian nations as the first act in the age of invasions began, and the Romans prepared to face the Visigoths at Adrianople.

THE VISIGOTHS EXPLOITED

Although the story of the battle is relatively well known, some elements of it are controversial, and in any event it bears retelling. The fearsome Huns from the Asiatic steppes of South Russia, riding on their fat-headed, peculiar-looking plains horses, swept down on the Ostrogoths living north and east of the Black Sea. In one of the few genuine examples of 'billiard-ball history' this set in motion a chain reaction as the Ostrogoths fled in panic westward against the Visigoths who were driven hard against Rome's Danubian frontier. Two Visigothic chieftains, Fritigern and Alavivus, sought Valens' permission to settle in the Empire, and on condition that the Visigoths give up their arms the emperor agreed to let them cross the border. Valens hoped that they would farm deserted land in Thrace and expected to recruit heavily from them for the imperial army.

Late in 376 the river crossing began. The Visigoths, perhaps 200,000 strong, were starving, and insensitive, grasping Roman officials exploited them unmercifully. To avoid starvation the Visigoths traded their children into Roman slavery for dog's meat at the rate of one child per dog. There were other stories of rape and robbery by Roman officials, one of the sorriest chapters

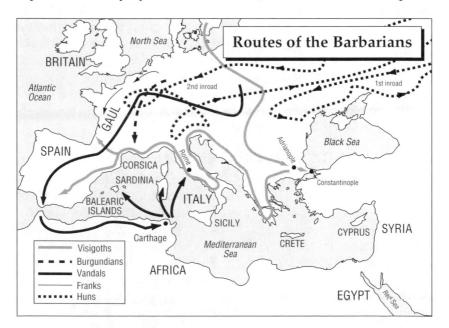

in the long history of governmental exploitation. Possibly the truth is less dramatic than the legend. Surely some Romans tried to alleviate the distress of the Goths, but clearly the crossing of the Danube was badly mishandled.

In the meantime some Ostrogoths, who did not have permission to cross the river, did so anyway, and to add to the confusion the Roman Field Marshal of Thrace, Lupicinus, killed some of the followers of Fritigern and Alavivus during a truce with the Visigoths. This was more than the barbarians could bear, and they began to ravage the area and then to gather in the general vicinity of Adrianople where they had been resisted and denied food by the local authorities. Vainly the Goths tried to storm the walls of the city until Fritigern returned them to the plunder of the countryside, reminding them that he kept peace with walls, a reasonable policy for a warrior with no capacity for siege warfare.

In Antioch the Emperor Valens decided that the problem required his imperial presence, and after sending up troops to Constantinople, he arrived there himself on 30 May 378. Earlier Gratian had despatched troops from the West, and in 376 and 377 the Romans had conducted a desultory campaign in which they won and lost some battles and skirmishes but generally succeeded in their strategy of sealing the Visigoths into Thrace, thereby protecting Moesia and Macedonia.

The Goths are sometimes assumed to have been a mounted, nomadic people, but in fact they are unlikely to have had many horses. That there were some is certain, but Ammianus' account of the skirmishes leading up to the battle of Adrianople suggests that for the most part Gothic warriors fought on foot as infantry. To the extent that Fritigern deployed cavalry, it was a small force used mainly for scouting, skirmishing, and, presumably, pursuit. The old view that Adrianople was a 'medieval' battle involving large numbers of cavalry is simply not sound. Indeed, one recent authority has said categorically that the Gothic victory was essentially infantry over infantry.

THE EMPEROR'S OVERCONFIDENCE

Valens moved out of Constantinople in the summer of 378 and headed for Adrianople where he stopped to wait for the arrival of the slow-moving Western emperor, Gratian. There were reports that only ten thousand Goths were under arms, and though Gratian was at last nearby, Valens decided to attack immediately and win all the glory for himself. Thus it came to pass that one of the world's most decisive battles was fought by a Roman emperor driven by jealousy into a hasty and precipitous assault. Our sources agree that the day, 9 August 378, was a 'scorcher', and from the descriptions it sounds as if the temperatures must have been near 100°F, as they often are in August in the same vicinity to this day.

In this terrible heat Valens led his army of nearly sixty thousand in line of column over uneven terrain with cavalry in front and rear. Around two in the afternoon, before the Roman forces had eaten their midday meal, they were as surprised as the Goths when the two armies began to come together. The Roman army had not yet deployed from line of column into line of battle. Such a failure of military intelligence on the part of the Roman army is nearly incredible, but it seems to have occurred, perhaps through overconfidence on Valens' part.

The Visigoths had formed their wagons into the traditional circular laager (a 'perfect' circle according to Ammianus), and Fritigern, caught equally by surprise, sent out a call for his mounted Ostrogothic and Alan allies who were probably foraging nearby. Both sides began negotiations to gain time for the proper deployment of their forces, but it was not long before fighting began.

DISASTER AT ADRIANOPLE: ROME'S DOWNWARD SPIRAL BEGINS

AMMIANUS MARCELLINUS

The Roman defeat at Adrianople (in Thrace) in 378 was a catastrophe for the Empire. As many as 40,000 Roman troops, along with their commander, the eastern emperor Valens, met their doom at the hands of the Visigoths; and afterward, Rome's military decline proceeded at an accelerating pace. This vivid description of the battle is by Ammianus Marcellinus (ca. A.D. 330–395). The finest Latin historian produced in the Later Empire, he was born a Greek at Antioch and served in the army in Gaul and Persia under the future emperor Julian. In 378, Ammianus settled down in Rome and began writing his now famous history, which covered events from 96 to 378 (but which survives only in sections). His honesty, balanced judgment, and elegant writing style rank him with the likes of the great first-century A.D. Roman Tacitus, to whom he is often compared. Following is a major portion of Ammianus's moving account of Rome's darkest day.

W hen dawn came on the day marked in the calendar as 9 August, the army was put in rapid motion. All its impedimenta and baggage were left near the walls of Adrianople under an adequate guard, and the praetorian prefect and members of the consistory remained inside the town with the treasure-chests and the imperial insignia. After a march of eight miles over rough country under a burning mid-day sun our troops came within sight of the enemy's waggons, which, as our scouts had reported, were drawn up in a regular circle. While the enemy in their usual way were raising a wild and doleful yell, the Roman generals marshalled their line of battle. The cavalry on the right wing were furthest advanced, and the greater part of the infantry were some way to their rear. But the cavalry of our left wing were still straggling along the road, making what speed they could but under serious difficulties. . . .

[Just when it appeared that a truce might be arranged] the archers and Scutarii [on the Roman side] commanded by Cassio and by the Iberian Bacurius impulsively launched a hot attack and engaged the enemy. Their retreat was as cowardly as their advance had been rash, a most inauspicious start to the battle. This untimely proceeding . . . brought on an attack by the Gothic cavalry under Alatheus and Saphrax, who had now arrived supported by a party of Alans. They shot forward *like a bolt from on high* and routed with great slaughter all that they could come to grips with in their wild career.

Amid the clashing of arms and weapons on every side, while Bellona [Roman goddess of war], raging with more than her usual fury, was sounding the death-knell of the Roman cause, our retreating troops rallied with shouts of mutual encouragement. But, as the fighting spread like fire and numbers of them were transfixed by arrows and whirling javelins, they lost heart. Then the opposing lines came into collision like ships of war and pushed each other to and fro, heaving under the reciprocal motion like the waves of the sea. Our left wing penetrated as far as the very waggons, and would have gone further if it had received any support, but it was abandoned by the rest of the cavalry, and under pressure of numbers gave way and collapsed like a broken dyke. This left the infantry unprotected and so closely huddled together that a man could hardly wield his sword or draw back his arm once he had stretched it out. Dust rose in such clouds as to hide the sky, which rang with frightful shouts. In consequence it was impossible to see the enemy's missiles in flight and dodge them; all found their mark and dealt death on every side. The barbarians poured on in huge columns, trampling down horse and man and crushing our ranks so as to make an orderly retreat impossible. Our men were too close-packed to have any hope of escape; so they resolved to die like heroes, faced the enemy's swords, and struck back at their assailants. On both sides helmets and breast-plates were split in pieces by blows from the battle-axe. You might see a lion-hearted savage, who had been hamstrung or had lost his right hand or been wounded in the side, grinding his clenched teeth and casting defiant glances around in the very throes of death. In this mutual slaughter so many were laid low that the field was covered with the bodies of the slain, while the groans of the dying and severely wounded filled all who heard them with abject fear.

In this scene of total confusion the infantry, worn out by toil and danger, had no strength or sense left to form a plan. Most had had their spears shattered in the constant collisions, so they made do with their drawn swords and plunged into the dense masses of the foe, regardless of their lives and aware that there was no hope of escape. The ground was so drenched with blood that they slipped and fell, but they strained every nerve to sell their lives dearly, and faced their opponents with such resolution that some perished at the hands of their own comrades. In the end, when the whole field was one dark pool of blood and they could see nothing but heaps of slain wherever they turned their eyes, they trampled without scruple on the lifeless corpses.

The sun, which was high in the sky (it was moving into the house of the Virgin after traversing Leo), scorched the Romans, who were weak from hunger, parched with thirst, and weighed down by the burden of their armour. Finally, our line gave way under the overpowering pressure of the barbarians, and as a last resort our men took to their heels. . . .

The barbarians' eyes flashed fire as they pursued their dazed foe, whose blood ran cold with terror. Some fell without knowing who struck them, some were crushed by sheer weight of numbers, and some were killed by their own comrades. They could neither gain ground by resistance nor obtain mercy by giving way. Besides, many lay blocking the way half dead, unable to endure the agony of their wounds, and the carcasses of slaughtered horses covered the ground in heaps. At last a moonless night brought an end to these irreparable losses, which cost Rome so dear.

Soon after nightfall, so it was supposed, the emperor was mortally wounded by an arrow and died immediately. No one admitted that he had seen him or been near him, and it was presumed that he fell among common soldiers, but his body was never found. A few of the enemy were hanging about the field for some time to strip the dead, so that none of the fugitives or local people dared to approach. . . . According to another account, Valens did not expire on the spot, but was taken with a few of his guards and some eunuchs to a farmhouse nearby, which had a fortified second storey. While he was receiving such rude treatment as was available he was surrounded by the enemy, though they did not know who he was. But he was spared the shame of being taken prisoner. His pursuers tried to break down the doors, which were bolted, but came under arrow-fire from the overhanging part of the building. In order not to let this delay rob them of their chance of spoil, they piled up bundles of straw . . . set fire to them, and burned the house with all who were in it. One of the guards escaped through a window and was taken prisoner. He told them what they had done, which greatly vexed them, because they had lost the glory of taking the ruler of Rome alive. . . .

It is certain that hardly a third of our army escaped. *No battle in our history except Cannae was such a massacre,* though more than once the Romans have been the playthings of fortune and suffered temporary reverses, and many disastrous struggles are recorded with grief in the legendary sagas of Greece.

DECLINE OF THE ROMAN ARMY

PAT SOUTHERN AND KAREN R. DIXON

One of the main contributing factors to the disintegration of the western Roman Empire was the steady deterioration of its army in its last century. Simply put, the military was eventually inadequate to the task of defending the realm, which as a result quite literally fell apart. Scholars Pat Southern and Karen R. Dixon, both of the University of Newcastle upon Tyne, provide this informative analysis of the imperial army's decline. Citing various ancient writers, including Ammianus (fourth-century Latin), Vegetius (late fourth-century Latin), Zosimus (early fifth-century Greek), and Eugippus (fifth-century Latin), they examine several causes for this decline. Among these are the steady barbarization of the military ranks and an increasing lack of resources to pay and equip the soldiers. Perhaps most telling of all, after the huge battles fought at Adrianople (in Thrace, in 378) and the Frigidus River (northeast of Italy, in 394), most of the soldiers in subsequent generations were poorly trained.

I t look three years of fighting before Theodosius brought the Goths to terms in 382, when he allowed them to settle in Thrace. The treaty which he made with them has not always been viewed in a favourable light, either by his contemporaries or by modern scholars, who censure Theodosius for his leniency towards the Goths. They were settled on the very lands they had ravaged, unsupervised by the Romans and permitted to live according to their own laws. . . .

The text of Theodosius's treaty (*foedus*) of 382 is unknown, and therefore the terms of military service exacted from the Goths also remain unknown. The exploitation of barbarian manpower was not unusual, but it seems that the terms laid down in the negotiations of 382 departed from normal practice. Before it can be stated how these terms differed, it is necessary to enquire what constituted normal practice. Usually, after the conclusion of a war, a treaty was made stipulating that the enemy should contribute a number of men to the Roman army, either *en masse* and annually thereafter, or by some similar arrangement. It was at one and the same time a means of removing potentially dangerous young men, of increasing the size of the army, and of gradually Romanizing the barbarians. The soldiers raised in this way could be distributed among existing units, thus diluting their barbarian influence, or they could be kept together, organized and trained as a regular unit, and sent to distant provinces to reduce the likelihood of their deserting to the enemy if rebellion should break out. This sort of treaty was made with tribes who remained outside the Empire and was a time-honoured method of raising men for the army.

Wholesale immigration of tribesmen into the Empire was a matter demanding a different response. Sometimes defeated tribesmen *(dediticii)* were settled inside the Empire in fairly large numbers. Other groups of barbarians entered voluntarily. Tribes had clamoured to be allowed to cross the frontiers since the Empire came into being, and had sometimes been admitted and given lands. . . . Under Augustus 50,000 Getae settled in Moesia; Tiberius allowed 40,000 Germans into Gaul and the Rhineland; Marcus Aurelius received 3000 Naristae into the Empire; Probus admitted 100,000 Bastarnae and Constantine settled 300,000 Sarmatians on lands in Thrace, Italy and Macedonia. The numbers are . . . suspect, but they serve to illustrate the magnitude of the problem. In the late Empire the numbers of barbarians seeking admission dramatically increased. . . .

WHO WERE THE BARBARIAN "FEDERATES"?

The employment of barbarians from beyond the frontiers, by means of an alliance with a tribal leader or a client king, had always been accepted as a method of increasing the size of the army for campaigns. Such troops fought under their own leaders, attached to the army for the duration of the war, then on the conclusion of peace they would return to their homes. On occasion, they might be recruited into the regular army to fill gaps in the ranks, or sometimes whole bands of them might be transformed into regular units, but most often they remained outside the army. Their chiefs would normally be strongly supported by Rome, sometimes subsidized, and kept in power in order to ensure that the frontiers were protected at least in part by tribes who had every reason to be on friendly terms with the Empire.

The term *foederati* ["federates"] is not an easily definable one, since it covers several different kinds of troops. In the late Empire, it denoted troops raised from barbarians settled within the frontiers as well as those raised from outside. The practice of settling barbarians by treaty arrangement on lands inside the Empire became more common from the end of the third century, when many frontier areas were devastated. Such settlements were widespread and frequent. . . .

Foederati could also describe conglomerations of men, not all of the same ethnic background, who had gathered around a leader. The bands of Goths following Alaric probably contained an ethnic mixture of different tribesmen. There can be no direct link with the original Goths who crossed the frontier in 376. . . . [Was] Alaric leading a nation or something more properly described as an army[?]

The distinctions between these *foederati* and the *bucellarii* are probably blurred. *Bucellarii* were private armies composed of retainers of a powerful . . . general like Stilicho. . . . The men who joined these private armies perhaps did so because their particular leader could guarantee them long-term employment.

Whatever their origin, the *foederati* attached to the army would be answerable to the Roman high command, but like the earlier *foederati*, their immediate commanders would be their own leaders. They were not part of the regular army.

By the sixth century, the *foederati* in the eastern army were quite different. These were regular troops, paid, trained and disciplined, like the rest of the army. The change presumably came about at some unknown date in the fifth century. These units were recruited exclusively from barbarians at first, then in the sixth century Romans were also admitted. . . .

In addition to individual recruitment of tribesmen to fill gaps in existing units, enrollment of large groups of barbarians in the army had been common practice since the early Empire. Marcus Aurelius used Germans to fight against Germans. . . . Claudius II enrolled Goths after defeating them. . . . Constantine's army at the battle of the Milvian Bridge was full of Germans, Gauls and Britons. . . .

The barbarian soldiers were, with few exceptions, loyal to Rome, and served her well. There was little sense of nationality among the Germanic tribes, and no unity, so that the dichotomy which modern readers might read into the labels German and Roman did not necessarily exist for the men who signed up for 20–25 years' service. Although the numbers of barbarians in the army may have seemed excessive, the cultural and moral superiority of the Romans ensured their subjection. The settlements of tribesmen were supervised by Roman officials, usually called *praepositi*, and the barbarians in the army were under the command of Roman, or thoroughly Romanized, officers. The Germans who attained positions of authority in the army and in civilian office were more Roman than the Romans, attuned to Roman civilization and ways of life.

EASTERN AND WESTERN RESPONSES TO BARBARIZATION

The process of barbarization of the army was already well under way by the time Theodosius made his treaty with the Goths, and the settlement of groups of tribesmen on Roman soil was nothing new. The crucial factor in the settlement of 382 concerns the status of the Goths, and their obligation to provide soldiers. Whereas other tribes inside the Empire were subject to Roman supervision and to Roman law, the Goths were governed by their own chiefs, and were therefore more or less autonomous. . . .

In the eastern Empire, the Gothic threat was dealt with summarily on more than one occasion. Immediately after the Roman defeat at Adrianople, sealed orders went out to the commanders of the eastern troops to summon the Goths in the army to a pay parade, and then to put them all to death. . . . Further purges of the army were carried out in 386 when another group of Goths were massacred at Tomi, and there was more slaughter after the revolt of Gainas in Constantinople. . . . Thereafter, in an attempt to reduce the proportions of Germanic tribesmen in the army, the eastern army began to recruit from the indigenous population, especially from the hardy tribes of Isaurians. It did not prove possible to maintain the army without recruitment of barbarians, but the numbers were kept small and more easily controlled. As mentioned above, by the sixth century troops with the title *foederati*, raised from barbarian tribes, were part of the regular army, subject to the same discipline as all other troops.

For some time the eastern army was weakened, since by purging it of the Goths, some of the best fighting elements had been removed. Fortunately, the Huns were temporarily defeated, albeit with great difficulty, in 408–9, and Theodosius also managed to resolve the Persian question. There were only two wars on the eastern frontier in 421–2 and 441–2, so that the government was able to concentrate on the defence of the Danube. . . . Territorially, the east was not so difficult to defend as the west. This gave the eastern emperors an opportunity to build up a dual system of defence, utilizing both the army and clever diplomacy . . . which the Byzantines developed into an art.

The western army did not find it so easy to meet the barbarian challenge by purging itself of undesirable elements. When an attempt was made to do so, the timing was faulty. On 13 August 408, the Romans in Honorius' court massacred the Germans among the Emperor's followers, and finally sacrificed Stilicho, to their immediate disadvantage. However dubious his motives may have been, Stilicho was a capable general, and the soldiers would follow him. By removing him and also weakening the army at the wrong time, the western Roman court found itself almost defenceless. The respite granted to the east did not occur in the west, and there were fewer opportunities for indigenous recruitment. When Alaric sacked Rome, the necessity of coming to terms with him meant that the anti-German elements of the court had to be silenced. . . . The western army never ceased to recruit barbarians, and never succeeded in removing them as the east had done. All that could be achieved was to preclude barbarians from the high commands. On the other hand, and perhaps more significantly, although the Western Empire accommodated the barbarians, it failed to assimilate them properly, and with this vacillating state of affairs it sealed its own doom.

A SHORTAGE OF TRAINED MANPOWER

Barbarization alone does not wholly explain the changes in the army which were detectable to fourth- and fifth-century authors, but the concomitant factors which resulted from the process were harmful. After Adrianople, and then the battle of the Frigidus, there was an urgent need to rebuild the armies of east and west. The two armies did not completely disappear, but when they were eventually reconstructed, it could be said that most of the links with the Roman armies of the past had been severed. It was not necessarily a question of shortage of manpower; it was a shortage of trained manpower, which is vastly different. This is one of the reasons why the apparent recovery after the disastrous battles of the late fourth century was not as effective as, for example, the seemingly effortless recovery after the loss of two expeditionary armies in the Dacian campaigns under Domitian [in the first century]. Military disasters had occurred in the early Empire without leading to collapse, and ravaged lands had been restored, but that was before the decades of exhaustion that the late Empire had experienced without respite.

The sources are deceptive. The poems of Ausonius and the letters of Sidonius attest to a reasonably settled life in late Roman Gaul, given that the circumstances were not ideal. But the recovery of Gaul after the ravages of the Frankish and Alamannic raids was probably far from complete. Similarly neither east nor west fully recovered from the effects of Adrianople and the Frigidus. The army had diminished in public esteem, as indicated by the marked reluctance of most men to serve in it. . . . This reluctance among Romans meant that the soldiers were mostly barbarians on both sides whenever so-called Roman armies clashed in civil wars, but Roman tradition, discipline, training and fighting methods had not yet been entirely extinguished in the early 370s. . . . At the end of the fourth century this changed, and the process of decline already apparent in the army took a firmer hold, making it impossible to reverse the trends towards complete barbarization. . . .

The law codes bear witness to the measures to which Theodosius was driven to refurbish troops from 378 onwards. Many of the laws were designed to unmask those who sought to avoid military service by one method or another. In 380, there was an effort to enforce the rule that sons of veterans must enlist. . . . Then there were penalties for those who offered slaves for the army instead of suitable recruits . . . and stronger measures against men who mutilated themselves to avoid service. In order to discourage the practice, it was declared that two mutilated men would be taken in place of one whole one. . . . By 406, all scruples about the unsuitability of slaves had been abandoned in the west, and the emperors were calling them to arms. . . .

It may have seemed that the shortages of manpower could be solved instantly by filling the ranks of the army with barbarians and by negotiating with various allied chieftains for temporary contingents of tribesmen to fight in specific wars. But the losses of Adrianople were not to be counted simply in numerical terms of manpower. What had been lost were experienced men, disciplined and trained to Roman standards. If, in the past, it had always proved possible to rebuild the army systematically and methodically, the situation now was too precarious and the danger too widespread to allow for anything other than rapid, piecemeal responses, which differed in each half of the Empire.

The Eastern Empire conducted its successive purges and endangered itself by reducing the size of its army, but it survived by a combination of good fortune and good management, and remained Roman by tradition even if it became Oriental in fact. Its territory was more homogeneous and easier to defend, and even though it was bordered by the Persian Empire, the threat posed by this sophisticated enemy did not cause the disintegration that the barbarians caused in the west.

The Western emperors never appointed a German *magister militum* after the removal of Stilicho. With the exception of Ulfilas and Sigisvult, who were Goths, after 408 all the *magistri* were Romans. But if the high-ranking officers were no longer barbarians, the troops were still recruited from tribesmen. The West retained an effective army under Aetius, but its lack of Romanization became more and more apparent. . . . Barbarians were not naturally disciplined. . . . It was unusual that the barbarians stayed at their posts, did not pillage and loot, and did not cause confusion. Ammianus had no very elevated opinion of barbarians; in scattered references . . . he describes them as inhuman and vicious, using all the stock epithets. With more insight from a military point of view, he says they are discouraged by the slightest set-back, disorganized, incapable of following any coherent plan, and unable to foresee a train of events. In other words, they were thoroughly unmilitary from a Roman point of view.

Zosimus has another point to add, which may concern only one army at one particular time, but is none the less deeply significant. He says that no record was kept of those enrolled in the army, and the deserters whom Theodosius had reinstated could go home whenever they felt like it, substituting other men in their places. Granted that modern armies are much more highly trained in various special tasks than was the Roman army, chaos would have resulted if, for instance, a tank driver in Normandy in 1944 had decided to go home, substituting the nearest garage mechanic to do his job for a few months. Such a lack of central control and lapse of disciplinary standards was nothing less than disastrous. Combined with the lack of a cadre of trained men to hand down tradition, and the lack of active training to remedy this defect, the downward spiral accelerated alarmingly and could not be stopped. . . .

In these circumstances the process of training and of Romanization could not operate. Lack of training would cause irreparable harm in a very short time. . . . With the disappearance of discipline and training, Roman combat methods also disappeared as a matter of course. It can be no accident that Vegetius, in the very first chapter after his preface and fulsome dedication, perhaps to Theodosius I, points out that it was discipline and training which enabled the Roman armies to conquer all peoples. He goes on to say that 'a small force, highly trained, is more likely to win battles than a raw and untrained horde'. . . .

Training is eased when there is a cadre of experienced soldiers round which to build up each unit, so that the original ethnic background of the new recruits is hardly of any significance. Romanization of tribesmen in the army is similarly eased when Roman culture is in the ascendancy. Neither of these elements applied after the battles of Adrianople and the Frigidus, and the situation was compounded by other serious factors. . . . At a time when both dynamic commanders and lots of money were needed, the Roman Empire had neither. If the army could have been Romanized and trained as it had been in the early Empire, the Western Empire may have survived longer. But the procedure for training an army and for Romanization of the barbarians required a commodity which was never granted to the west: time.

THE ARMY EVENTUALLY CEASES TO EXIST

The break up when it came proceeded rapidly, from the first decade of the fifth century. The inability of the western government to defend the Empire arose from lack of centralized administrative control and impoverishment of resources. Civil wars between usurpers accelerated the decline. Constantius II withdrew troops from Britain in 407; three years later Honorius decided against trying to regain the island. The army was withdrawn from Spain in 411. The Western Empire shrank to a shadow of its former self. Italy was naturally the first priority, the second was Gaul, virtually the only other province that was defended. Even the Rhine frontier was allowed to be overrun. The *magister militum* Aetius, though a Roman, had been a hostage among the Huns, and increasingly used these ties of loyalty to recruit Huns for his army, with which he successfully fought Burgundians and Visigoths in Gaul. Appeals for help from the other provinces were ignored. . . .

The exact date when the Western Empire ceased to exist is hard to ascertain. There are successive stages, all equally qualified for the honour, but even after the widely accepted date of 476, Roman forms of law and military institutions were not completely dead, surviving as they did in the barbarian kingdoms. The date at which the western Roman army ceased to exist is no less problematic. There was no formal disbandment centrally directed from Ravenna or Rome. It could be said that even the soldiers serving in the army were not really sure of their demise as an institution. A famous passage from Eugippius' *Vita Sancti Severini* best illustrates this. He describes how, while the Romans were in power, soldiers were maintained in many towns at public expense to guard the frontier. But when this custom ceased, several whole units of soldiers disappeared. The men at Batava (modern Passau, at the junction of the rivers Inn and Danube) remained at their posts, and sent a delegation to Italy to find out why they had received no pay. Some days later, their bodies floated down-river and came to rest on the banks, silent testimony to the end of Rome's ability to keep her Empire intact and to defend her frontiers.

THE LAST ROMAN EMPERORS IN THE WEST

J.B. BURY

After the emperor Valentinian III was murdered in 455 in retaliation for his own killing of the popular general Aëtius, and later that year the Vandals sacked Rome, western Rome's political deterioration accelerated. Another general, Ricimer, set up a number of what were in effect puppet emperors who all recognized that he held the real power. Then, after he died, still another powerful military man, the German-born Odovacar (or Odoacer), rose to prominence; and it was he who deposed the last western Roman emperor, Romulus Augustulus. As the late distinguished classical historian J.B. Bury explains here, technically speaking another imperial claimant, Julius Nepos, was still recognized as the legitimate western ruler by the eastern Roman court. But Nepos died before he could press his claim. Bury also points out that at the time no one viewed these events as catastrophic or fancied that the western Empire had collapsed; for Odovacar and other Germans continued to administer a very much intact Rome. The idea of the year 476 being a great historical turning point did not become fashionable until much later.

T he forty years succeeding the collapse of the Empire of the Huns, from about 454 to 493, were marked by the gradual advance of the German power in Gaul and Spain; while before 493 Italy itself had become a German kingdom. Now the steady increase of the barbarian power, and the steady decline of

From *Invasion of Europe by the Barbarians*, by J.B. Bury (New York: Norton, 1967). Reprinted by permission of Palgrave.

the imperial power, in the west during these years was largely conditioned . . . by the existence and hostility of the Vandal power in north Africa. The Vandal king Gaiseric had formed a strong fleet with which he was able to attack and plunder Italy, as well as to occupy Sicily and Sardinia. . . . The presence of this enemy in Africa . . . immeasurably weakened the Roman power in all the western provinces. It had the direct result of controlling the corn supply of Italy, and it prevented the Roman government from acting with effectual vigour in either Gaul or Spain. If the Romans had continued to hold Africa—if the Vandals had not been there—there can be little doubt that the imperial power would have maintained itself for a far longer period in Italy, and would have offered far more effective opposition to the expansion of the Germans in Gaul and Spain. In my view, therefore, the contribution which the Vandals made to the shaping of Europe was this: the very existence of their kingdom in Africa, and of their naval power in the Mediterranean, acted as a powerful protection for the growth of the new German kingdoms in Gaul and Spain, and ultimately helped the founding of a German kingdom in Italy, by dividing, diverting, and weakening the forces of the Empire. The Vandals had got round, as it were, to the rear of the Empire; and the effect of their powerful presence there was enhanced by the hostile and aggressive attitude which they continuously adopted.

RICIMER THE GERMAN

Even if there had been united councils in Italy, the task of ubiquitous defence would have been beyond the power of the government; but the government went to pieces, and thereby hastened the dismemberment [of the realm]. I need not here enter at all into the history of the short-reigned emperors who were set up and knocked down in Italy after the murder of Valentinian III in 455. I would invite your attention to two main points: first, the Vandal danger which embarrassed the Italian government during these years; and secondly, the power behind the imperial throne. This power behind the throne is of great significance. . . . It was wielded by a German general, Ricimer, of Suevian race. He was the successor of the German Stilicho and of the Roman Aetius as the defender of the Empire. The circumstances in which Ricimer had to act were indeed different from the circumstances of Stilicho and of Aetius. They differed in two main particulars. First, . . . while the activity of Stilicho and of Aetius reached beyond Italy to the other western provinces, the activity of Ricimer was practically confined to Italy and the Italian seas: this was due to the powerful hostility of the Vandals. Secondly, Stilicho and

Aetius had been the ministers of emperors who belonged to the well-established dynasty of Theodosius; and although those emperors, Honorius and Valentinian III, were personally weak and worthless, yet their legitimacy gave their thrones stability; so that Stilicho and Aetius could feel that, though they might fall themselves, they had a secure throne behind them. It was not so in the case of Ricimer. The male line of Theodosius was extinct; Valentinian III had left no sons: and it devolved upon Ricimer to provide the imperial authority which he was to serve. He became through circumstances an emperor-maker; and his difficulty was this. If he set up too strong a man, his own power would have probably been overridden; his own fall would have been the consequence; while on the other hand weak upstarts were unable to maintain their position for any length of time, since public opinion did not respect them. In estimating the part played by Ricimer, I think that hard and unjust measure is sometimes dealt out to him. The difficulties of his position can hardly be overstated, and he may be held to have made a serious and honest attempt to perform the task of preserving a government in Italy and defending the peninsula against its formidable enemies.

Now you must observe that the fact of Ricimer's being a German was a significant and determining factor in the situation. If he had not been a German, the situation would have been much simpler; for he could have assumed the imperial purple himself; the real and the nominal power would have been combined in the same hands; and the problem of government would have been solved. His German birth excluded this solution. This is a very remarkable thing. Germans like Stilicho and Ricimer, who attained to the highest posts in the imperial service, who might even intermarry with the imperial house, could not venture to take the last great step and mount the imperial throne. Just so much, just at the pinnacle, they were still outsiders. And they fully recognised this disability themselves. . . .

ENTER NEPOS AND ORESTES

It is also to be noted that in the intervals between the reigns of the emperors whom Ricimer set up and pulled down, when there was no emperor regnant [ruling] in Italy, it did not mean that there was no emperor at all. At such times the imperial authority was entirely invested in the eastern emperor who reigned at Constantinople, the Emperor Leo; and this, too, was fully acknowledged by Ricimer, who indeed selected two of his emperors by arrangement with Leo.

Ricimer died in 472 and the march of affairs after his death shows how difficult his task had been. The events of these next few years have often been misconceived in respect of the exact nature of their importance. Ricimer's nephew Gundobad seemed marked out to succeed to the place of his uncle—as the head of the military forces in Italy, and as the power behind the throne. Gundobad belonged to the royal family of the Burgundians and was a son of the reigning Burgundian king; but he had entered the imperial service. The Emperor Olybrius, Ricimer's last creation, recognised Gundobad's position and raised him to the rank of patrician. But Olybrius died before the end of the year, and a crisis ensued. For Gundobad and the Emperor Leo could not agree as to who should succeed to the purple. Leo's candidate was Julius Nepos, and Gundobad set up an obscure person named Glycerius. . . .

But hardly had the deadlock arisen between Gundobad and the Emperor Leo, when Gundobad disappeared from the scene. A new ambition was suddenly opened to him. . . . His father had died, and Gundobad withdrew to Burgundy to endeavour to secure his own election [to the Burgundian throne]. He succeeded. . . . After his departure the Emperor Julius Nepos, Leo's candidate, landed in Italy and deposed Glycerius. But Nepos was not equal to the situation. He very wisely negotiated a peace with Euric, king of the West Goths, . . . and he then appointed a certain Roman, Orestes by name, to be commander-in-chief, *magister militum*, in Gaul, to defend the Roman territory there. Orestes had been in Attila's service: he had lived much with barbarians of all kinds, and Nepos thought that he was making a very clever choice in selecting Orestes to command an army of barbarian soldiers. I may point out that after the break-up of Attila's empire there had been an immense influx of barbarian mercenaries into the Roman service. The army which Orestes now commanded was composed not only of Germans drawn from families long settled in the Empire but also of these new adventurers who had drifted into Italy through Noricum and Pannonia. Nepos was deceived in Orestes; Orestes was ambitious, and instead of going to Gaul, as he had been told, he marched on Ravenna. Nepos immediately fled to Dalmatia. Italy was for the moment in the power of Orestes. He did not seize the Empire himself, he preferred the double arrangement which had prevailed in the time of Ricimer. . . . Keeping the military power himself, he invested his child-son Romulus Augustulus with the imperial purple.

RISE OF ODOVACAR

But before Orestes had established his government he was surprised by a new situation. His host of barbarian soldiers, who were largely Heruls, suddenly formulated a demand. They were dissatisfied with the arrangements for quartering them. Their wives and children lived in the garrison towns in their neighbourhood, but they had no proper homes or hearths. The idea occurred to them that arrangements might be made in their behalf in Italy similar to those which had been made in Gaul, for instance, in behalf of the Visigoths and the Burgundians. Why should not they obtain permanent quarters, abiding homes, on the large estates . . . of Italy? This feeling prevailed in the host, and the officers formulated a demand which they laid before Orestes. The demand simply was that the normal system of *hospitalitas* should be adopted in Italy for their benefit, *i.e.* that a third part of the Italian soil should be divided among them. The sympathies or prejudices of Orestes were too Roman to let him entertain this demand; Italy had so far been sacrosanct [safe] from barbarian settlements. He refused, and his refusal led to a revolution. The mercenary soldiers found a leader in an officer who was thoroughly representative of themselves, an adventurer who had come from beyond the Danube to seek his fortunes, and had entered the service of the Empire. This was Odovacar: he was probably a Scirian, possibly a Rugian (there is a discrepancy in the authorities), at all events he . . . now undertook to realise the claim of the soldiers, and consequently there was a revolution. Orestes was put to death, and his son the Emperor Romulus Augustulus abdicated. The power in Italy was in the hands of Odovacar. We are in the year 476.

ODOVACAR NEGOTIATES WITH CONSTANTINOPLE

There was, constitutionally speaking, nothing novel in the situation. There were two legitimate emperors, the Emperor Zeno at Constantinople, and the Emperor Julius Nepos (who was in Dalmatia). In the eyes of the government of Constantinople, Romulus Augustulus was a usurper. This usurper had now been deposed by a military revolution; the leader of that revolution, Odovacar, had shown no disloyalty to the eastern emperor, whose authority he fully acknowledged. There was no thought here of any dismemberment, or detachment, or breaking away from the Empire. Odovacar was a Roman officer, he was raised by the army into the virtual position of a *magister militum*, and his first thought, after the revolution had been carried through, was to get his position regularised by imperial authority, to gain from Zeno a formal recognition and appointment. Odovacar was in fact the successor of the series of German commanders who had supported the Empire for eighty years: and when he came to power in 476, there was not the least reason in the actual circumstances why the same kind of regime should not have been

continued as in the days of Ricimer. But Odovacar had states-
manlike qualities, and he decided against the system of Ricimer,
which had proved thoroughly unsatisfactory and unstable. His
idea was to rule Italy under the imperial authority of Constantinople, unhampered by a second emperor in Italy, whom recent
experiences had shown to be worse than useless. There would
have been no difficulty for Odovacar in adopting this policy, if
there had existed no second emperor at the time; but Julius
Nepos was still alive, and, what was most important, he had
been recognised at Constantinople. Odovacar was determined
not to acknowledge the authority of Nepos. It is very important
to understand this element in the situation, because it directly led
to the peculiar position which Odovacar afterwards occupied.
He first addressed himself to the Roman senate, and caused that
body to send envoys to Constantinople, bearing the imperial insignia, and a letter to the Emperor Zeno. The purport of the letter was to suggest that one emperor, namely Zeno himself and
his successors at Constantinople, sufficed for the needs of the
whole Empire, and to ask that Zeno should authorise Odovacar
to conduct the administration in Italy, and should confer on him
the title of Patricius, which had been borne by Ricimer. The Emperor was not a little embarrassed. Julius Nepos was at the same
time demanding his help to recover Italy, and Nepos had a legitimate claim. The Emperor wrote a very diplomatic reply. He insisted, in the most definite and correct terms, on the legal claim
of Nepos; he, however, told Odovacar, whom he praised for the
consideration he had shown in his dealings with the Italians after the revolution, that he would confer upon him the title of
Patricius, if Nepos had not already done so.

ODOVACAR'S REVOLUTION

This limited recognition was not what Odovacar had hoped for;
the express reserve of the rights of Julius Nepos was most unsatisfactory; there was always a chance that those rights might at
a favourable moment be enforced. Accordingly, while he accepted the patriciate from Zeno, and so legitimised his position
as an imperial minister in the eyes of Italy, he fortified himself by
assuming another title which must have expressed his relation
to the barbarian army, viz. the title of king, *rex*. We do not know
what solemnity or form accompanied the assumption of this title. But its effect was to give Odovacar the double character of a
German king as well as an imperial officer. . . . So Odovacar was
king of the Germans who through him obtained settlements in
Italy, while he was also a Patricius, acting under the authority of
the Emperor Zeno. There was thus theoretically no detachment

of Italy from the Empire in the days of Odovacar. . . . The position of Odovacar was still further regularised a few years later (480) by the death of Julius Nepos.

The death of Julius Nepos is an event which has some significance; it marks the cessation of a separate line of emperors in the west. But if I have made clear the circumstances of the revolution headed by Odovacar, you will perceive that this event, though of importance in the history of Italy, has not the importance and significance which has been commonly ascribed to it. The year 476 has been generally taken as a great landmark, and the event has been commonly described as the fall of the Western Empire. This unfortunate expression conveys a wholly erroneous idea of the bearings of Odovacar's revolution. . . . This event concerns specially the history of Italy, in the same way as the settlements of the Visigoths and Burgundians concerned the history of Gaul; and the settlement of the Germans in Italy does not directly affect the western provinces as a whole. It is then a misleading misuse of words to speak of a fall of the Western Empire in 476: the revolution of that year marks but a stage, and that not the last stage, in the encroachments of the barbarian settlers in the western provinces.

CHRONOLOGY

B.C.

ca. 500–323

The years of Greece's Classical Age, in which Greek arts, architecture, literature, and democratic reforms reach their height.

490

The Athenians defeat a force of invading Persians at Marathon (northeast of Athens).

ca. 486–473

Death of the Indian wise man Siddhartha, who became known as the Buddha, or "Enlightened One." Buddhism subsequently spreads throughout India and then to southeast Asia, China, and Japan.

480

The Athenian statesman-general Themistocles engineers a major naval victory over the Persians at Salamis (southwest of Athens).

472

The Athenian playwright Aeschylus first produces *The Persians*, which includes an eyewitness account of the recent Greek victory at Salamis.

431

The disastrous Peloponnesian War, which will engulf and exhaust almost all the city-states, begins.

429

A deadly plague strikes Athens, killing a large number of residents, including its most able leader, Pericles.

415

The Athenians send a large military expedition to Sicily in hopes of conquering the Greek city of Syracuse.

413

The Athenians are disastrously defeated in Sicily; most of the survivors are condemned to slave labor in the local quarries.

404

Athens surrenders to Sparta, ending the great war; the Spartan hegemony of Greece begins.

359

The young Philip II takes charge of the disunited, culturally backward Greek kingdom of Macedonia; within just a few years he will turn it into a strong nation with a formidable standing army.

338

Philip and his teenaged son, Alexander, defeat a temporary Greek alliance led by Athens and Thebes at Chaeronea (in central Greece).

334

After Philip's recent assassination, Alexander invades Persia; in the next few years he overruns Persian territories, spreading Greek language, ideas, and political administration across the Near East.

323

Having created the largest empire the world has yet seen, Alexander dies in the former Persian capital of Babylon.

ca. 323–30

The years of Greece's Hellenistic Age, in which Alexander's generals, the so-called "Successors," war among themselves and carve up his empire into several new kingdoms, which then proceed also to fight among themselves. During the second half of this period, Rome gains control of the Greek world.

321

The Maurya Dynasty creates India's first large empire.

305–304

Alexander's former general Ptolemy declares himself king of Egypt, formally establishing the Ptolemaic Dynasty.

280

Three large Greek monarchies (the Macedonian, Seleucid, and Ptolemaic kingdoms) have by now emerged from the chaos of the long wars of the Successors; Pyrrhus answers a call for help from Tarentum, a Greek city in southern Italy that has been threatened by Rome; Pyrrhus narrowly defeats the Romans at Heraclea (near Tarentum).

275

Having failed to make decisive headway against the Romans, Pyrrhus abandons Italy.

ca. 268–233

The life of Asoka, a skilled and enlightened Indian ruler who converts to Buddhism and attempts to govern by that faith's ethical concepts.

265

Having secured control of the Greek cities of southern Italy, the Romans are the masters of the Italian peninsula.

241

The Romans defeat the maritime empire of Carthage, ending the First Punic War.

ca. 238

The Parthians seize control of the Seleucid territory of Parthia and begin a period of expansion that will eventually absorb most of the Seleucid Empire.

221

The Ch'in, a vigorous, authoritarian group of rulers based in western China, overrun the numerous other warring states of China and unify the country under a central administration.

202

After a brief period of political chaos, another Chinese dynasty, the Han, replace the Ch'in and largely adopt their imperial system.

201

The Second Punic War ends with another resounding Roman victory.

200–197

Rome prosecutes and wins the Second Macedonian War against Macedonia's King Philip V, who had allied himself with Carthage in the Second Punic War.

171–168

Rome wins the Third Macedonian War and dismantles the Macedonian Kingdom.

146

The Romans destroy Carthage at the close of the Third Punic War; a Roman general destroys the once-great Greek city of Corinth as an object lesson to any Greeks contemplating rebellion against Rome.

58

The gifted Roman general Julius Caesar initiates his now famous conquest of Gaul (the area that later became France and Belgium).

53

The Parthians disastrously defeat the Roman general Marcus Crassus in Mesopotamia.

44

Caesar is assassinated in the Roman Senate.

31

Cleopatra VII, queen of Ptolemaic Egypt, and her Roman lover/ally, Mark Antony, are defeated by another powerful Roman, Octavian, at Actium (in western Greece); the following year, the legendary queen, last of the Hellenistic and independent Greek rulers of antiquity, takes her own life.

ca. 30 B.C.–A.D. 180

Approximate years of the so-called *Pax Romana* ("Roman Peace"), a period in which the Mediterranean world under the first several Roman emperors enjoys relative peace and prosperity.

27

With the blessings of the Senate, Octavian takes the name of Augustus. Historians usually mark this date as the beginning of the Roman Empire, with Augustus as its first emperor (although he himself never used that title, preferring to call himself "first citizen").

ca. 4

Jesus, who will later become the focus of a major world religion, is born in Roman-controlled Palestine.

A.D.

14

Augustus dies and is succeeded by the second emperor, Tiberius.

ca. 30–33

Jesus is crucified by order of the Roman governor of Judaea.

66

The Jews in Palestine launch a major rebellion against the Romans, who in the following few years besiege Jerusalem and other Judaean cities and crush the rebels; at this same time, far to the south, in what is now Ethiopia, the African kingdom of Axum is rising to prominence, in large part because of its trade contacts with the Greco-Roman Mediterranean sphere.

98–117

Reign of the emperor Trajan, in which the Roman Empire reaches its greatest size and power. During the later years of the reign, in distant Central America, the Maya, who have inhabited southern Mexico for several centuries, begin building many new towns, each with an impressive ceremonial center containing large stone temples and other public buildings.

116

Trajan defeats the Parthians and marches to the shores of the Persian Gulf.

180

Death of the emperor Marcus Aurelius, marking the end of the *Pax Romana* era and the beginning of Rome's steady slide into economic and political crisis.

212

The emperor Caracalla extends Roman citizenship rights to all free adult males in the Empire.

224

The last Parthian (or Arsacid) ruler is overthrown by Ardishir, who establishes the Persian Sassanid Dynasty, whose members see themselves as the successors of the Persian rulers defeated centuries before by Alexander the Great.

235–284

The Roman Empire nearly collapses under the strain of terrible political anarchy and civil strife.

284

Military man Diocletian becomes emperor and initiates sweeping political, economic, social, and military reforms, in effect reconstructing the Empire under a new blueprint.

307–337

Reign of the emperor Constantine I, who carries on the reforms begun by Diocletian.

312

Constantine defeats his rival, the usurper Maxentius, at Rome's Milvian Bridge. Constantine credits the Christian god for his victory.

313

Constantine and his eastern colleague, Licinius, issue the so-called Edict of Milan, granting religious toleration to the formerly hated and persecuted Christian sect.

ca. 320–ca. 540

The years during which the Gupta Dynasty unites and rules most of India, encouraging religious tolerance, the arts, literature, and philosophy.

330

Constantine founds the city of Constantinople, on the Bosphorus Strait, making it the capital of the eastern section of the Roman Empire.

375

The Huns, a savage nomadic people from central Asia, sweep into eastern Europe, pushing the Goths and other "barbarian" peoples into Rome's northern provinces.

378

The eastern emperor Valens is disastrously defeated by the Visigoths at Adrianople (in the Greek region of Thrace).

395

The emperor Theodosius I, the Great, dies, leaving his sons Arcadius and Honorius in control of a permanently divided Roman Empire.

ca. 407

As Rome steadily loses control of several of its northern and western provinces, Britain falls under the sway of barbarian tribes.

410

The Visigoths, led by their war chief, Alaric, sack Rome.

455

Rome is sacked again, this time by the Vandals, led by Gaiseric.

476

The German-born general Odoacer deposes the young emperor Romulus Augustulus. Later historians came to see this event as the "fall" of Rome and the end of the classical world.

FOR FURTHER RESEARCH

Ancient Africa (Including Egypt)

David T. Adamo, *Africa and the Africans in the Old Testament.* San Francisco: International Scholars Publications, 1998.

John Addison, *Ancient Africa.* New York: John Day, 1970.

Basil Davidson, *African Empires.* New York: Time-Life, 1966.

Nicolas Grimal, *A History of Ancient Egypt.* Oxford, England: Blackwell, 1992.

Serge Lancel, *Carthage: A History.* Trans. Antonia Nevill. Oxford, England: Blackwell, 1992.

Naphtali Lewis, *Greeks in Ptolemaic Egypt.* Oxford: Clarendon Press, 1986.

————, *Life in Egypt Under Roman Rule.* Oxford: Clarendon Press, 1983.

Harold G. Marcus, *A History of Ethiopia.* Berkeley: University of California Press, 1994.

Don Nardo, ed., *Cleopatra.* San Diego: Greenhaven Press, 2000.

Roland A. Oliver, *Africa in the Iron Age, ca. 500 B.C. to A.D. 1400.* New York: Cambridge University Press, 1975.

Desmond Stewart, *The Pyramids and the Sphinx.* New York: Newsweek Book Division, 1971.

L.A. Thompson and J. Ferguson, *Africa in Classical Antiquity.* Nigeria: Ibadan University Press, 1969.

Ancient Central America and the Maya

Cottie Burland, *The People of the Ancient Americas.* London: Paul Hamlyn, 1970.

Leonard E. Fisher, *Gods and Goddesses of the Ancient Maya.* New York: Holiday House, 1999.

William T. Hanks and Don S. Rice, eds., *Word and Image in Maya Culture: Explorations in Language, Writing, and Representation.* Salt Lake City: University of Utah Press, 1989.

Timothy Laughton, *The Maya: Life, Myth, and Art.* New York: Stewart, Tabori, and Chang, 1998.

Mysteries of the Ancient Americas. Pleasantville, NY: Reader's Digest, 1986.

Linda Schele and David Freidel, *A Forest of Kings: The Untold Story of the Ancient Maya.* New York: Morrow Quill, 1990.

Ancient China and Far East

Patricia B. Ebrey, *The Cambridge Illustrated History of China.* New York: Cambridge University Press, 1996.

Jonathon Fryer, *The Great Wall of China.* South Brunswick, NJ: A.S. Barnes, 1977.

L. Carrington Goodrich, *A Short History of the Chinese People.* New York: Harper and Row, 1969.

Valerie Hanson, *The Open Empire: A History of China to 1600.* New York: Norton, 2000.

Kenneth S. Latourette, *A Short History of the Far East.* New York: Macmillan, 1964.

H. Maspero, *China in Antiquity.* Amherst: University of Massachusetts Press, 1978.

Franz Schurmann, ed., *The China Reader.* New York: Random House, 1967–1974.

Ancient Greece

Aeschylus, *The Persians,* in *Aeschylus: Prometheus Bound, the Suppliants, Seven Against Thebes, the Persians.* Trans. Philip Vellacott. Baltimore: Penguin Books, 1961.

Arrian, *Anabasis Alexandri,* published as *The Campaigns of Alexander.* Trans. Aubrey de Sélincourt. New York: Penguin Books, 1971.

Peter Connolly, *Greece and Rome at War.* London: Greenhill Books, 1998.

Charles Freeman, *The Greek Achievement: The Foundation of the Western World.* New York: Viking/Penguin, 1999.

Michael Grant, *The Classical Greeks.* New York: Scribner's, 1989.

————, *From Alexander to Cleopatra: The Hellenistic World.* New York: Charles Scribner's Sons, 1982.

Peter Green, *The Greco-Persian Wars.* Berkeley: University of California Press, 1996.

————, *The Parthenon.* New York: Newsweek Book Division, 1973.

N.G.L. Hammond, *The Genius of Alexander the Great.* Chapel Hill: University of North Carolina Press, 1997.

————, *Philip of Macedon.* Baltimore: Johns Hopkins University Press, 1994.

W.G. Hardy, *The Greek and Roman World.* Cambridge, MA: Schenkman Publishing, 1962.

Donald Kagan, *The Outbreak of the Peloponnesian War.* Ithaca: Cornell University Press, 1969.

————, *Pericles of Athens and the Birth of Democracy.* New York: Free Press, 1991.

John Lazenby, *The Defense of Greece.* Bloomington, IL: David Brown, 1993.

Thomas R. Martin, *Ancient Greece: From Prehistoric to Hellenistic Times.* New Haven: Yale University Press, 1996.

Don Nardo, ed., *Complete History of Ancient Greece.* San Diego: Greenhaven Press, 2001.

————, ed., *The Decline and Fall of Ancient Greece.* San Diego: Greenhaven Press, 2000.

John G. Pedley, *Greek Art and Archaeology.* New York: Harry N. Abrams, 1993.

Plutarch, *Parallel Lives,* excerpted in *The Rise and Fall of Athens: Nine Greek Lives by Plutarch.* Trans. Ian Scott-Kilvert. New York: Penguin, 1960; also excerpted in *The Age of Alexander: Nine Greek Lives by Plutarch.* Trans. Ian Scott-Kilvert. New York: Penguin, 1973.

Sarah B. Pomeroy et al., *Ancient Greece: A Political, Social, and Cultural History.* New York: Oxford University Press, 1999.

C.E. Robinson, *Hellas: A Short History of Ancient Greece.* Boston: Beacon Press, 1957.

George D. Wilcoxon, *Athens Ascendant.* Ames: Iowa State University Press, 1979.

Ancient India

A.L. Basham, *The Wonder That Was India.* New York: Taplinger Publishing, 1967.

William T. de Bary, ed., *Sources of Indian Tradition,* Vol. 1. New York: Columbia University Press, 1958.

B.G. Gokhale, *Asoka Maurya.* New York: Twayne, 1966.

John Keay, *India: A History.* New York: Atlantic Monthly Press, 2000.

Vincent A. Smith, *The Oxford History of India.* New York: Oxford University Press, 1981.

Percival Spear, *India: A Modern History.* Ann Arbor: University of Michigan Press, 1961.

Mortimer Wheeler, *Early India and Pakistan to Asoka.* New York: Praeger, 1959.

Ancient Near East

Maria E. Aubert, *The Phoenicians and the West.* Trans. Mary Turton. New York: Columbia University Press, 1993.

M.A.R. Colledge, *The Parthians.* New York: Praeger, 1967.

John Curtis, *Ancient Persia.* Cambridge, MA: Harvard University Press, 1990.

Roberta L. Harris, *The World of the Bible.* London: Thames and Hudson, 1995.

Samuel N. Kramer, *Cradle of Civilization.* New York: Time-Life, 1967.

Don Nardo, *Empires of Mesopotamia.* San Diego: Lucent Books, 2001.

———, *The Persian Empire.* San Diego: Lucent Books, 1997.

Georges Roux, *Ancient Iraq.* New York: Penguin, 1980.

Emil Schürer, *History of the Jewish People in the Age of Jesus.* Edinburgh: Clark, 1987.

Daniel C. Snell, *Life in the Ancient Near East, 3100–332 B.C.* New Haven: Yale University Press, 1997.

Ancient Religions: Their Rise, Struggles, and Tenets

Max I. Dimont, *Jews, God and History.* New York: New American Library, 1962.

Will Durant, *Caesar and Christ: A History of Roman Civilization and of Christianity from Their Beginnings to A.D. 325.* New York: Simon & Schuster, 1944.

Charles Eliot, *Hinduism and Buddhism.* 3 vols. Boston: Routledge and Kegan Paul, 1968.

Josephus, *The Jewish War.* Trans. G.A. Williamson. New York: Penguin Books, 1981.

Howard C. Kee, ed., *The Origins of Christianity: Sources and Documents.* Englewood Cliffs, NJ: Prentice-Hall, 1973.

Ramsay MacMullen, *Christianizing the Roman Empire, A.D. 100–400.* New Haven: Yale University Press, 1984.

Don Nardo, *The Rise of Christianity.* San Diego: Lucent Books, 2001.

Paul W. Roberts, *In Search of the Birth of Jesus.* New York: Riverhead Books, 1995.

John Romer, *Testament: The Bible and History.* New York: Henry Holt, 1988.

H.J. Rose, *Religion in Greece and Rome.* New York: Harper and Brothers, 1959.

E.P. Sanders, *The Historical Figure of Jesus.* New York: Penguin Books, 1993.

Byron E. Shafer, ed., *Religion in Ancient Egypt.* Ithaca: Cornell University Press, 1991.

A.K. Warder, *Indian Buddhism.* Delhi: Motilal Banarsidass, 1970.

Robert L. Wilken, *The Christians as the Romans Saw Them.* New Haven: Yale University Press, 1984.

A.N. Wilson, *Paul: The Mind of the Apostle.* New York: W.W. Norton, 1997.

Ancient Rome

Ammianus Marcellinus, *History,* published as *The Later Roman Empire, A.D. 354–378.* Trans. and ed. Walter Hamilton. New York: Penguin Books, 1986.

J.P.V.D. Balsdon, *Life and Leisure in Ancient Rome.* New York: McGraw-Hill, 1969.

Arthur E.R. Boak and William G. Sinnigen, *A History of Rome to A.D. 565.* New York: Macmillan, 1965.

Averil Cameron, *The Later Roman Empire: A.D. 284–430.* Cambridge, MA: Harvard University Press, 1993.

Dio Cassius, *Roman History: The Reign of Augustus.* Trans. Ian Scott-Kilvert. New York: Penguin Books, 1987.

Tim Cornell and John Matthews, *Atlas of the Roman World.* New York; Facts On File, 1982.

Arther Ferrill, *The Fall of the Roman Empire: The Military Explanation.* New York: Thames and Hudson, 1986.

Michael Grant, *Caesar.* London: Weidenfeld and Nicolson, 1974.

———, *Constantine the Great: The Man and His Times.* New York: Scribner's, 1994.

———, *The Roman Emperors.* New York: Barnes and Noble, 1997.

———, *The World of Rome.* New York: New American Library, 1960.

A.H.M. Jones, *Constantine and the Conversion of Europe.* Toronto: University of Toronto Press, 1978.

———, *The Decline of the Ancient World.* London: Longman Group, 1966. Note: This is a shortened version of Jones's massive and highly influential *The Later Roman Empire, 284–602.* 3 vols. Norman: University of Oklahoma Press, 1964, reprinted 1975.

Anthony Kamm, *The Romans: An Introduction.* London: Routledge, 1995.

Naphtali Lewis and Meyer Reinhold, eds., *Roman Civilization, Sourcebook I: The Republic,* and *Roman Civilization, Sourcebook II: The Empire.* Both New York: Harper and Row, 1966.

Don Nardo, *The Decline and Fall of Ancient Rome.* San Diego: Greenhaven Press, 2000.

———, *Games of Ancient Rome.* San Diego: Lucent Books, 2000.

———, *Life of a Roman Slave.* San Diego: Lucent Books, 1998.

———, *Life of a Roman Soldier.* San Diego: Lucent Books, 2000.

Plutarch, *Parallel Lives,* excerpted in *Plutarch: Makers of Rome.* Trans. Ian Scott-Kilvert. New York: Penguin Books, 1965.

Polybius, *Histories,* published as *Polybius: The Rise of the Roman Empire.* Trans. Ian Scott-Kilvert. New York: Penguin Books, 1979.

Justine Davis Randers-Pehrson, *Barbarians and Romans: The Birth Struggle of Europe, A.D. 400–700.* Norman: University of Oklahoma Press, 1983.

Henry T. Rowell, *Rome in the Augustan Age.* Norman: University of Oklahoma Press, 1962.

Chris Scarre, *Chronicle of the Roman Emperors.* New York: Thames and Hudson, 1995.

William G. Sinnigen, ed., *Sources in Western Civilization: Rome.* New York: The Free Press, 1965.

L.P. Wilkinson, *The Roman Experience.* Lanham, MD: University Press of America, 1974.

General Ancient Times

Paul G. Bahn, ed., *The Cambridge Illustrated History of Archaeology.* New York: Cambridge University Press, 1996.

Lionel Casson, *The Ancient Mariners.* New York: Macmillan, 1959.

———, *Travel in the Ancient World.* Baltimore: Johns Hopkins University Press, 1994.

Peter Clayton and Martin Price, *The Seven Wonders of the Ancient World.* New York: Barnes and Noble, 1993.

L. Sprague de Camp, *The Ancient Engineers.* New York: Ballantine Books, 1963.

Charles Freeman, *Egypt, Greece, and Rome: Civilizations of the Ancient Mediterranean.* New York: Oxford University Press, 1996.

Chester G. Starr, *A History of the Ancient World.* New York: Oxford University Press, 1991.

John Warry, *Warfare in the Classical World.* Norman: University of Oklahoma Press, 1995.

Tim Wood, *Ancient Wonders.* New York: Penguin Books, 1991.

INDEX

ABOUT THE EDITOR

Historian Don Nardo has written extensively about the ancient world. His studies of ancient Greece and Rome include *Life in Ancient Athens, The Age of Augustus, Greek and Roman Sport, Life of a Roman Soldier,* and the *Encyclopedia of Greek and Roman Mythology;* he is also the editor of Greenhaven Press's massive *Complete History of Ancient Greece.* In addition, Mr. Nardo has produced volumes about ancient Egypt and Mesopotamia. He lives with his wife, Christine, in Massachusetts.

DATE DUE

6/17/12			
GAYLORD			PRINTED IN U.S.A.